WITHDRAWN

HARVARD LIBRARY

WITHDRAWN

*Deism, Masonry,
and the Enlightenment*

Alfred Owen Aldridge

Deism, Masonry, and the Enlightenment

ESSAYS HONORING
Alfred Owen Aldridge

EDITED BY
J. A. Leo Lemay

Newark: University of Delaware Press
London and Toronto: Associated University Presses

© 1987 by Associated University Presses, Inc.

Associated University Presses
440 Forsgate Drive
Cranbury, NJ 08512

Associated University Presses
25 Sicilian Avenue
London WC1A 2QH, England

Associated University Presses
2133 Royal Windsor Drive
Unit 1
Mississauga, Ontario
Canada L5J 1K5

The paper used in this publication meets the requirements
of the American National Standard for Permanence of Paper
for Printed Library Materials Z39.48-1984.

Library of Congress Cataloging-in-Publication Data

Deism, Masonry, and the Enlightenment.

"Alfred Owen Aldridge, a bibliography to 1986": p.
Bibliography: p.
Includes index.
1. Deism—History. 2. Freemasonry—History.
3. Enlightenment. 4. Aldridge, Alfred Owen, 1915–
I. Aldridge, Alfred Owen, 1915– . II. Lemay,
J. A. Leo (Joseph A. Leo), 1935– .
BL2758.D45   1987   211'.5'09033   86-40585
ISBN 0-87413-317-3 (alk. paper)

PRINTED IN THE UNITED STATES OF AMERICA

Contents

Alfred Owen Aldridge: A Sketch	7
Introduction	11
Latitudinarianism and the English Deists ROGER L. EMERSON	19
Spinoza, Stillingfleet, Prophecy, and "Enlightenment" GERARD REEDY, S.J.	49
Deism, Immortality, and the Art of Theological Lying DAVID BERMAN	61
The Amerindian in the Early American Enlightenment: Deistic Satire in Robert Beverley's *History of Virginia* (1705) J. A. LEO LEMAY	79
Defoe, the Occult, and the Deist Offensive during the Reign of George I MAXIMILLIAN E. NOVAK	93
Clio Mocks the Masons: Joseph Green's Anti-Masonic Satires DAVID S. SHIELDS	109
The Secret Fall of Freemasonry in Dr. Alexander Hamilton's *The History of the Tuesday Club* ROBERT MICKLUS	127
Radicalism in Joel Barlow's *The Conspiracy of Kings* (1792) CARLA MULFORD	137
The Age of Reason versus *The Age of Revelation*. Two Critics of Tom Paine: David Levi and Elias Boudinot RICHARD H. POPKIN	158
Alfred Owen Aldridge: A Bibliography to 1986	171
Works Cited	181
Notes on Contributors	199
Index	201

Alfred Owen Aldridge
A Sketch

Owen Aldridge was born on 16 December 1915 in Buffalo, New York, to Abel and Jane (Ette) Aldridge; attended Indiana University from 1933 to 1937, taking a B.S. in education in 1937; journeyed to the University of Georgia the following year where he was awarded an M.A. in English in 1938; and then went to Duke University for his Ph.D. in English (1942). He taught at the University of Buffalo from 1942 to 1947, advancing from instructor to associate professor, and then, at age thirty-two, moved to the University of Maryland in 1947 as professor of English.

His articles in the *Journal of the History of Ideas, PMLA, Philological Quarterly, Studies in Philology, American Literature,* and other scholarly journals during the period before moving to the University of Maryland established Owen Aldridge as an expert in eighteenth-century English and American literature, with a special expertise in the history of ideas. (Since Owen has written over one hundred essays and since they are categorized and listed in the bibliography, I will not enumerate them here, except to mention that from his earliest writings to the 1985 "Shaftesbury's Rosicrucian Ladies," many of his essays bear upon this volume's specific subjects.) His first monograph, *Shaftesbury and the Deist Manifesto* (Philadelphia: American Philosophical Society) appeared in 1951. In 1952–53, he had a Fulbright fellowship to France, teaching at the University of Toulouse in 1952 and at the University of Clermont-Ferrand in 1953. He studied at the Université de Paris in 1953–55, taking a Docteur Littérature comparée there in 1955.

The publication of *Benjamin Franklin and His French Contemporaries* (New York University Press) in 1955 (reprinted, Greenwood Press, 1976), with a revised, expanded version in French in 1963 (Paris: Didier), marked Franklin as a favorite scholarly subject. Owen Aldridge taught at the University of Rio de Janeiro as a visiting professor in 1957–58 and received a Smith-Mundt fellowship for Brazil in 1958. In addition to being a professor of English at the University of Maryland, he also became a professor of comparative literature there in 1958, the director of the comparative literature program in 1960, and the head of the department of comparative literature in 1964.

His standard biography *Man of Reason: The Life of Thomas Paine* (J. B. Lippincott) appeared in 1959, has been translated into French (1964), Arabic (1964), Bengali (1965), and Urdu (1967), and has been reprinted in England (1960) and in the States (1963). As a result of this biography and numerous specialized articles on Paine, he has been elected an honorary vice president of the International Thomas Paine Society. In 1960, he published *Essai sur les personnages des "Liaisons Dangereuses" en tant que types littéraires* (Paris: Les Lettres Modernes).

Adriana Garcia Davila and Owen Aldridge married on 7 June 1963. That same year he founded the journal *Comparative Literature Studies* and has edited it from 1963 to the present. For the Great American Thinkers Series, he wrote *Jonathan Edwards* (Washington Square Press) in 1964. He served on the advisory board of the American Comparative Literature Association from 1965 to 1971 and again from 1974 to 1977.

His biography of Franklin, *Benjamin Franklin: Philosopher and Man* (J. B. Lippincott) appeared in 1965, and his study of the deism and other aspects of Franklin's religious thought, *Benjamin Franklin and Nature's God* (Duke University Press), appeared in 1967.

The University of Illinois called him to be professor of French and comparative literature in 1967. He edited a volume entitled *Comparative Literature: Matter and Method* in 1968 and another on *The Ibero-American Enlightenment* (both University of Illinois Press) in 1970. The Institute of Ibero-American Enlightenment elected him vice president for 1969–70. He served on the advisory board of the American Society for Eighteenth-Century Studies from 1970 to 1975 and on the advisory board of the International Comparative Literature Association, 1970 to 1976. The National Endowment for the Humanities awarded him a senior fellowship in 1973. His critical and intellectual study of Voltaire, *Voltaire and the Century of Light* (Princeton University Press), appeared in 1975. The American Comparative Literature Association elected him its vice president for 1977–80 and its president for 1980–83.

In accordance with his developing interests in Oriental languages and literatures, he visited Nihon University in Japan in 1976 and 1982. He wrote in Japanese *Comparative Literature: Japan and the West* (Tokyo: Nan'un Do) in 1979, and, again in Japanese, *Fiction in Japan and the West* (Tokyo: Nan'un Do) in 1985. The Rockefeller Foundation sponsored a stay at Villa Serbelloni, in Bellagio, Italy, for a period in 1980; and he taught at Kuwait University as a visiting professor in 1983.

With *Early American Literature: A Comparatist Approach* (Princeton University Press) in 1982, he returned to a favorite subject and then examined the origins and intellectual background of Paine's ideas in 1984 with *Thomas Paine's American Ideology* (University of Delaware Press). His most recent book is *The Reemergence of World Literature: A Study of Asia and the West* (University of

Delaware Press, 1986). He is currently writing a comparative study of Benjamin Franklin and Voltaire. In 1986, he became professor emeritus at the University of Illinois. For the academic year 1986–87, he has accepted the Will and Ariel Durant Professorship of Humanities at Saint Peter's College, Jersey City, New Jersey.

Let me conclude with a personal testimony to Owen Aldridge. When I began graduate school at the University of Maryland in the fall of 1959, I was working full time and was not certain either that I wanted to return to a student's life or that I wanted to take advanced degrees in English. I therefore decided to test my own inclinations and resolve by signing up for what I then considered to be the two most dreadful-sounding courses that the University of Maryland's English department offered in the fall of 1959. (As an undergraduate, my favorite English courses had been in modern American literature, modern poetry, and Shakespeare.) Those two courses were Bibliography and Methods and Colonial American Literature. To my surprise, I enjoyed them both enormously; and in the latter course, Owen Aldridge made me a colonialist.

J. A. Leo Lemay

Introduction

It is fitting that a festschrift honoring Professor Alfred Owen Aldridge should focus on "Deism, Masonry, and the Enlightenment," for Professor Aldridge has devoted much of his scholarly career to studying English, American, and European aspects of the Enlightenment. His major books on Anthony Ashley Cooper, the third earl of Shaftesbury, on Thomas Paine, on Benjamin Franklin, and on Voltaire all specifically address deism and/or Freemasonry and of course explore Enlightenment thought. Although these areas of investigation do not begin to encompass all of Professor Aldridge's interests, they are sufficiently limited for the contributors to produce a volume with a relatively well-defined focus, and at the same time, they are broad enough to accommodate a diverse group of individuals from different disciplines.

The first two essays deal primarily with the Restoration period. Professor Roger L. Emerson's wide-ranging essay "Latitudinarianism and the English Deists" surveys the connections between the latitudinarians and the deists asserted by several prominent scholars; defines what *deism* meant in the late seventeenth century; argues that deism and the English deists belong to the European tradition of epistemology—i.e., of debates concerning the sources of knowledge—rather than to the native English tradition of debates over social and political order; proves that the leading latitudinarian John Tillotson preached a doctrine based upon belief in the Bible as revealed religion and rooted in the liturgy and *Book of Common Prayer* of the Anglican church; and concludes by recommending that deism be studied within the contexts of seventeenth- and eighteenth-century intellectual thought. His essay valuably discriminates the fundamental differences between the latitudinarians and the deists and provides a critical bibliographical survey of the recent historical literature on deism.

Father Gerard Reedy's "Spinoza, Stillingfleet, Prophecy, and 'Enlightenment'" begins by questioning the meaning of *Enlightenment*, stressing that it is necessary to recognize differences as well as similarities between key Enlightenment figures. He then briefly recapitulates key elements of Benedictus de Spinoza's argument in his *Theologico-Political Treatise;* informs us that Edward Stillingfleet replied to Spinoza in an unpublished sermon delivered on 23 February 1682/3; stresses that Spinoza and Stillingfleet differed in the methodological tools they applied to Scripture (Stillingfleet held that revelation and reason went hand in hand, whereas Spinoza relied only upon a rigorous logical methodology); questions how both these thinkers share Enlightenment ideology, pointing out that both attempt to liberate divinity from superstition and from reliance on inner light as a means of verification; shows that for Spinoza the only sense of Scripture that survives rational analysis is the moral sense, whereas for Stillingfleet the historical and typological approaches, as well as the tropological (or moral) are valid; and concludes that although the concept of Enlightenment as sometimes used may be too inclusive, it is nevertheless useful to see the similarities as well as the differences between Spinoza and Stillingfleet. Indeed, Reedy argues that both the similarities and the differences between the two figures must be appreciated in order to understand the real nature of the controversy.

Dr. David Berman's essay "Deism, Immortality, and the Art of Theological Lying" spans a period from the late seventeenth to the mid-eighteenth century, from Charles Blount to David Hume. Berman argues that the (so-called) foremost British deists (Charles Blount, John Toland, Anthony Collins, and Matthew Tindal) only pretended to believe in a future life; like David Hume they were actually mortalists who suggested their true meanings by indirection. Berman subsumes the various names for their rhetorical method under the new and inclusive rubric, "the Art of Theological Lying." Since the freethinkers could not openly speak or write their opinions, they had to remain silent or resort to artful lying. Although these writers all claimed to be Christian fideists, Berman shows that they elsewhere refuted that position. He also argues that in some instances, only external evidence reveals that the writers were actually lying; the internal evidence of irony and tone is at times an insufficient guide to the deists' covert meaning. He concludes that in reading their writings we are not really dealing with the shallow, superficial deism that intellectual historians from the time of Leslie Stephen have ascribed to them but with a deep, covert atheism. As Berman writes, "The *onus* of proof now lies with those who claim that they were sincere deists to show that they were." I personally believe that only Berman's thesis adequately explains the horror with which the contemporaries of these deists greeted their opinions.

My own contribution, "The Amerindian in the Early American Enlightenment: Deistic Satire in Robert Beverley's *History of Virginia* (1705)," argues that one of the best-known and most widely cited passages in Beverley's *History*, his exploration of an Amerindian house of worship, is actually fictitious. I provide evidence indicating that a close reading of the key passages reveals they are fictions; show that Beverley's description was inspired by De Bry's print in Thomas Hariot's *Brief and True Report* (1590); point out that the print itself (which Beverley adapted and reprinted) is regarded as a fake and does not accurately represent any known gods of

Virginia Indians or any other American Indians; and maintain that Beverley's purpose in this passage and elsewhere in the book was to advocate both critical and constructive deism. In concluding, I briefly glance at other American writers who used the Amerindian to advocate deism.

Professor Maximillian E. Novak, probably the greatest Defoe scholar of this generation, contributes "Defoe, the Occult, and the Deist Offensive During the Reign of George I," focusing on several works by Defoe written in 1726 and 1727. In sketching the background of Defoe's works against the deists, Novak makes a new attribution to Defoe of the anonymous pamphlet *Some Remarks upon the Late Differences among the Dissenting Ministers and Preachers* (London: Boreham, 1719). He traces Defoe's replies to the deists (especially to John Toland and Anthony Collins) in *An Essay on the Original of Literature* (1726); *Mere Nature Delineated* (1726); *New Family Instructor* (1726); *The Political History of the Devil* (1727)—incidentally explaining the underlying reasons for Defoe's attack on Milton in that work; *A System of Magick* (1727); and *An Essay on the History and Reality of Apparitions* (1727). Novak concludes by explaining how the orthodox dissenter Defoe could seem to adopt and even to praise deistic beliefs in some of his fictions, while attacking them in polemical works.

Two essays examine the influence of Freemasonry on mid-eighteenth-century American writers. Professor David S. Shields claims in "Clio Mocks the Masons: Joseph Green's Anti-masonic Satires" that the Boston poet's scurrilous satires, written from 1739 to 1755, constitute the most elaborate poetic examination of a cultural institution in colonial America. In the course of describing Green's milieu, Shields expertly attributes several anonymous and pseudonymous poems to him; identifies for the first time another pseudonymous Boston poet, "V.D.," as John Hammock; explains why the New England "Old Light" Joseph Green objected to Freemasonry; and argues that Green's poems prefigure the personal satires that dominated Revolutionary American literature.

Professor Robert Micklus argues that Freemasonry was first and foremost a form of clubbing in the great age of clubs. His "The Secret Fall of Freemasonry in Dr. Alexander Hamilton's *The History of the Tuesday Club*" shows that Hamilton (who organized the Freemasons' society in Annapolis, Maryland, in 1749, served as its grand master and published a masonic "Discourse Delivered from the Chair in the Lodge-Room" recommending *"Charity, Benevolence,* and *Brotherly Love")* burlesques the trappings and the ideals of Freemasonry throughout his masterpiece, *The History of the Tuesday Club*. Micklus concludes that Hamilton felt secure enough about the role of Freemasonry in eighteenth-century society that he not only played upon the many popular misconceptions about it in his *History* but also constructed the book itself as a narrative that mockingly subverted its principles. Micklus's essay is, in many ways, the best testimony to the enormous influence of Freemasonry in the eighteenth century that I know.

INTRODUCTION

Two essays deal with writers who flourished at the end of the eighteenth century. Professor Carla Mulford's "Radicalism in Joel Barlow's *The Conspiracy of Kings* (1792)" shows the extent to which Barlow engaged in propagandizing radical social and political philosophy in support of the French Revolution. After supplying the contemporary political contexts for Barlow's poem, Mulford explains that in Barlow's radical view the old political and religious beliefs are now known to be lies (conspiracies by kings and other authorities); examines the sources of *The Conspiracy*, maintaining that Barlow echoes Constantin Volney's *Ruins* in the poem; shows how Barlow casts Edmund Burke in the role of a lying antichrist; explains the revolutionary mythology underlying the poem; suggests that William Blake's *America, Song of Liberty,* and *Visions of the Daughters of Albion* all reveal Barlow's influence; and indicates that Barlow's adaptation of the *Translatio Studii* to *Translatio Libertatis* characterized the later radical writings.

In the volume's final essay, "*The Age of Reason* versus *The Age of Revelation*. Two Critics of Tom Paine: David Levi and Elias Boudinot," Professor Richard H. Popkin argues that the two most significant replies to Paine's *Age of Reason* were written by the leading Anglo-Jewish scholar, David Levi, and by the sometime president of America's Continental Congress, Elias Boudinot. Popkin, a standard authority on the history of skeptical thought, points out that Levi and Boudinot were both erudite scholars who nevertheless believed they were living in providential history. He characterizes the main thrust of Levi's *Defense* (that the Pentateuch reports a series of prophecies by Moses that have been exactly fulfilled); presents the religious beliefs of Boudinot, pointing out that for both Levi and Boudinot the fulfillment of prophecies was offered as the strongest answer to Paine; and briefly sketches the background for Paine's skepticism. Popkin points out that although Thomas Paine's view that we are living in a secular rather than providential history has been dominant since the Enlightenment, the interpretation of events as part of providential history was an important aspect of the eighteenth century; and he notes that the resurgence of fundamentalism in the modern political world has a continuous history from Levi and Boudinot to the modern political states of Israel and the United States of America. While granting that it is impossible to understand the religious history of England and America without studying their evolution in the writing of Thomas Paine, Popkin also claims that it is equally impossible to understand the religious history of England and America without studying their evolution in the writings of Thomas Paine's opponents: "We are again living in the Age of Reason versus the Age of Revelation, and need to understand both sides." Like the opening essay by Roger L. Emerson, Richard H. Popkin's study shows that there is no possibility of agreement on the nature of reality without first defining the basic epistemological methodology of knowledge.

While rereading all of these essays, I was struck by the difference in the reputation of the British and the American writers. The British writers discussed in the volume are familiar to every student of the Enlightenment, but Robert Beverley, Joseph Green, Dr. Alexander Hamilton, and even, to some degree, the Americans of the Revolutionary period, Joel Barlow and Thomas Paine (and his opponents) are comparatively unfamiliar. That fact had much greater significance for Americans of the generation of the Revolution than it has for modern scholars—who are used to seeing some of their friends and colleagues pursue obscure byways through strange thickets. But what American intellectual of the Revolutionary generation could expect his contemporary British opponents to recognize the earlier colonial writers? Colonial and Revolutionary Americans primarily knew the writers and orators in their local newspapers, pamphlets, books, and legislature. In Virginia, people like Robert Beverley, Sir John Randolph, and Richard Bland were far more influential upon Robert Bolling, Patrick Henry, Thomas Jefferson, George Mason, and James Madison than were John Locke, Francis Hutchinson, Lord Bolingbroke, the classical republicans of the seventeenth century, and the opposition writers of the eighteenth century. But Bolling, Henry, Jefferson, Mason, and Madison could hardly cite the writings or the lives of their Virginia predecessors in their writings to their British intellectual opponents—or even in their writings for their contemporaries from other provinces of British America. To have a dialogue, the terms of reference must be held in common. Therefore the Revolutionary Americans almost always ignored their own most formative intellectual origins and cited the British and Continental authors so that they could be understood—and so that they would not be thought of as absolute provincials. But the preceding local writers and orators were more important in creating their beliefs and attitudes than all the British writers of the past. Because writers of the Revolutionary generation were forced to ignore their most important intellectual heroes and role models in their writings, subsequent students of American intellectual history have also generally ignored them. Scholars studying American culture, institutional history, and such details of legal history as impeachment in the United States Constitution, have shown that the colonial American background was the most important single influence upon the making of Revolutionary America; and I think that future intellectual historians of the Revolutionary period will also come to recognize the importance of the colonial period for the intellectual history of the American Revolutionary and early national periods.

Numerous topics relating to deism, masonry, and the Enlightenment are not treated in the following pages, but all of these essays make, I believe, valuable new contributions to the knowledge of English and American literature and culture during the Enlightenment. And all of them complement—and are also meant to compliment—the work in these areas done by our friend, fellow investigator, and teacher, Alfred Owen Aldridge.

J. A. Leo Lemay

Deism, Masonry,
and the Enlightenment

Latitudinarianism and the English Deists

ROGER L. EMERSON

During the last two decades studies of English deism and particular deists often have related that movement and its adherents to Anglican thought, particularly to latitudinarianism as it was expounded by John Tillotson and his friends. This paper seeks to explore some of the alleged connections between deism and liberal Anglican theology.

One old interpretation of deism as the culmination of heretical developments begun in the Reformation period has recently been restated by James O'Higgins, S.J. (1970, 50). Deism is inseparable from extreme Protestantism. Luther's defense of conscience and Christian freedom had strange consequences. In England these included the peculiar Christianity of Anthony Collins, whose natural religion could have been derived from Anglican rationalists such as John Tillotson (O'Higgins 1970, 46ff.). After considering the influences which Collins's books and library catalogue suggest at work in his thought, Father O'Higgins concluded in his excellent study of this deist:

> Collins therefore represents an extreme product of a long process. As far as can be gathered from his writings, and from his library, it was not English Socinians, whom in many ways he resembled, not the scientists, who had the greatest influence on him. Bayle had a great deal. But the most important was that of a long chain that leads from Hales to Chillingworth and the Cambridge Platonists to the Latitudinarians and such men as Locke even though these would not have agreed with his conclusions. Varaisse and Tyssot de Patot might have affinities with him but he had reached his position mainly through a different, and that an English route. (50)

The liberal Anglicans of Collins's time had produced a church and an intellectual ambience in which this so-called deist could be a practicing Anglican "ambiguous [and] anti-Christian though his later works were" (234). Where others have painted a hypocrite and unbelieving freethinker, Father O'Higgins has given us a portrait of Collins that is more nuanced and finely drawn:

His death-bed remarks confirm its ambiguity. He believed in God and a future life. There was something which he considered to be true religion and he associated himself with it. He was a member of the Established Church, and he did not like to be accused of hypocrisy because he so belonged. He was just on or just over the fringe of protestant Christianity. In spite of his books against Revelation and his defence of natural religion, it is doubtful if he had ever really analyzed and defined his position. It was one that had grown out of the Christianity of Locke and the Latitudinarians. (234)

The long tradition running from Hooker to Locke ended in the latitudinarianism, Socinianism, deism, or free thought of Anthony Collins.[1] But what was true of him, O'Higgins suggests, was also true of others as well because Collins was a rather typical radical intellectual (1, 2, 236). A case has recently been made for considering John Toland's work in a similar manner.

The Reverend Robert Sullivan's fine book, *John Toland and the Deist Controversy: A Study in Adaptations*, places Toland in a latitudinarian and Socinian context (109, 139, 174). From that he moved not only to deism but to pantheism (17, 204), the esoteric doctrine of wise men who should reform the Anglican church to its true national role of "fostering moral instruction and general peace, order and happiness" (170). Father Sullivan writes, "In his critique of Christian orthodoxy, Toland systematically developed arguments which Socinians had broached and Anglican rationalists were to accommodate. At the same time he was the only putative deist who openly embraced a coherent materialism."[2] Toland, like Collins, is at the margin of Anglican thought. To call him a deist is not to describe his views but to assert a distinction between free thought and liberal Christianity that is ultimately unreal, without much meaning, or at best "elusive" (Sullivan 1982, 274–77; cf. O'Higgins 1970, 52).[3]

Dr. Sullivan's chapter on the "elusiveness of deism" (204–34) argues that attempts to define deism have failed mainly for two reasons. The definitions have been too general and unable to exclude "nominal or rational Christianity" (215) and its adherents. Second, they have failed to delineate a set of opinions consistently held by so-called deists (213, 215). Toland and Collins never explicitly acknowledged their alleged deism; Matthew Tindal did so only very late in his career (215). All three may have called themselves Christians mainly because, like Toland, they "accepted membership in the Church of England as an element of citizenship" (17). What may be of greater importance is Sullivan's claim that "until his death Toland would be treated as a Socinian" (109). Even enemies, such as Daniel Defoe, were "reluctant to accuse Toland of deism" (109). At best, definitions of deism such as those offered by Günter Gawlick only "credibly describe the purposes of [the deistical] writers" (Sullivan 1982, 215, 233). These purposes unfortunately were little different from those that "most Anglican rationalists eventually adopted" and incorporated into a "Georgian Anglicanism" (275). That, ironically, was close in content, structure, and outlook to what Sullivan describes as Toland's "civil theology" (170–72, 269–73). Dr. Sullivan advises us to recognize *deism* as "a convenient term to describe the revision of traditional Christian formulas which occupied so many English writers between the Civil War and the French Revolution" (274). He sees its supporters as "engaged in a theological conversation" (273) with Anglican rationalists, Socinians, and Unitarians. While this comment is not likely to clarify the debate or identify the deistic debaters, it at least concentrates attention on religious issues and not upon the materialism and politics of thinkers who were seen first and foremost as engaged in debates over theological doctrines and clerical institutions. Deism for Sullivan is a synonym for "freethinking or rational theology." He also says that "habit is powerful enough to ensure that [historians] will continue to use deism" (274) as an alternative to those terms. Incoherent though it may have been, deism was an historical force that shaped "the Georgian civil religion" (271) until that was destroyed by the Oxford Movement (272). Deism was not refuted by liberal antideists whose works "shared presuppositions and a common discourse" (273).

Richard Westfall has also seen Enlightenment deism as "the religion of reason which grew to maturity in the tradition that Newton completed" (1958, 218–19). Anglican apologists for a *via media*, learned *virtuosi* needing to assuage their own doubts and relieve their anxieties about their orthodoxy as they pursued the new sciences, those seeking irenic grounds for Christian unity—all these produced a natural religion "meant to supplement Christianity, to provide it with a rational foundation" (106). They produced instead a natural religion that displaced Christianity and "omitted its spiritual teachings" (144):

> While the virtuosi concentrated vigorously on the demonstration of natural religion and proved to their own satisfaction that the cosmos revealed its Creator, they came to neglect their own contention that natural religion is only the foundation. The supernatural teachings of Christianity received little more that a perfunctory nod, expressing approval but indicating disinterest. Although the absorption in natural religion and the external manifestations of divine power did not dispute any specific Christian doctrine, it did more to undermine Christianity than any conclusions of natural science. (106–7)

Deism, which to so many orthodox divines was not better than atheism, was promoted by the work of Anglican scientists and apologists. Their natural religion became the deism of the Enlightenment and the rational Christianity of unspiritual men of the eighteenth century: "Change only the attitudes, remove the reverence for Christianity that the virtuosi maintained, in a word move only from the religious 17th century into the doubting 18th and deism, the religion of reason, steps full grown from the writings of the Christian virtuosi" (219). Voltaire was the heir of latitudinarians.

Margaret Jacob has put forth a similar view (1976, 28–71). For the latitudinarians, as for the deists, "rational argumentation and not faith is the final arbiter of Christian belief and dogma" (34). Anglican rational religion became the Whiggish deism of organized Grand Lodge Freemasonry and the somnolent Georgian church of England (1981, 65–108). Like Westfall she sees Anglican rationalism as a response to the fears of atheism and the violence of enthusiastic sectaries. At the same time she describes another form of deism that drew not only on the Anglican apologists but also upon the "atheists" and sectaries whom the former were concerned to refute and control. This second kind of wild deism was compounded not only from Renaissance naturalism, pantheism, Hobbist materialism, Spinozism, and other philosophic errors but also from religious and political heresies rampant during the period 1640–60 (1981, 109–15):

> During the English Revolution particular natural philosophies came to be associated with particular political and social theories, or occasionally with political behavior. For instance, radicals such as the Levellers preached and wrote about nature in a way that can best be described as pantheistic and materialistic. (1976, 23–24)

After 1660 Anglicans sought to control the expression of such errors by the construction of a broad if repressive church whose doctrinal commitments would be few. They insisted upon moral behavior as the true expression of faith. Controlled at the popular level but not at court, these heresies threatened to revive after 1688. The Glorious Revolution lit again the hopes of sectaries and those who regarded civil society as a mere contrivance of human power and wisdom for the satisfaction of the more basic human wants. Correctly, she thinks, Anglicans discerned a cabal of deists and freethinkers (Leslie 1694, 14, 26) bent on "merging the republicanism of the English Revolution with religious and philosophical radicalism" (1976, 202).[4] Pantheists participating equally in a material God would by right pursue their selfish interests (1976, 227; 1981, 72–73). In this world churches were mere engines of repression and religions a contrivance for civil order or the true but esoteric beliefs of the enlightened. This ideological deism was hardly conservative and sedate. Not Voltaire but Holbach was to be its exponent in France among the major *philosophes* (1981, 256–66). There were, however, others who made of this complex of beliefs the core of a radical enlightenment that was institutionalized in clubs and unregulated lodges of speculative Freemasons (1981, 23–27). Among these Masons Jacob finds Toland, Collins, and a number of Dutch and French publishers, men of letters, and artists (1981, 143–76). As the conservative deists were Newtonians, so these men had a science that found matter not inert but active, and the world less mechanical than vital and organic. Nature was not composed of the dead, inert material required by the Newtonian system. While Sullivan and Westfall saw the controversies between the orthodox and the deists as curiously inconclusive, Professor Jacob sees the Anglican apologists, the Christian deists, as having won the ideological war if not the war of truth. Newtonian ideology triumphed. No leveling republicans came to power. The world was kept safe for property owners to pursue a new "possessive individualism."[5] The wild deists were driven underground and out of England. The tame ones became Grand Lodge Freemasons, Voltairean deists, or Anglicans who regarded a short rational creed and a good life as the marks of the Christian. That is pretty much what O'Higgins and Sullivan find institutionalized in the Georgian church. Shaftesbury's religion of all wise men, supplemented by Newtonianism, provided the antidote against wild deism and atheism. One might do well to remember that among Professor Jacob's principal exponents of this creed were Richard Bentley, Samuel Clarke, and William Whiston, none of whom was an orthodox Anglican (Westfall 1980, 649–53). Indeed, all of them were denied promotion because of their heterodoxy. It is unlikely that most Anglicans were of their persuasion. Certainly the Lower House of Convocation was not.

All four of these authors have asserted links between liberal Anglicanism, latitudinarianism, and deism that seem questionable and would not have been accepted by most writers in 1700. Perhaps we too should look at them more carefully.

Déiste has been in use since 1564 while *déisme* dates from 1660. The more pious English had no use for their cognate words until 1621 and 1682 (Sullivan 1982, 205–215). Early writers did not sharply separate deists from atheists but they did tend to attribute to the former a disbelief in revealed religion. Pierre Viret's deists of 1564 believed in God "comme les Turcs & les Juifs" but not all of them could have believed in revelation since some thought "la doctrine des Evangelists, & des Apostres" only "fables & reveries." Recognizing a creator, some deists treated him in an Epicurean fashion: "there are among them some who believe in immortality of souls: others think like the Epicureans [on this subject] and similarly about the providence of God in human affairs: as if He does not involve himself in the government of things human, but that they are governed either by chance or by the folly of men as the case may be" (Viret 1594, 2: Epistle Dedicatory; my translation).[6] Viret's deists seem to have called themselves Christians but they clearly had a religion that all men could share and one that in some cases did not rest on revelation but upon ancient rational speculations about God.

There are other sixteenth-century figures who seem to share these characteristics. Roger Ascham's "Italinate Englishmen" and the Italians they aped were "atheists" who denied the "Fables, the holie misteries of Christianity" because they were "Epicures," made such by the extravagancies of Rome:

> And yet, thies men, in matters of Divinitie, openlie pretend to great knowledge, and having priuately to them selues a verie compendious vnderstanding of all, which neuertheless they will vtter when and where they liste: And that is this: All the misteries or *Moses*, the whole lawe and Cerimonies, the Psalmes and Prophecies, Christ and his Gospell, GOD and the Deuill, Heauen and Hell, Faith, Conscience, Sinne, Death, and all they shortlie wrap vp, they quicklie expounde with this one halfe verse of Horace. *Credat Judaeus Appella*. (Ascham [1563–68], 78–83)

Ascham's well-born and traveled unbelievers had their counterparts at all social strata by about 1600. Learned "atheists" like Giordano Bruno or Lucilio Vanini were contemporary with allegedly blasphemous loose-living Englishmen such as Thomas Nashe and Robert Greene whose works, like Cyril Tourneur's *The Atheist's Tragedy* (1611), were known in less erudite circles. So too were pieces like the Ballad of Jasper Coningham (Roxburghe 1869–99, 3:103–110; Pepys 1929, 3:183), which appeared in print around 1600.[7] Indeed, there was a constant and growing stream of allegations that atheism and deism were flourishing at every social level. In England by 1621 there was no lack of what Robert Burton classed as "religious melancholy in defect":

> . . . in defect march those impious Epicures, Libertines, Atheists, Hypocrites, Infidels, worldly secure, impenitent, unthankful, and carnal-minded men that attribute all to natural causes, that will acknowledge no supreme power; that have cauterized consciences, or live in a reprobate sense; or such distrustful persons as are too distrustful of his mercies. (Burton 1621, 873; 925)

Sick, melancholy and preyed upon by the Devil, this legion of the irreligious sometimes held "all Religion a fiction" and "Nature but God" (929). In 1621 Burton called the deists, "Couzin-germans to these men" and remarked that "too much learning makes them mad" (929). From the very appearance of the word *deist* it was usually taken as denoting someone who denied revelation but affirmed some set of ideas not unlike those which Dr. Jacob assigned to the deists who came to prominence in the 1690s (1976, 205). Perhaps deism was promoted by the apologists' discussion of it and Socianism.[8]

Between the 1620s and the late 1670s no works arguing for deism appeared in England, for Lord Herbert of Cherbury was no deist, however much he believed in natural theology.[9] Deists may have existed but blasphemy laws, censorship, and prudence kept them silent.[10] It was left to others to define their views. By the late 1670s one man who later acknowledged the label then coming into use (Welsh 1956, 165) did begin to publicly express the ideas of the rakes and freethinkers among whom he moved. Charles Blount's works and publications comprised the best-known examples of deism and were refuted by latitudinarian writers (Allen 1964, 192–200; Berman 1983, 379; Redwood 1974, 490–98). They thought, quite correctly, that their natural religion differed profoundly from that of Charles Blount or his protégé Charles Gildon.

For Blount reason was the only source of man's knowledge. Dependent upon the senses, passions, and desires of man, it functioned mainly as a calculating faculty relating ends and means. It also sought and was properly guided by clear and self-evident truths. There was no higher source of authority: "REASON, therefore, being the Supream and Primitive Director of every Man, to infringe its Liberty of directing, is to invade the Common Charter of Nature, and every Man's Right and Property; so that those that do so, are justly to be look'd on as Enemies of Humane-kind" (1695, unnumbered pp. 7–28, 27). Among these enemies were the crafty priests and politicians who had, like Moses and Mahomet, pretended to have revelations. Reason knew only "Nature, or that Sacred and Supream CAUSE of all Things, which we term GOD" (unnumbered p. 25) but which we could not call triune or expect to intervene in the affairs of men. Blount's religion was unambiguously anti-Christian. By 1679 Blount had questioned the reality of spirits and revelation in blasphemous works that likened "most of the Christian Churches to the Muskmelons from the Dunghill . . . [which] were raised out of the filthy Corruption and Superstition of Paganism" (1679, 122). In 1680 he produced an un-Christian gloss on the Pauline account of Diana of the Ephesians (Acts 19:23; 1680a). And he published a translation of *The Two First Books of Philostratus, Concerning the Life of Apollonius Tyaneus*, a Neoplatonic mystagogue whose life resembled that of Christ. From 1680 until his death by suicide in 1693 Blount continued to write and sometimes clandestinely published short works that bore out Gildon's claim that "he kept all profane Notions of God at a distance and prefer'd those writ by the finger of the Almighty Creator in the minds of all mankind, to the *Obscure, unintelligible* and impious Doctrines, devis'd by men to serve some turn or particular Faction or Nation" (1695; unnumbered p. 7). Blount's works contain a potpourri of critical ideas drawn from many sources—the classics, Erasmus, Chillingworth, Hobbes, Spinoza, and Bayle. His pieces form a pandemonium in which the unifying theme is the rejection of all revealed religion and Christianity in particular. Often covert (Allen 1964, 192–200), this position is clear in *A Summary Account of the Deists Religion* in which Blount condemned the "Idolatry" of even the Socinians (1695, 87–90).[11] This and other squibs, including some not by him, were reprinted by Charles Gildon in *The Oracles of Reason* (1693) and in the *Miscellaneous Works* (1695). Gildon was to recant similar views in the *Deist's Manual* (1705) and in his *Miscellanea Aurea* (1720).

Blount and Gildon defined deism or "atheism" (Berman 1983, 378–83) for the generation writing ca. 1675–1700 (Harth 1968, 56–94; Nicholls 1696–97, preface). It was a view which held that a set of principles of natural religion can be known by reason to be true or at least probable (Harth 1961, 21; 1968, 58–61). These principles included a rejection of all religious beliefs dependent upon grace dispensed in some supernatural or mysterious way as in revelation (Gildon 1705, passim). The deists were Pelagians. Attendant upon these views were a variety of others that criticized religious beliefs and practices or that often tried to explain them. The explanations involved a variety of metaphysical propositions, some of which led to an identification of God with nature. These were the beliefs that Blount and Gildon owned and that they claimed others shared (Gildon 1720, 235). They called themselves *deists* and applied to their beliefs and themselves terms used by them and their contemporaries as synonyms for *deist* and *deism*. When Gildon later abandoned deism and became an Anglican, he called the deists "Free-Thinkers" whose beliefs were based upon "a Sort of dogmatical *Ipse dixit*" (1720, 235). They were, he then thought, "fools" and atheists but his characterization of them as deniers of revealed religion did not change (235–40).

The essence of Blount's definition of a deist is, then, the claim that only natural knowledge was possible and that all true or correct belief had to be based on reasons that were self-evidently true (e.g., O'Higgins 1970, 52–53). Those claims allowed for a wide diversity of beliefs but they made the heart and center of deism an epistemological claim spelled out in a religious context. Such a definition of deism has been too often rejected. The result has been an unhelpful blurring of distinctions between deists and those who opposed them. Without retaining this distinction it is difficult to make sense of the Anglican apologetics that were aimed at establishing the reasonableness of Christians' belief in Christ's message of hope and in the act of sacrifice related in the New Testament (Harth 1968, 95–173). After the 1690s no one was apparently more successful in this venture than the various Boyle Lecturers, many of whom sought to refute the deists. To do so they had to define or characterize the position they attacked.

The Boyle Lecturers may have "created the Newtonian ideology as a justification for the pursuit of self-interest, for a Christianized capitalist ethic" (Jacob 1976, 160), but their official obligations were "to preach Eight Sermons in the Year for proving the Christian Religion against notorious Infidels, *viz.* Atheists, Deists, Jews and Mahometans, not descending to Controversies that are among Christians themselves."[12] The mandate of the lecturers was thus restricted in many ways not usually noticed. Doctrinal exposition, bound to be contentious, was to be and was more or less avoided (Dahm 1970, 172–74). One cannot then use these sermons as tests of what really constituted Anglicanism or latitudinarianism. Second, the sermons had to give reasons to believe in revealed Christianity to those upon whom the mere preaching of the Word was likely to make no impression (Kroiter 1960, 512). The logic of the apologists' situation made it imperative for them to address their infidels in terms upon which both sides might agree. In the late seventeenth and early eighteenth centuries, as for Richard Hooker a hundred years earlier, those terms were set out in rational religion and in the theories of knowledge that make it possible. That Anglican divines should stress these aspects of their thought in the Boyle Lectures should not surprise us nor lead us to conclude that Anglicanism was no more than a Christianized deism. It had mysteries, revelations, and miracles that every lecturer defended. Finally, the early lecturers did indeed address themselves to atheists, deists, Jews, and Moslems.[13] As they did so, they frequently discussed deism. This they tended to see principally as the rationally defended belief in the existence of God accompanied by a denial of all revealed religion and by various other doctrines that varied from deist to deist and from lecturer to lecturer. Among the early writers Blount was the chief bogey man; it was his and Gildon's specification of deism that was accepted.

Richard Bentley in 1692 alluded to Blount when he wrote that deists "understand [God to be] no more than some inanimate Matter, some universal Nature, and Soul of the World, Void of all Sense and Cogitation, so far from being endowed with infinite Wisdom and Goodness" (Boyle Lectures 1739, 1:3). Nature's religion was not revealed but rational and had as little a place for active matter in Bentley's scheme as in those of the Cambridge Platonists. In the lectures given between 1694 and 1702 the principal deist was still Blount. He, like others, was said to have had bad and immoral reasons to hold his views. Antideistical polemics resumed in earnest with the lectures of Samuel Clarke in 1704. He too thought deists claimed to have all their knowledge "by the light of Nature alone" (2:77). After Clarke's lectures the cast of deists increased but the definition of their essential beliefs remained the same. Even William Berriman in 1730–32, writing against Jews, Toland, Tindal, and Collins, says that *"Deism if taken in the best Sense, admits all the Principles of Natural Religion, and lays such a Foundation, upon which we might easily convince Men of the Truth of Christianity, when brought into a proper Light"* (3:596). Deism for the Anglicans was indeed rational but not enough. It attributed too much ability and certainty to men. For Berriman and others this confidence masked evil ends: "But it is greatly to be feared that they who pretend to *Deism* at present, do take it only in the negative Sense, as it disclaims the Truth of Revelation; and do not so much acknowledge the Existence of a God, as deny what is fit to be believed concerning Him." He went on to say that *"Deism* and *Atheism* are but two Names for one and the same Thing"* (3:596). Even at midcentury Henry Stebbing spoke of the deists as men who denied the possibility of revelation. They were upholders of natural religion but not of the Fall or any revealed truth. In words reminiscent of Tillotson's, Stebbing wrote:

> I think the proper Work of a Defender of *Christianity* is to defend it upon the foot that Christ taught it, that is, upon the foot of *Natural Religion*. Natural Religion is and must be the Foundation of all Religions; and in this Sense *Jesus Christ* was a Teacher of Natural Religion as he required the Practice of it. But his *Message* was *Pardon* and *Reconciliation* to Sinners, which is the proper Subject of his Revelation. (1720, vi)

The meaning of deism does not seem to be so elusive after all. By 1700 deists thought of it as including a denial of revealed religion. Their Anglican opponents had claimed since the 1620s that this is what deism entailed. They desperately sought to show the necessity of revelation in work after work. Perhaps here we should agree with Peter Gay:

> To remote observers, the distance between radical Protestants and deists might seem negligible, but to contemporaries it was decisive. It made all the difference if one accepted revelation, no matter how attenuated, or the Christian God, no matter how remote, or rejected both revelation and the Christian God altogether. The deists might be religious men but in their natural religion, nature was primary and religion evaporated. (1968, 11–12)

Gay says that deism stood in an "intimate" but "dialectical" relationship "to its environment," but that it was also "remote" because it had ceased to possess a supernatural and revealed dimension (12). This seems a fair statement of the case and one that applies to the works of Collins and Toland for whom there were no mysteries in religion. Throughout its early history deism has been principally associated with the denial of revealed religion. To see it as little different from Anglican liberalism is to overlook a history still real to the polemicists of the early 1700s and to make light of their evaluations of their own beliefs and apologetic positions. It is, in short, to wrench the deistic controversy out of context. Deism did not emerge as a reaction to the disorders of the English Civil War. It had a character that was already formed by the 1640s and that was retained well into the eighteenth or even the nineteenth century.[14] The development of latitudinarianism was not necessary for the emergence of deism in England and it is not sufficient to account for it. The numerous references to Epicurus, to other classical sources, to Erasmus, Spinoza, and Bayle show that. They also show that deism and the English deists belong to a European debate about knowledge more than to an English debate about social and political order. To that question we should now turn.

Deism, like the moralism of Anglicans after 1660, was in part a response to the extravagancies of Rome, Geneva, and various sectaries. Pierre Viret's deists were men, who, he thought, abused the liberty given them to criticize idolatry and superstition. Their Protestantism had gone too far, just as Ascham's Englishmen had gone too far in their reactions to Catholicism.

Both men believed that among the inducements to go too far were various selfish interests such as "present pleasure and private profit." That explanation of deism came rather naturally to men who believed in the reality of the Fall and in the sinfulness of men. But Viret also noticed that the intellectuals who became deists were well educated and clever men:

> I am horrified when I think that among those who bear the name of Christian there are such monsters. But my horror is even redoubled when I consider that many of those who make a profession of learning and humanistic [rational] philosophy and who are often times esteemed the most knowing and of most acute and subtle minds, are not only infected with this Atheism but also hold and teach it in the schools and infect others with this poison. (n. 6; my translation)

They resembled the philosophers whom Burton thought learning and the Devil had made mad. All three commentators recognized that deism and the so-called atheism to which it was related arose in a context formed by Reformation controversies, revived classical philosophy, which now included skepticism, and the thought of moderns such as Machiavelli, Bruno, Vanini, Lord Herbert, and others who sought a replacement for decadent and exhausted scholastic philosophies. In short they placed the deists in a context well described in English by R. H. Popkin (1964), Walter Rex (1965), Brian Armstrong (1969), H. G. Van Leeuwen (1970), and Barbara Shapiro (1983). What characterized that intellectual scene was an earnest search for the criteria of truth, certainty, and correct belief, for what Locke was to tag "the Original, Certainty, and Extent of human Knowledge; together with the grounds and degrees of Belief, Opinion and Assent" (1700, 43). What was at stake was not merely epistemological theories or social questions but the rule of faith—as Chillingworth said, salvation and a safe way to it. Deism belongs to this debate because it held with Blount, Toland, Collins, and others that all knowledge is merely human and that the grounds of belief include none that are miraculous. All that is or can be known is known empirically or rationally and tells us nothing supernatural. Its opponents recognized what we should remember—that this denial of the possibility of revealed knowledge was indeed a significant and radical change in the epistemological revolution of the seventeenth century. Deists, unlike the latitudinarians, were prepared to take that step and to eliminate the realm of grace both from man's consciousness and from the world (Harth 1961, 41). That was a shocking thing to do. It fundamentally altered the conception of the intellectual world. To oppose it for religious, philosophical, and dialectical reasons was perfectly natural for Christian apologists. They needed no social, economic, political, or ideological motives for doing so.

Anyone who has looked at the schematized philosophical systems diagrammed in some editions of the works of Bacon, Locke, Wolff, or in various eighteenth-century encyclopedias should recognize that the systems there laid out contain or imply both realms of nature and grace. Natural philosophy leads up to God; rational theology leads to revealed and dogmatic theology or at least to a discussion of their claims. These systems are also holistically related. No part exists in isolation from another. In a priori and deductive systems everything flows from a few metaphysical propositions. In more empirical constructions, one mounts analytically but expounds the system synthetically in a deductive fashion. In nature all is related. Change one portion of the system and the whole structure requires modification and amendment. The task of latitudinarian writers in seventeenth-century England was largely to defend the probability of revelation and their conceptions of its meaning for the Anglican church. In doing so they had to adjust to profound shifts in the character of natural knowledge and its relation to the realm of grace. How they did this has been nicely summarized by Barbara Shapiro. To reintegrate human knowledge both natural and revealed, to defend it against skeptics, and to bring coherence to philosophy was the aim of every notable thinker of the time. It had been the goal of the pansophists (Manuel 1979, 205–21) and it remained the aspiration of the fellows of the Royal Society of London, of Newton and Locke. In this process of adjustment it was important to show that the tenets of natural religion were still supported by natural philosophy and that both justified the Anglican *via media*. It required no special motives rooted in changing social, economic, or political circumstances. Some Catholics and Protestants and most skeptics had denied that this task could be accomplished. The latitudinarian contribution to this task was great and complex but it had its continental counterparts and was not unique.[15] Moreover, it was an activity that remained within the realm of natural knowledge, as did the moral philosophy of the period.

Natural religion and its attendant moralism might constitute a deist's religion but they did not constitute the substance of the Christianity that latitudinarians professed (Sykes 1959, 146–52). The hope and promise of salvation through Christ rested upon revelations and mysteries that had no place in the realm of natural knowledge but did find a niche in the systems of the pious but not in those of the deists (181–86; Reedy 1978–79, 238–240). It is hardly fair to say of men like the Boyle Lecturers or other Anglican polemicists against deism that they, like "English religious thinkers in the late seventeenth century[,] came to assign meaning to religion in so far as it served a social function" (Jacob 1976, 185). Religion did indeed do so and had always done so because religion was held to be closely related to morality. Christians could not discuss one without the other. This was hardly new. Indeed, Burton in 1621 seems to deplore those things that Dr. Jacob finds the latitudinarians condemning in the 1690s (52–61):

Our love in spiritual things is too defective, in worldly things too excessive. . . . We love the world too much; God too little, our neighbour not at all, or for our own ends. . . . The chief thing we respect is our commodity: and what we do, is for fear of worldly punishment, for vain-glory, praise of men, fashion, and such by-respects, not for God's sake . . . we involve ourselves into a multitude of errors, we swerve from the true love and worship of God which is a cause unto us of unspeakable miseries. (1938, 929)

Where religion is lacking, there is no virtue; where there is no morality, there is no binding obligation to civil order. Political and social questions were related to religious ones within a system of natural knowledge used and presupposed by Anglican apologists. "Religion," as Dr. Jacob writes, "performed the task of contributing order to society, of checking greed and avarice, or ensuring stability within the society it served to cement" (185). All that was trite in 1621 and recognized as a function of both natural and revealed religion. Indeed, one might think it would come to mind rather naturally among divines who read the Old and New Testaments, the Apocrypha, or just the catechetical injunctions to do one's duty to God and to honor and obey civil authorities by submitting to governors, masters, and all one's betters. Religion might be social cement but it was also the promise of pardon and redemption, a promise unavoidably tied to the mysteries of the Incarnation and the Trinity. To confine religion merely to its natural and moral roles is to make nonsense of the structures of thought used by deists and orthodox alike (Sykes 1959, 156–69; Harth 1961, 13–51). The deistic controversy was about the shape, size, and character of the intellectual world and about how one was to know it. For the latitudinarians that world was more than a moral and rational one (McAdoo 1965, 158–240). It remained a world still committed to a traditional Anglicanism that emerges in the sermons of John Tillotson, the man who has often seemed to be no better than a deist to historians.[16]

Dr. Sullivan's reading of the latitudinarians and of Tillotson seems fairly typical but wrong in its insistence that they were unfaithful to Christian orthodoxy and did not preach Christ and Him crucified. He begs too many questions when he says that latitudinarians did not find a place for "the necessity of and act of faith, an individual's recognition and acceptance of the incarnate God [which] was the redoubt of the God of history in the Augustan religious sensibility" (63). By "insisting on both the fallibility and naturalness of Christian assent [Tillotson] tended to limit the range and efficiency of the Spirit's activity. He had always to work within the confines of order and propriety" (64). Supervenient grace as the mark of a true Christian tended to be replaced by sincere obedience to moral laws proclaimed to all men by a secular reason and merely republished with emphasis and ceremony in the Old and New Testaments. Tillotson and his like had "transformed grace from a divine gift into a human attainment" (66). In doing so they had become Pelagians and had shown again that "[it] was impossible to be consistently rational and still remain doctrinally orthodox" (55). Their errors were shared by Dutch Arminians and English Socinians, in whose camp Tillotson and his colleagues found friends (51–53). All three groups reduced the Christian message to a natural morality separable from revealed religion. This rational religion became the basis for a policy of broad church comprehensiveness providing "easy terms of submission" (59) to all who prized religious peace and unity. A short creed, tolerance, and a polite abstention from asserting contentious theological or ecclesiastical doctrines in systematic theologies (65) marked the outlook of a church unfaithful to historical and scriptural Christianity. It justified a church "seen as an expression of nationality" (59) and one that provided social stability in a world made dangerous by resurgent Catholicism manipulated by Louis XIV. Because the latitudinarians were bad Christians, they could be useful to men like Toland and Collins. They accepted the latitudinarian outlook and could even remain within the Anglican church because it was no longer very Christian. That its leaders were still committed to further reformation made it easy for the deists to propose means to that end (131, 171).

Tillotson's own doctrinal shortcomings are summed up by Father Sullivan in the following way:

> The specific challenge "But whom say ye that I am?"[17] perplexed the Anglican rationalists. At times Tillotson referred to "the depravation of our nature." Still, by failing clearly to relate the Incarnation to original sin and insisting that Christianity is compatible with ordinary reason, he blunted such references. He could paint so bleak a picture of man's natural condition that the weakest sign of rational or moral life amounted to a reflection of divine energy. As he neglected to shade his portrait with Calvin's contempt for every merely human activity, he managed to turn all helpful actions into tokens of divine favor. A coherent soteriology eluded him. Once the juridical events of Calvary were over, well-intentioned individuals were able to "aspire so much as is possible to become like" Christ in the assurance of receiving divine assistance in proportion to their own enterprise. Tillotson was vague about the role of a mediator in creating such aspirations. Notwithstanding his vagueness he was confident that the question contained little mystery. By identifying justification with "the whole Christian religion" after having reduced Christianity to the disciplinary promptings of the moral sense, he virtually guaranteed that he would achieve clarity. (67–68)

Late-seventeenth-century Anglican theology, as Father Sullivan sees it, was untraditional, unscriptural, incoherent, and too naturalistic to be truly Christian. It tried to square a circle. But "in trying to square this circle Latitudinarians virtually reduced Christianity to morality, first by treating as natural what had always been seen as supernatural, then by ignoring, redefining, or eliminating all refractory elements" (55). Latitudinarianism led logically to deism. We should test these claims before we accept them. Specifically, we should look more closely at Tillotson's views of reason, natural theology, faith and revelation, the role of Christ and the sacraments he established. In doing so it helps to remember the polemical context in which he wrote (Reedy 1978–79, 239).

Tillotson's sermons were the great rhetorical exemplars of latitudinarianism. They were widely read, republished well into the nineteenth century, and used throughout the eighteenth by students, preachers, literati, and ordinary Anglicans. Constituting as clear and important a source of latitudinarian ideas as there is, they ought not be approached with the belief that one must make a leap of faith in order to understand. The archbishop was no Tertullian, no Pascal, no Kierkegaard (Carroll 1975, 1–3).[18] It does help to remember that, like most sixteenth- and seventeenth-century Anglicans, Tillotson was arguing against skeptics, Catholic and Protestant fideists, and sectaries who believed direct inspiration was the basis of their religion. The sermons are for the most part polemical, with Catholics being his chief concern. In this respect they resemble many other expressions of the Anglican *via media* during times when Catholicism and particularly Catholic fideism was seen as a menace. But other skeptics, even Socinians (Reedy 1978–79, 239), were never far from his thoughts. Tillotson's demonstrations of the existence of God were also rooted in dialectical motives not so different from those of Descartes. They were designed to show that a natural religion is possible and that worship and morality are entailed by it. In this respect Tillotson's tradition on the one hand ran back through Chillingworth, Hooker, and Jewel to Saint Thomas; on the other it owed a debt to Calvin and in the end to Augustine. Tillotson, like many of his friends, was something of a scholastic theologian. He still believed that reason constituted the most important means for the construction of a theology. But that theology was dual in nature, being both natural and revealed.

Natural theology comes from man reflecting upon the natural and moral world (Tillotson 1722, 1:343, 404, 559). This view was quite traditional and can be found in the scholastics, notably in the works of Aquinas. His natural theological conclusions Saint Thomas called "not articles of faith, but . . . preambles to the articles; for faith presupposes natural knowledge, even as grace presupposes nature and perfection the perfectible" (Aquinas 1948, 24).[19] Reason can establish the existence of God, analyze his moral, physical, and, perhaps, his intellectual powers. It can show that we are bound by his moral law and have duties to him and to his other creatures (Tillotson 1722, 1:570). Reason also knows what it does not and cannot know. That establishes the need for revelation (2:321). Revelation addresses our ignorance but it will not contradict the truths of natural religion (1:343). God is not of two minds although he may reveal mysteries that we cannot understand (1:744). What we can do is: test what is testable by the truths of natural theology; be critical in our acceptance of facts concerning alleged revelations and test revealed messages by those we take to be authentic. In all this Tillotson was saying things that were believed by many of his opponents.

Seventeenth-century Jesuits shared in the scholastic heritage and found a place for natural religion in their systems. Indeed, most Catholics were not heretical fideists (Harth 1968, 99), but held that "since right reason was itself the word of God no one who understands right reason was wholly ignorant of divine law" (Palmer 1961, 42) or of natural religion. Calvin too had said as much. Fallen though we be, we have a natural knowledge of God and of the principles of natural theology. An awareness of God "exists in the human mind, and indeed by natural instinct [we have] some sense of deity." Calvin went on to say that "this belief is naturally engendered in all, and thoroughly fixed as it were in our very bones." There can be no real atheists although "scarcely one in a hundred is found who cherishes [this knowledge and fears God] in his heart, and not one in whom it grows to maturity, so far is it from yielding fruit in its season" (Calvin 1962, 1:40–44). Tillotson shared the premises but not the pessimistic conclusion. Likewise, he shared Calvin's belief that "the visible worlds [are] as images of the invisible (Heb. XI.3), the elegant structure of the world serving us as a kind of mirror, in which we may behold God, though otherwise invisible" (1:51–52). From this natural knowledge of God should come fear, worship, and a moral life (Tillotson 1722, 1:699). While our knowledge—compared with that of unfallen Adam—is imperfect, it suffices to give us a natural knowledge of God, of his law written on our hearts, and of our inability to keep it. Calvin noted, as Tillotson was to do, that "it is one thing to perceive that God our Maker supports us by his power, rules us by his providence, fosters us by his goodness, and visits us with all kinds of blessings, and another thing to embrace that reconciliation offered to us in Christ" (Calvin 1962, 1:40). That has been provided for sinners who are heedless of what nature shows. Consequently reconciliation has been offered to us by God who "supplement[ed] these common proofs by the addition of his Word, as a surer and more direct means of discovering himself" (1:65). This he has done in successive dispensations until the time of Christ and the apostles (1:68). The Gospel then, is a republication of the pristine religion lost by Adam to which have been added promises of redemption. Believing in this Gospel, we may be saved by God's grace and by faith but it cannot be known to be certainly true (1:72). Proofs from miracles, prophecies, the witness of martyrs, the testimony of the Church, the harmony of the evangelists, or the survival of Christians in a sinful world "cannot of themselves produce a firm faith in Scripture until our heavenly Father manifest his presence in it, and thereby secure implicit reverence for it" (1:83). Tillotson's views, so often held to be untraditional, are but a semi-Pelagian version of this position set out more blandly but with equal assurance. They also very much resemble those of dissenters like Richard Baxter who also knew that

> The Spirit of God supposeth Nature and worketh on Man as Man; by exciting your own Understanding and Will to do their parts.
> The Spirit worketh not on the Will but by the Reason; He moveth not a man as a beast or stone, to do a thing he knoweth not why; but by illumination giveth him the soundest Reason for the doing of it.
> He works on man as man, and causeth him to believe nothing but what is credible.
> Where is it that the Spirit giveth light, but into our own Understandings? And how perceive we that light but by the rational apprehensions and discourses of these Understandings. (Nuttall 1965, 121; Armstrong 1969, 177–78, 273–75)

To argue against some Catholics and some dissenters by appeals to reason was to speak a common language. That this language was not wholly secular is often overlooked.

Reason for Tillotson is not only the ability to calculate, compare, and to perceive the self-evident, but it is also "the candle of the Lord" (Yolton 1956, 25–42; Shapiro 1983, 75–118) flickering in fallen people. As such it is that set of God-given mental abilities shared by all people and known to be both shared and God-given (Van Leeuwen 1970, 34–48; Tillotson 1722, 1:17–19, 307). It can attain to human, natural, or rational belief, if not certain knowledge: "the frame of our understandings is not a cheat, but that our faculties are true" (Van Leeuwen 1970, 34). Here even nature and reason are involved with God's grace since God allows humanity to prove or render probable his existence, which then guarantees the proofs. As Aquinas said, people need and get "divine help in order that the intellect may be moved by God to its act" (Aquinas 1948, 653). The rational theology of the latitudinarians depends upon God's prevenient grace, without which there would be no common sense of mankind (Raven 1953, 111–12). Such a conception of reason is hardly secular and it saved the Anglican latitudinarians from being mere rationalists. Indeed, their use of reason in natural philosophy was a godly activity, enveloped in grace and properly leading to faith and sanctity. Running to and fro to increase knowledge (Daniel 12:4) was not unrelated to the pansophic millennialism that Tillotson shared with others accused of reducing Christianity to natural religion. Reason for Tillotson was, however, a less reassuring faculty than it was for most deists. It could give grounds for belief or show errors but it could not produce certainty: "But no human understanding being absolutely secur'd from possibility of mistake by the perfection of its own nature . . . it follows that no man can be infallible in any thing, but by supernatural assistance" (quoted in Van Leeuwen 1970, 36). With Tillotson we have entered a world in which probability is the guide to life.[20] Effective against Catholic views of infallibility, this position still required that the true Christian exhibit a faith that was given by God and not the faith that Tillotson equated with probability (Carroll 1975, 80–83, 100). The natural religion that comes from such an outlook is probable and believable just as it is necessary to prepare us to accept God's pardon for the sins we commit (1722, 1:229, 307, 667; 2:673).

Tillotson's natural religion, unlike that of some deists, is not certain. It was based upon facts (Shapiro 1983, 103), those of natural history and the new sciences that showed design in nature and the highly probable existence of a designer (68). Tillotson also appealed to ontological and cosmological arguments for the existence of God and to a theory of innate ideas and principles (1722, 1:405–7; 2:433) but a priori arguments were increasingly less at home in an outlook such as his. Moreover, Christianity as a religion rooted in the facts of revelations occurring at a particular time and place had to be justified in a similar way. Reasoning could establish the credibility of Christianity (2:256, 447–48, 495) but it could not judge mysterious doctrines propounded in the Gospels (1:17). That was the message of his *Rule of Faith* (1666) and of numerous sermons (2:441, 451). Probabilities lead us to accept the beliefs of natural theology that show us our sinful nature and prepare us to accept God's pardon (1:229, 307, 667; 2:673):

> Unless we are first persuaded of the providence of God, and his particular care of mankind, why should we believe that he would make any revelation of himself to men. Unless it is naturally known to us, that God is true, what foundation is there for the unbelief of his work. And what signifies the laws and promises of God, unless natural light do first assure us of his sovereign authority and faithfullness. So that the principles of natural religion are the foundation of that which is revealed; and therefore in reason nothing can be admitted to be a revelation from God, which plainly contradicts his essential *perfection;* and consequently, if any pretends divine revelation for this doctrine [double predestination] I am as certain that this doctrine cannot be of God, as I am sure that God is good and just: because this grates upon the notion that mankind have of goodness and justice. (1722, 1:579)

Probabilities, then, justified belief in Christianity. But true faith in Christ's promises is not for any who have it a wholly natural achievement:

> There is a divine power and efficacy goes along with the gospel, to make way for the entertainment of it in the hearts of men, where they put no bar and obstacle to it. But if men will resist the motions of God's blessed Spirit, and quench the light of it, and obstinately hold out against the force

of truth; God will withdraw his grace and holy Spirit from them. (1722, 1:307)

To speak of such faith was to come closer to the sectaries whose claims to inspiration he was at pains to refute. Their miracles, visions, and revelations did not accord with the truths of natural religion or with others implied by them. They could not pass tests of probability easily met by events recounted in the Bible or reported in accounts of the early and uncorrupted Church (2:495–502). They also did not square with Christian teaching, which had been set forth once and for all time by Christ, whose word endures forever. Miracles might possibly occur to bear witness to sound doctrine but none had been wrought since the days of the primitive Church (1:151). Tillotson's discussion was not only rather traditional in an Anglicanism devoted to a middle way (Reedy 1977, 298–301) but it was also one that showed him committed to supernaturalism.

God's revelations had been experienced by those who received them as clear and evident ideas and principles of action that were neither illogical nor contradictory or contrary to natural or previously revealed truths. Those who had them, like Simon Peter, had "a clear and vigorous perception," one which gave "an undoubted assurance," "a supernatural Effect evident and wonderful to Sense." We cannot "explain the particular way how it is done, it being a thing not to be expressed in words, but to be felt and experienced." Repeatedly he says that revelations to those who truly received them were "such a clear and overpowering Light as shall discover to us the Divinity of them, and satisfy us beyond all doubt and scruple" (2:441; Van Leeuwen, 1970, 34–40). There is an order of causation rather different from that of the everyday world. God, angels, and the devil are all still at work in the souls of men in much the same fashion (2:495–96). The Spirit still works upon our minds; ministering angels encourage us; devils tempt and entice us away from God and sanctity (1:152–61). Every true Christian has his or her mere belief in the Christian message vivified in this way.

No person in Tillotson's sermons is a Christian without being called. We can assent to the Christian message but only God's grace allows us to make it a reality in our lives. "It *is God that works in us both to will and to do of his own goodness*; that is, who both inclines and excites us to that which is good, and enables us to do it" (1:503). The sincere Christian acts "with regard to God, and out of Conscience to our Duty to him, and in hopes of the reward which he hath promised, and not for any low, and mean and temporal end" (2:369). Christianity should become an existential faith in which mere probable belief becomes Christian faith manifest in continual actions glorifying God in this world (1:368, 393; 2:364). As Tillotson more sedately put it, our Christian faith ought to be the "habitual and settled intention of mind to glorify God in the course of our lives" (2:370). The end of this moral, or better, religious life is equally traditional in conception. It is that "holiness, which reunites us to God, and restores our souls to their primitive and original state, [and which] can make us *happy*, and give peace and rest to our souls" (1:667) here and hereafter. To imitate Christ by living a life of repentance and sanctity requires special grace (2:243). The Christian who believes the Christian message and who makes of it an existential faith is enabled to do so by the special intervention of God:

> ... the holy Spirit of God conducts and manageth this great work of our sanctification and salvation from first to last, by opening our hearts to let in the light of divine truth upon our minds, by representing to us with advantages such arguments and considerations as are apt to persuade us to embrace and yield to it; by secret and gentle reprehensions softening our hard hearts and bending our stiff and stubborn wills to a compliance with the will of God, and our duty. ... Thus the Spirit of God carries on the work of our sanctification and makes us *partakers of a divine nature*, by way of inward efficacy and assistance. (1722, 1:304–5)

That is facilitated by the preaching of the Word of God and the administration of the two sacraments instituted by Christ for his Church. The sacrifice of Christ is not only remembered by the Church but preached as the basis of our hope and redemption (2:298–310; 1:227). That depends not upon ourselves but God.

If the truths of natural and revealed religion are known, so too is the fact of men's natural inability to conform to their requirements (1:375, 503–10). Just as we cannot know God without prevenient grace, neither can we repent and turn to God without his help (1:304–7, 376, 386). When we attend to rational arguments and when we strive to be good, we are able to do so because his grace is given to all who will accept it (1:298–99). At best this obedience is imperfect and our assurance of pardon and continued favor but weak and improbable: "but yet because it is the utmost that we can do in this state of infirmity and imperfection, the terms of the Gospel are so merciful and gracious, as that God is pleased for the sake of the meritorious obedience and sufferings of our blessed Saviour, to accept this *sincere*, tho' *imperfect* obedience, and to reward it with eternal life" (1:501). It is not our efforts that justify us but God's free grace and the mediation of Christ (2:298–325). The "real renovation of our hearts and lives depends on the faith', the hope and promises of further grace and the mediation of Christ who has justified us before the Father by his death which has bought our Pardon, or Remission of Sins" (1:392, 498; 2:298–365). The natural man has "the gift of God" (1:503) in prevenient grace; the convinced Christian is supported by the working of God within him (1:502–10). This is abetted by the Church that preaches the Gospel and administers the sacraments.

The good news for John Tillotson was not just the impressive republication of the truths of natural religion in a world falling further into sin. Tillotson's Christ is of course a preacher whose moral message was contained in the simplest version of the law and the prophets and in the beatitudes. That Jesus the Messiah and moralist ranks above Saint Paul the theologian should not be held against the archbishop. We would do well to remember the answer to the Pharisee who asked, "Master, which is the greatest commandment in the law?" (Matthew 22:37–40). It had nothing to do with mysteries. It was, however, followed by Christ's assertion of his messiahship, a matter to which Tillotson devoted several published sermons (1:116–24, 447–57). For Tillotson as for Matthew, "Jesus Christ the Son of God came in our nature to save us, by revealing our duty more clearly and fully to us, by giving us a more perfect example of holiness and obedience in his own life and conversation and by dying for our sins, and rising again for our justification; these are the things which men may easily understand; and yet for all that they are difficultly brought to the practice of religion" (1:417). What this understanding involved was something reason could make probable but not fathom and something that only grace and faith could bring to fruition in good works.

> [Christ] is *the Author of eternal salvation*, as he hath purchased it for us, by the *merit of his obedience and sufferings*, by which he hath obtained eternal redemption for us; not only deliverance from the wrath to come, but eternal life and happiness. When by our sins we had justly incurr'd the wrath and displeasure of Almighty God, and were liable to eternal death and misery, he was contented to be substituted a sacrifice for us, *to bear our sins in his own body on the tree,* and to expiate the guilt of all our offences by his own sufferings. He died *for us*, that is, not only for our benefit and advantage, but in our place and stead: so that if he had not died we had eternally perish'd; and because he died, we are saved from that eternal ruin and punishment, which was due to us for our sins. . . . it is call'd *the price of our redemption:* for as sinners, we are liable and indebted to the justice of God, and our blessed Saviour by his death and suffering hath discharged this obligation. . . . Not that God was angry with his Son, for he was always well pleased with him; or that our Saviour suffer'd the very same which the sinner should have done in his own person, the proper pains and torments of the damned: but that perfect obedience and grevous sufferings, undergone for our sakes, and upon our account, were of that value and esteem with God, and his voluntary sacrifice of himself in our stead, so highly acceptable and well pleasing to him, that he thereupon was pleased to enter into a covenant of grace and mercy with mankind; wherein he hath promised and engaged himself to forgive the sins of all those who sincerely repent and believe, and to make them partakers of eternal life. And hence it is, that the blood of Christ, which was shed for us upon the cross, is call'd *the blood of the covenant;* as being the sanction of that new covenant of the Gospel, into which God enter'd with mankind; and not only the confirmation, but the very foundation of it; for which reason, the cup in the Lord's Supper (which represents to us the blood of

Christ) is call'd *the New Testament in his blood, which was shed for many for the remission of sins*. (1722, 1:498)

Christ, conceived by the Virgin (1:478), truly died as a propitiation for our sins and was miraculously resurrected, which is to Christians a promise of eternal life.[21] Upon Christ's death depends our salvation and the vivifying faith that leads to a holy life:

> [By His] perpetual intercession with the Father ... he procures all those benefits to be bestowed upon us, which he purchased for us by his death; the forgiveness of our sins, and our acceptance with God, and perfect restitution to his favour, upon our faith and repentance, and the grace and assistance of God's holy Spirit to enable us to a sincere discharge of our duty, to strengthen us against all temptations of the world, the flesh, and the Devil, to keep us from all evil, and to preserve us to his heavenly kingdom. ... And by virtue of this powerful *intercession* of our blessed Saviour and Redeemer, our sins are pardoned upon our sincere repentance, our prayers are graciously answered, our wants are abundantly supplied, and the grace and assistance of God's Spirit are plentifully afforded to us, to excite us to our duty, to strengthen us in well doing, to comfort us in afflictions, to support us under the greatest tryals and sufferings, and *to keep us through faith unto salvation*. (1:448–49)

Upon this mediation depends our faith and hope and from it flows our charity, which leads to sanctification.

Christianity was a republication of the tenets of natural religion but it also announced the deliverance of man from the bondage of guilt and sin. It grounded man's hopes and induced him to persevere in a life of good works or faith. The heathens who have a natural religion and who try to live a moral life know that they have failed. They are not the equals of Christians but subjects for missionary work that would bring them promises of hope and salvation. Had Christianity been merely the religion of nature in fancy dress there would have been less interest among the latitudinarians in missionary activities sponsored by the New England Company (1649), the Society for the Propagation of Christian Knowledge (1699), the Scottish SPCK (1700) and the Society for the Propagation of the Gospel in Foreign Parts (Dahm 1970, 172; Cremin 1970, 341–55). There would also have been no need for sacraments that convey grace.

Baptism and the Lord's Supper are for Tillotson means by which God's grace comes to the Christian. The first was an outward and visible sign of induction into the Church and of the acceptance of its beliefs. These make us "partakers of the Holy Ghost" (2:308). What "our Saviour" instituted "cannot be neglected or slighted, without great affront to the Christian Religion, and contempt of one of the greatest blessings promised in the Gospels" (2:308); that is, the "continual assistance of God's Holy Spirit residing and dwelling in us, which secures all the other blessings and benefits of the Gospel to us, and conducts us safely thro' all the temptations of this World, and the difficulties of a Christian course, to *the end of our Faith, the eternal salvation of our Souls*" (2:304). Tillotson's sermons say little about the Lord's Supper. He treated it as a commemoration of Christ's passion, one that should show us God's love and mercy as well as the "terms of the gospel" and our duty. It "should raise strange passions in us" leading to repentance, "resolutions of service and obediance" and thankfulness to God (1:227).[22] In his "Discourse to his Servants concerning the Sacrament" Tillotson called communion "the most solemn Institution of our Religion" and recommended that it be "frequent" (2:676). By its inward grace "we are confirmed in Goodness, and our Resolutions of better Obedience are strengthened; and the Grace of God's Holy Spirit to enable us to do his will is hereby conveyed to us" (2:676). The sacraments are supernatural aids to Christians who neglect them at their peril. The Church (for him still the "Mystical body") (2:319) administers them and preaches the gospel. It is no mere political institution to preserve the social order (Irene Simon 1967, 1:Chap. 3). Tillotson did not dwell upon these matters in sermons. They were too contentious, too irritating, too sensitive, too divisive. There is, however, no question about his own adherence to a view of the sacraments as important in the Christian life because they transmitted God's grace to people much in need of it. He was not the only latitudinarian who held such views.

Tillotson's theology had a doctrinal content that was rather traditional (McAdoo 1965, 212–39). It was still defined by one canon, two testaments, three creeds, four councils, and the practice of five centuries as these were understood by men whose outlook had been formed not only by Chillingworth and Hooker but also by Calvin and Jewel, Saint Thomas, Augustine, and other patristic writers. Those who say, as Professor Jacob does, that the latitudinarians made "rational argumentation and not faith . . . the final arbiter of Christian belief and dogma" (1976, 34) need to explain more clearly than they have how this statement squares with the creeds, the Articles of Religion, the mysteries or the gracious operation of God's Holy Spirit in the minds of people for whom reason is a kind of faith. Just as the archbishop's religion was scriptural, so also was it rooted more deeply in the liturgy and *Book of Common Prayer* than is sometimes appreciated. Tillotson does seem to have believed that we should "receive God's promises in such wise as they be generally set forth to us in Holy Scripture; and in our doings, that Will of God is to be followed, which we have expressly declared unto us in the Word of God" (Article 17). All the contradictions and perplexities of that Word we cannot unravel but we can sincerely try to imitate Christ's goodness and believe both his injunctions and promises (2:221–43). Tillotson's "Arminianism," like that of latitudinarians generally, should be seen as the view of men who held that the Bible, as well as philosophy, required us to think people capable of free choices and responsible acts. Those who too quickly reduce latitudinarian Christianity to morality also have failed to notice that its end was both sanctity here and salvation hereafter. They have also confused mere probable belief with Christian faith still seen as the gift of God and not solely as the product of reason. Tillotson's Christianity is not reducible to "a natural religion comprehensive enough to override doctrinal differences" (Jacob 1976, 49). It was an Anglicanism that could not include the Socinians or Arians although it could tolerate them. Perhaps we should also recall more often Tillotson's close relations with George Bull and Robert Nelson, whose high-church and nonjuring Anglicanism was probably as acceptable to him as Thomas Firmin's Socinianism. Neither was latitudinarianism dedicated to making "the actions of the prosperous compatible with Christian virtue and with the very mechanism of the universe." Tillotson's Christianity belongs more to a traditional and scholastic exposition of the synoptic gospels, Acts, James, Daniel, and Revelation. If we overlook these dimensions of latitudinarian thought we do scant justice to Tillotson and we underrate the boldness of the deists, who in England and elsewhere wanted no truck with supervenient grace.

No one would argue that John Tillotson was a great theologian. In his own time that distinction was given to his friend Edward Stillingfleet, who shared and better expressed most of what the archbishop believed. Both men were more orthodox, traditional, and scriptural than Westfall, O'Higgins, Sullivan, Jacob, and others have believed. The obvious moralism of their thought had a scriptural basis and represented a view of Christian sanctity as a conscientious effort to live in accordance with the laws of God, Christ, or the Holy Spirit (2:478). This was to be exemplified in whatever sphere the Christian was called to act. It is rather a crude distortion of latitudinarian thought to see it as "[adapting] Christianity to a market society by transforming it into a natural religion which would serve the needs of self-interest and make them compatible with the dictates of providence" (Jacob 1976, 69–70). Tillotson and others still insisted upon notions of charity and upon principles of behavior that reflect not the conditions of the period c. 1660–1700 but that harked back to the *Book of Common Prayer* and to the catechisms. These antedate the editions issued in 1662. Moreover, latitudinarianism was absorbed by its audience principally in sermons and polemical works that expounded the Bible, used proof-texts, and exhibited a regard for the Anglican Articles of Religion. Men like Tillotson or the Boyle Lecturers and their readers believed they were dealing with Christian and revealed truths that went well beyond the confines of rational theology. The temptation to distort their religious views comes because we pay too little attention to the way they thought, to the substance of their doctrinal Christianity, and to their views of reason and faith and how they functioned. We pay too much heed to their moralism and to the principles that they offered as a basis for policies of comprehension or toleration. In doing so we overlook those revealed truths they held to be necessary but whose exposition in theology or sermons was bound to be contentious. We also see them in a setting that is too English. Latitudinarianism had its foreign counterparts and English deism belonged perhaps as much to Europe as to England (Soman 1967, 597–600; Barnard 1971, 221–46).

Placing the English deists in a European context is one of the interesting features of Professor Jacob's discussion of deism. Burton saw them there. So too did those who wrote against Toland and Collins. That context is still not well enough known. The contributions of Spinoza, Richard Simon, and the authors discussed so long ago by I. O. Wade have been recognized, as have those of Radicati di Passerano (Colie, Bredvold, Wade, Venturi). Others too contributed to the English controversy over deism but not much seems to have appeared concerning them. English readers knew of the rational religions of the Sevarambians (Vairresse), the Australians (de Foigny), and those peoples met by Jacques Massé and Pierre de Mesange (Rosenberg). The same audience bought numerous editions of the *Turkish Spy* (Williams) and was titillated by Adario, the rational Huron of the Baron De Lahontan's *Dialogues Curieux*.[23] The deism purveyed by such works was different in source from that discussed by Sullivan and O'Higgins and suggests that men like Toland and Collins perhaps relied less upon latitudinarian thought than has been claimed. Such sources need more investigation. We also need to know more about men like Thomas Johnson, the Hague bookseller (Rosenberg 1972, 232; Jacob 1981, 307; O'Higgins 1970, 264), who published works by Socinians, Shaftesbury, Collins, probably the *Voyage et avanture de Jacques Massé* and the *Journal literaire* for which Pierre Desmaizeaux wrote. Johnson was not only a publisher of risqué books but a supplier of publications to Collins and Scottish gentlemen. Likewise, we need more information on others who spread deistical ideas in Europe such as Ludvig Holberg (1970, 152–53, 193–98). By reminding us of the European context in *The Radical Enlightenment* Professor Jacob has well served the interests of scholars of deism. That she has correctly described the context is less clear.

In her book Dr. Jacob has sought to connect the political and religious views of Toland and Collins with those of various Dutch, French, and German publishers, writers, intellectuals, political activists and Free Masons. At present this enterprise looks rather shaky. Collins, the Whig *Custos rotulorum* of Essex, was hardly a leveling commonwealth man. Toland's politics may have been more republican but they were also more affected by mercenary motives. Her Toland is not Sullivan's; her Collins is not O'Higgins's. Other deists had political views carefully analyzed by Caroline Robbins. Of Robert Molesworth and his friends—among whom were to be found Tindal, Shaftesbury, Toland, Trenchard, Gordon, and Asgill—she wrote:

> Fundamental questions about social distinctions were hardly raised. Discussions like those about the distribution of wealth, occasionally found even in Temple as well as in the works of the Commonwealthmen, were pretty closely limited to the relation of wealth to empire, that is, to the old question of the stable state, and were not much concerned with the welfare of the individual as such. The Commonwealthmen within the terms of their age, their class and their education asserted liberty, talked about equality, and assumed the possibility of progress at a time when most Englishmen thought of the constitution as sacrosanct and change as dangerous if not sacrilegious. (1961, 90–91)

Not very radical, all that. Deists were alleged to be republicans (Emerson 1968, 9–14; Jacob 1981, 78–81) but the republic most approved by them was ruled by William, Anne, and George. Even Trenchard and Gordon, the two deists whose political works were of greatest use to genteel American revolutionaries, refused the republican label (Robbins 1961, 121). Deists do not seem to have been so politically radical as Dr. Jacob would have them be.

To link the diverse deistic metaphysics to leveling politics was traditional but it is not so evident in the deistic texts. We should, therefore, be suspicious of Dr. Jacob's claims concerning radical, speculative Freemasonry, especially that of Toland and Collins. Dr. Sullivan cannot place Toland in any lodge (1982, 202–3). Father O'Higgins seems to have found no evidence for Collins's involvement in Masonry in either England or Holland.[24] G. C. Gibbs has examined Dr. Jacob's evidence for their Masonic connections in a devastating review of *The Radical Enlightenment.* He rejected her claims about their Masonic activities and her views of the philosophic outlook of their Dutch friends.[25] At present the relation of English deism to European thought remains an intriguing but unsettled matter. There is, however, little reason to think that as it is explored the alleged connection between the deists and latitudinarians will not be weakened. That is also probably to be expected from further studies of deism as it appeared in British periodicals after 1695. We know far too little about that topic.

This paper originated in dissatisfactions; let it end with recommendations. We should, I think, return to a simple analytical definition of *deism* even though it will not capture every belief held by particular deists. Such a definition does the one thing needful—it concentrates attention upon deists' religious beliefs and upon the grounds for asserting them. Doing this again places the deists' religious beliefs in their European intellectual context. It has the added advantage of widening our views of the plausible reasons people had for holding or combatting deistic beliefs. These were hardly merely English or social. Deists and Anglicans can still be seen as sharing much but their differences would also be made more apparent. If I am correct about how the Boyle Lectures are to be read, then liberal Anglicans and deists were farther apart than most recent commentators have appreciated. Latitudinarians were doing a particular kind of apologetic work within intellectual structures whose validity we do not recognize and often forget. Relating English to Continental deistic thought will perhaps overcome the parochialism of English historians. It ought also to help us see ways in which the English not only promoted the Enlightenment but remained essential for its Whiggish and radical expressions. Viewing deism in this way, we also return to a definition and a context that Professor Aldridge has done much to make familiar.

NOTES

1. David Berman in a series of articles dealing with Collins has added to the list of publications attributable to him, modified O'Higgins's assessment of his philosophy, and placed Collins more securely in the deists' camp although allowing for his Anglicanism.

2. That statement is at odds with Sullivan's view of Charles Blount (1982, 224, 223) and with Margaret Jacob's belief that Toland belonged to a coterie that accepted "pantheistic materialism" (1976, 248–49; 1981, 216–17, 248–49, 262). O'Higgins calls Collins a materialist but denies he was a thorough one (1970, 6, 69–76). See also John Yolton's *Thinking Matter* for a bibliography and a discussion of the controversies between deists and Christians over this and related matters.

3. That conclusion is more or less shared by Professor Gerard Reedy, S.J. (1977, 285–304). He shows how Toland had gone beyond Socinian arguments by 1696. Reedy sees "Toland's deism" as "rooted in and a variation of Socinian thought" rather than in and of latitudinarianism (289). His view of the latter is that given by Phillip Harth in *Swift* and *Contexts*—two fine studies that have been ignored by students of English deism even though they are, as Reedy says, "the best available accounts of Anglican rationalism" (286).

4. Much more work needs to be done on these circles. Harth and Allen have described the group centered on Blount while Dr. Jacob and others have noticed clubs somewhat later. Robert Wodrow (1842–43b, 95) in 1700 assumed that London deists were holding meetings and that they believed in the "tenets . . . we have in Blount's Oracles." William Stephens, Charles Gildon, Charles Leslie, George Berkeley, and other Anglican apologists have also referred to groups of deists from the 1690s to the 1730s but no one has yet sorted out the evidence for believing they were organized or systematically traced the relationships among them and in the various periodicals with which they were associated.

5. C. B. MacPherson's account of the phenomenon has, I think, been rightly dismissed by Alan MacFarlane 1978, 58–61, 164–88.

6. Pierre Bayle accurately quotes the relevant sections from Viret's "Epistle Dedicatory" to volume 2 of the *Instruction* but altered their form in minor ways. *Déiste* is used in a similar sense in Henri Estienne's *Apologie pour Herodote* (1566). For similar figures see discussions in Van Gelder, Febvre, Busson, Charbonel, Pintard, Spink, and Kocher. See also C. J. Betts 1984, 3–42.

7. For restoration stage plays depicting such practical and speculative atheists see Van Lennep; for a comparable figure in prose see Richard Head's *The English Rogue*.

8. Alan Kors in a forthcoming book will persuasively argue that the apologists

promoted atheism in France. The English experience with atheism and deism was probably similar. Socinianism in France has been discussed by R. E. Florida.

9. R. D. Bedford has perhaps come closest to describing Herbert's views: "And yet in Herbert himself this advanced rationalism was tempered by a sense of worship, actively exercised; a passionate religious instinct which could see the superfluity of proliferating Churches and professions; and, despite his warnings about revelations, by such a sense of the numinous that this extraordinary 'deist' has even been described as an animistic sun and star worshipper" (256).

10. Phillip Harth's account of the deists of this period (1968, 56–94) is based on some marvelous detective work. To the list he gives should perhaps be added the Cambridge Platonists to whom Anthony Tuckney referred as "sublimated Deists" (Greene 1981, 234). Among earlier figures we may ultimately find Blount's father, Sir Henry Blount, whose anticlericalism and ideas about imposture, superstition, and the political uses of religion were clearly inherited by his son (1636, e.g., 30, 47–50, 68, 119; Redwood 1974, 491). Sir Thomas Blount also used the word *deist* to describe Socinians (1656) and un-Christian rationalists (1670) (Welsh 1956, 160–62).

11. Harth believed Blount was not so much a deist as a freethinker interested in the freedom to think and publish. He shows him to have been a circulator of clandestine tracts including the *Summary Account of the Deists Religion* (1968, 77, 91–94). Gildon's preface to Blount's *Works* and his own later recantations suggest to me that Blount's name should remain upon the deists' roll. It is of some interest that *The Oracles of Reason* in 1693 were also circulated clandestinely and that they found interested purchasers in Cambridge who did not wish to be known to the Beadles (Levine 1977, 57).

12. This is the wording given in *A Defence of Natural and Revealed Religion;* Dahm quotes the codicil to Boyle's will that reads, "Atheists, Theists, Pagans, Jews and Mahometans" (172). Dahm also notes that Bishop Thomas Tenison exercised the major influence in the selection of the early Boyle Lecturers. He seems to have picked or supported Bentley, Gastrell, Bradford, Samuel Clarke, Derham, and Ibbot (174–76). Rather than expressing the viewpoint of the controlling minority of the Anglican church ca. 1691–ca. 1705, these men may have spoken for a much smaller coterie. About as many had their careers blocked because of heretical tendencies as became bishops.

13. The Boyle Lectures were directed to this motley set of unbelievers but they were also to "assist and encourage all companies for propagating the Gospel in foreign parts" (Dahm 1970, 172). The foundation had aims similar to those expressed by Grotius in *The Truth of the Christian Religion* (1815, 3); (Bedford 1979, 152–53). He had hoped to be useful in the conversion of pagans, infidels, Moslems, Jews, and "profane persons, who upon occasion, are ready to scatter their poison amongst the weak and simple" (Grotius 1815, 3). The early Lecturers did indeed address infidels and atheists (1691–93), Jews (1694), Jews and deists (1695–96), deists (1697–98), "Atheists, Deists, Pagans, Jews and Mahometans" (1699), and Jews and deists (1700–1702). Most arguments about the necessity and sufficiency of the Christian revelation would have been seen as refutations of Jews, Moslems, or pagans as well as atheists or deists. This suggests that the context given these lectures by Dr. Jacob may in reality have been rather different (1976, 196).

14. A topic that merits attention is the continuing republication of deistic and antideistic pamphlets during the nineteenth and twentieth centuries by atheistic or evangelical tract societies. This is important for the history of deism in America and certainly for its social meaning everywhere after 1789.

15. Charles Webster has admirably studied the complexities of a story that Christopher Hill and those who follow him have sought to make too simple (Webster 1975, 496–507; Jacob 1981, 4–5).

16. Louis Locke, Tillotson's biographer, notes his subject's supernaturalism but

says that his "religious thought is not at all characteristically theological" but practical. That practical theology was, however, rooted in both Calvinist and Anglican theology deriving from the early and mid-seventeenth century. It also shared in a general pattern marking European Protestantism (L. Locke 1954, 108; Allison 1966, passim; Rex 1965, 77–120). Tillotson's work was orthodox enough to appeal to New England Calvinists, as Norman Fiering has pointed out (1981, 307–44). His essay in my opinion stresses too much the "autonomy of reason" (337) and the relation of Christianity to the social utilities of London merchants (341) but it does assert "that Tillotson was not a skeptic or deist in disguise." However, "his logical intelligence, inventiveness, and perceptiveness again and again carried him unwittingly beyond the limits of his mission as a churchman" (337). It is easier to agree with the first claim than the second.

17. Tillotson's explication of that text comes in a sermon entitled "Religious and Divine Faith." There he says Simon Peter had revealed to him by "my Father which is in Heaven" the messiahship of Jesus. Tillotson characterized the manner of such a revelation as "various and arbitrary." Its authenticity was warranted "by the evidence it carries along with it" and by its compatibility with the "Natural and Essential Notions of his Mind and Understanding." It is therefore not delusional or devilish but it does show "that it is a Foreign Impression, and doth not spring from his own Mind" (1722, 2:435, 441–45). The messianic character of Christ is confirmed by his doctrine and miracles and by the "evidence" these produce in those who witness them and in whom we can reasonably trust. The revelation was a sense experience whose evidence is "so strong that even the strongest demonstration of the contrary is not sufficient to shake it" (Van Leeuwen 40). Tillotson made a similar argument concerning God's command to Abraham to sacrifice Isaac (1722, 1:11–21). For a comment on this and later deistic treatments see Gawlick 1967, 577–600.

18. Carroll's *Stillingfleet* spells out what I take to be the essentials of Tillotson's philosophy and theology. But see also Harth 1961, 42–50.

19. For a discussion of the place of scholasticism in latitudinarian thought see McAdoo 1965, 209–22; 1949, passim; and Urban 1971, 5–20.

20. Harth claims that the rationalism of the latitudinarians was short-lived (1961, 51) but it was this belief that furnished the basis for Joseph Butler's defense of Christianity in the *Analogy* (1736). See also Rurak 1980, 365–81.

21. The latitudinarians, including Tillotson, were indeed cautious about damning non-Christians. Their caution was rooted in their view of God's mercy more than in humanity's deserts, as much in the scriptures as in their assessment of our ability to do well (Harth 1968, 158–64). It was also a reflection of our ignorance (Tillotson 1722, 1:737, 765).

22. What McAdoo wrote of Isaac Barrow's practical Christianity applies here to Tillotson:

> The characteristic practicality of Latitudinarianism and devotion in the traditional mode are combined within a theological framework and are expressed with feeling and directness. "The consideration of our Lord's suffering in this manner is very useful in application to our practice" he writes, sounding the authentic Latitudinarian note. But there is more than this, for if Barrow stresses that "mediation on the cross" has this outward context so it has an inward and theological context also: "it indeed may yield great joy and sprightly consolation to us, to contemplate our Lord upon the Cross, exercising his immense charity towards us, transacting all the work of our redemption." (1965, 233–34)

23. Lahontan's work was discussed in London periodicals. See the forthcoming work by Elizabeth McCamus, Real Ouellet, and Georges Tissot; Marshall and Williams 1982, 54, 199–203.

24. Neither Father O'Higgins nor Berman discuss this topic. Professor Jacob's case for Collins's Masonic affiliations does not appear to depend upon manuscripts of

which O'Higgins had no knowledge; at least she cites none (Jacob 1981, 3, 176–81). A study by Robert Walters suggests that the iconographical evidence educed by Dr. Jacob for Bernard Picart's beliefs is also susceptible to other interpretations.

25. Gibbs says Dr. Jacob's reading of her subjects' papers has resulted in a "farrago of pretentious and portentous moonshine" (1984, 75). He concluded that the case she has made for the English origins of a radical enlightenment "not only has not been proved, it scarcely exists . . . and finally, the manner in which the case has been constructed instils little confidence in the validity of the rest of Professor Jacob's story" (79). Reviewers of her *The Newtonians and The English Revolution* have criticized its sections on politics, the latitudinarians, and the "social dimensions of her book." One, properly, I think, warns that "her thesis is far less watertight than its apparent buoyancy might suggest" (Holmes 1978, 168, 170).

Spinoza, Stillingfleet, Prophecy, and "Enlightenment"

GERARD REEDY, S.J.

In a 1975 essay, the British historian John Lough takes a severe look at the term *Enlightenment*. He notes its rather recent appearance in the vocabulary of historians of ideas of the eighteenth century, as well as the seductive imprecision that the term invites. "It is surely obvious," Lough writes, "that the greater the diversity of ideas which the term *Enlightenment* is stretched to cover, the less use it has as a scholarly tool. By the time the lowest common denominator can be discovered for ideas produced under such vastly different conditions, *Enlightenment* and *Lumières* become empty words" (1975, 12). Central to Lough's discussion are the geographical and temporal variations that *Enlightenment* strains to include; these variations, he argues, render the term a block to clear analysis.

I admit that some syntheses of the intellectual milieu of late-seventeenth-century England illustrate Lough's thesis. To lump together, as has been done, figures such as John Locke, John Tillotson, archbishop of Canterbury, and John Toland, the deist controversialist, as precursors of the Enlightenment—all of whom appealed for a wider play of reason in the interpretation of Scripture—obfuscates their individuality: how they agreed or disagreed, and how each changed his mind or approach under different intellectual stimuli and with different audiences in mind. To attempt, for example, to align Locke's *Essay Concerning Human Understanding* (1689) and his *Reasonableness of Christianity* (1695) with the posthumous *Essay for the Understanding of St. Paul's Epistles* is an acrobatic activity, perhaps prompted more by our desire for consistency than by Locke's. The late seventeenth century was not yet a time of specialization; individual thinkers ventured into many areas, were often disinclined to build a system of ideas, and followed their own inquisitiveness with a delight that now seems both refreshing and naive.

Much late-seventeenth-century English writing, moreover, expresses a thorough skepticism about the use of the metaphor of light for the workings of human knowledge. If any prominent thinker is of the Enlightenment in that era, it is John Locke. Locke only occasionally uses "light" as a metaphor for growth in true knowledge: "Sparks of bright Knowledge" undoubtedly occur, he writes in the 1689 *Essay*, but only initiate the rational search, the human groping in the dark, by discourse and reference, towards true knowledge (683–84). In his wariness of the metaphor, and in his insistence on painstaking, rational method, Locke enunciates a dominant theme of his time. For him and for many others, truth from "light" was a staple of "Enthusiasm." Locke parodies the enthusiast position in matters of divinity: "This Light from Heaven is strong, clear, and pure, carries its own Demonstration with it, and we may as rationally take a Glow-worme to assist us to discover the Sun, as to examine the celestial Ray by our dim Candle, Reason." Enthusiasts "are sure because they are sure"; they are lost in "Similes" that confound the hard work of thought (700). It would not be difficult to assemble texts from many other writers that agree with Locke's point. True understanding of the early Enlightenment in England might well begin with this bias against "light" as a metaphor for knowledge; only the extinguishing of the inner light of certitude lets Enlightenment happen.

Opposition to the doctrine of the inner light was so broad in England as to involve many parties and viewpoints, often in argument with one another about the extent of a core in divinity not susceptible to the rational analysis widely adopted; for this analysis for better or worse, one cannot avoid the term *Enlightenment*. One major source of contention was the privileged place of Scripture in forming a scheme of theological truths. It was highly disputed whether all of Scriptural doctrine was open to exactly the same kinds of rational analysis, what truths Scripture unambiguously taught, and what "sense" of Scripture taught the truth. The following essay concerns one such controversy, that conducted by Edward Stillingfleet, dean of Saint Paul's, and, later, bishop of Worcester, against Benedict de Spinoza, the great Dutch metaphysician and political philosopher, whose works began to be known in England in the 1670s and 1680s. My approach to the controversy is, first, to honor strictures such as Lough's and to look at it in terms of the differences between Spinoza and Stillingfleet. Such an approach yields, however, incomplete understanding, for Spinoza's and Stillingfleet's profound differences are accompanied by profound similarities. Only by also stressing common features of opposing arguments, by allowing a few accepted meanings of *Enlightenment* to have their way, is adequate understanding of the controversy achieved.

Spinoza published his *Theologico-Political Treatise* in Latin in 1670; though his name did not appear on the title page, his authorship did not remain secret. On the title page of Stillingfleet's own copy of the 1670 edition, now in Marsh's Library, Dublin, "Spinoza (Bened.)" is written, in what seems to be Stillingfleet's hand. Because Spinoza intended the work for philosophers and not "the multitude" (11), he resisted its translation into the vernacular. This may help to explain why the first English translation appeared only in 1689, although part of chapter 6 of the *Treatise*, on miracles, was published in English in 1683. Though it is generally noted that the *Treatise* caused public outrage, Rosalie L. Colie's research on the reception of Spinozism in England shows that the *Ethics*, published in 1677, after Spinoza's death, received somewhat more attention than the earlier work. In the early 1860s, Matthew Arnold published three short essays on the *Treatise*, with the implication that it was a forgotten classic; Arnold's essays still provide a readable and accurate introduction. The light of the *Ethics* must always fall on the *Treatise*. Even its first chapters on prophecy, with which Stillingfleet's reply is solely concerned, allude to wider frames of philosophical reference that only the *Ethics*, apparently written in the 1660s and 1670s, makes clear.

The first fifteen chapters of the *Treatise* deal with Scripture, the last five with religion and the state. The whole is densely argued. The first three-quarters conclude that Scripture has little to do with reason and philosophy, and should not be reconciled to them: "we may draw the absolute conclusion that the Bible must not be accommodated to reason, nor reason to the Bible" (195). Spinoza's knowledge of Scripture, particularly the Hebrew text of the Old Testament, was massive and exact. His guiding methodology was to understand Scripture in its own terms, in the categories it constructs, and in its own language. Like many late-seventeenth-century writers, Spinoza tried to free the Bible from doctrinal demands placed on it long after its composition. For him the Bible was of great use as an exhortation to a moral life, but of small use as sure knowledge. This established, philosophy could proceed unimpeded by the "superstition" that one book already contained all truth.

In the first two chapters of the *Treatise*, two synonymous terms, *prophecy* and *revelation*, signify that which is gained not by natural faculties but by special communication from God. Spinoza's use of the term *prophecy* is broader than the conventional use in two ways: prophecy includes foretelling the future, but only as one aspect of the larger phenomenon of divine communication, and prophecy is not limited to the contents of the major and minor prophetic books of the Old Testament. Isaiah and Micah were prophets in the Spinozan sense; so too were Moses, Jesus, and the apostles, who also claimed to communicate with various kinds of divine authority. For a number of reasons, we are forced to conclude that the prophets did not communicate true "knowledge of natural and spiritual phenomena" (27, 40). Prophets had strong imaginations and, often, weak intellects. Because they wrote in images, not in clear and distinct ideas, and because their revelations needed external signs for credibility, their writings can command only moral, not mathematical certainty (28–29). Prophets contradicted one another and laws of nature, for God measured the content of his revelation to them not by some absolute standard, but by their temperaments and living situations

(30). Thus prophets gloomy by nature received gloomy revelations. God did not intend to reveal natural truths through the prophets, yet an admirable piety and reverence are evident even in the contradictory truths they relate. Apparent ignorance on the part of these sacred authors should not lead us to devise strange hermeneutical principles to make them appear scientifically veracious (33); that the literal sense contradicts truth as we know it shows only that truth is not their purpose.

Leo Strauss calls attention to "the particular complexity of the argument of the *Treatise*. A considerable part of the argument is actually an appeal from traditional theology to the Bible, whose authority is questioned by the other part of the argument" (193). Such a dialectic explains how Spinoza could at times write of prophecy with what appears to be orthodox reverence. Especially in his first few paragraphs, he seems to indicate that prophecy might provide some kind of knowledge unavailable by ordinary means of knowing; yet these same paragraphs elevate all knowledge to a knowledge of the idea and nature of God—in the Spinozan sense—as those with "intellectual certainty" will attest (14). The subsequent analysis shows the inferiority of prophetic "knowledge" to that of the philosopher, and also the inferiority of prophetic morality to morality gained when freedom of inquiry establishes necessary causes between thought and action (39). The philosopher honors Scripture for its moral force, but it is a force that the multitude, not the philosopher needs.

Stillingfleet's reaction to these ideas of Spinoza was presented in a sermon he delivered on 23 February 1682/83 at Whitehall, presumably in a chapel of the royal palace that burned down in 1698. The text of the sermon is Luke 16:31: "And he said unto them, if they hear not Moses and the prophets, neither will they be persuaded though one rose from the dead." The context is the story of the rich man and Lazarus, one in hell for his selfishness and the other in the bosom of Abraham—a story chosen not without irony for a Whitehall congregation. Though the point of the sermon is repentance, the text's mention of Moses and the prophets leads Stillingfleet to digress to two recent works on these subjects, Richard Simon's *Critical History of the Old Testament* (translated into English in 1682) and Spinoza's *Treatise*. These books are named in the margins of the manuscript, though not in the written body of the sermon, which has never been published in full.

The Restoration sermon was a sophisticated genre written for attentive, intelligent, and patient congregations. The length, order, and learning of the many sermons that survive symbolize not only widespread interest in religion, but also, for their original audiences, the stability of a society that allowed the requisite leisure for enormous feats of research, composition, and hearing. The diaries of John Evelyn and Samuel Pepys indicate the centrality of sermon-going to their social and intellectual lives; like many others, they seem to have taken notes as they listened, to help them remember the lengthy development of ideas. Nevertheless, the capacity of an audience for an oral presentation is not the same as that for a written tract, and Stillingfleet narrows the *status quaestionis* of the first few paragraphs of Spinoza's *Treatise*. Stillingfleet calls the prophets "wise Physicians" (42r) who diagnosed the moral ills of their day, yet in the main stays to an idea of scriptural prophecy as an accurate foretelling of future events. He also reduces Spinoza's treatment of prophecy to two headings: that the prophets were men of vivid imagination and therefore incapable of truth, and that they received and enunciated only those revelations suited to their emotional temperaments.

Stillingfleet's entire defense of prophecy rests on its historical validity: Isaiah, Amos, Hosea, Daniel, and others accurately predicted future events such as the Babylonian captivity, the fate of Jerusalem, and the suffering of the Messiah. Their ability to do so proves their rationality; "no force of Imagination could extend itself to such particular Events as the Prophets foretold" (37r). Unlike Savonarola, for example, who also claimed the gift of prophecy, Old Testament prophets were not political, intriguing, or inaccurate (38r). The characters of the prophets as shown in their writings do not give us ethical reasons for suspecting their veracity. Stillingfleet brings up the possibility that his historical argument might be fallacious if it were proved that the prophecies were written after, not before the events they foretold; he dismisses this possibility as something that would "overthrow the Faith of all History" (39r–40r). This argument, which seems naive and uncritical today, is actually central to much Anglican writing about Scripture in the late seventeenth century. The divines after the Restoration insisted that the same moral certainty granted to the events of secular history—that they, in fact, happened—must be granted to the events of scriptural history as well. The methodology one assumes to establish the historicity of ancient texts, secular or sacred, should be uniform.

Ignoring Spinoza's evidence of inconsistency among prophecies, Stillingfleet twice asserts (but does not illustrate) the "consistency" and "uniformity" of prophetic teaching (41r, 43r). It is wrong, on the face of things, to say that temperament conditioned revelation, for individual prophets mixed gloomy predictions of disaster "with the most gracious & encouraging Promises of the Favours & Mercy of God to them, if they would yet Repent" (42r). On this point it is probable that Stillingfleet has the weight of textual evidence with him; it is likely that even the application of form criticism, of which Stillingfleet of course knows nothing, would reinforce his thesis of individual authors' several moods. Last, Stillingfleet knows his opponent: he says that the prophets' "busyness was not to read Lectures of Philosophy, or to resolve difficult Problems about Lines & Numbers; it was not to busy their Heads with Politicks and new Frames of Government" (43r). Thus he both grants and disagrees with a major Spinozan thesis. There are certain kinds of knowledge that prophetic Scripture will not provide; on the other hand, the prophet's plea for reform fortifies itself with exact knowledge of historical truth.

No understanding of the past, even of a small corner of late-seventeenth-century controversy, is presuppositionless; a hermeneutic, implied or stated, always highlights or screens parts of the object. In the preface to his *Philosophy of the Enlightenment*, Ernst Cassirer discusses two models that apply to understanding his topic. The writer might "string its various intellectual formulations along the thread of time and study them chronologically" (viii), a model Cassirer finds appropriate for seventeenth-century thought, but not for that of the high Enlightenment; there he pursues "a few great fundamental ideas expressed with strict consistency and in exact arrangement" (x). Both approaches, it seems to me, are useful in understanding the Spinoza-Stillingfleet encounter just described. By alternate arrangement of diachronic and synchronic, particular and general, and inductive and deductive evidence, one achieves an adequate knowledge of the facts and implications of the matter at hand.

In front of us are two texts, twelve years apart, one published and one not, one anonymous and one given in a most public way, for a court audience. The desire not to become personally involved in controversy seems to account for Spinoza's reluctance to commit his name to the *Treatise*, a desire soon frustrated by events; he appears to dissociate the objectivity of his findings on Scripture from the aura of freethinking already associated with his name in 1670. Stillingfleet twice avoided publishing his sermon: once immediately after its delivery, since Whitehall sermons were often published, and again in his collected sermons that appeared in the last four years of his life, from 1696 on. These lay the groundwork for the first volume of his *Works, Fifty Sermons*, published by his chaplain, Timothy Goodwin, in 1707. The 1682/83 sermon is by no means the only sermon in manuscript left unpublished in 1707. In this case perhaps Stillingfleet assessed the generic considerations of his work, felt that they had not allowed him room to explore Spinoza fully, and decided that no homiletic treatment would suffice to do this. Later in his life, Stillingfleet did engage Spinoza's thought more fully, but then in closely argued tracts, a genre more suited to philosophical reasoning.

At least in the 1680s, Stillingfleet was not as comfortable with controversy with the rationalist side as he was with Roman Catholic or other non-Anglican theology. Having committed himself to a "rational theology," at least from his *Origines Sacrae* (1662) onward, he tended to become shrill when confronted by thinkers whose concept of reason was bolder than his own. One may also admit the possibility that Stillingfleet simply did not understand Spinoza's thought in 1682/83; historians of philosophy stress that no part of Spinozism—such as his remarks on prophecy—is intelligible without reference to the whole of his system. Demands of time and the desire for a prompt response to newer thought on Scripture by a member of the Anglican establishment may have urged precipitate response, at least in oral if not printed form. The immediate cause of the digression to Richard Simon and Spinoza was the English version of Simon's *Critical History* that was published in 1682. Stillingfleet tacked on a response to Spinoza, not wanting to miss the opportunity that might not later have presented itself.

In 1670 and 1682, Spinoza and Stillingfleet had different conceptions of the scriptural text. As Rosalie L. Colie writes, Spinoza makes a "calm consideration of Scripture as an historical rather than as an eternal document" (1963, 185). This consideration involved a strict investigation of the possible inferiority of biblical to philosophical thought. Spinoza also makes a fresh venture into questions of authorship; in chapter 10 of the *Treatise*, his research leads him to conclude that the present prophetic books represent a fraction of Jewish prophetic writing, and that there is evidence of multiple authorship of individual books. Without greatly exploring the matter, Spinoza distinguishes "the compiler of the prophetic books" from the original author-prophets (149). This was still a radical idea, if not completely a new one in 1670.

Stillingfleet was not ignorant of textual and authorial problems. He admitted some "literal mistakes," "varieties of Readings," and "some few additional passages injected to compleat the History" (30r–30v). This aside was meant to address the objections of Spinoza and others to gross improbabilities in the Pentateuch, such as Moses' writing an account of his own death in the last chapter of Deuteronomy. Stillingfleet was committed to preserving the integrity of as much of the text as he could. The truth of Scripture rested for him on a sure sense of who its authors were; their credibility was proved by the miracles God let them perform. A two-stage process of composition, involving prophets and later editors, seemed the first step towards probative chaos. Likewise, his awareness of the whole of Scripture, of the interrelatedness of its parts, was acute. Since Jesus frequently referred to the books of Moses, the Christian apologist must assume a methodology that worked towards proving the integrity of Jesus' referent.

Scriptural apologetics implied, then, not only different conclusions about Scripture but also different definitions of methodological tools, especially reason. Spinoza was a rationalist in a pure sense of the term; "no other philosopher," writes Stuart Hampshire, "has ever insisted more uncompromisingly that all problems, whether metaphysical, moral or scientific, must be formulated and solved as purely intellectual problems, as if they were theorems in geometry" (1951, 21). Scripture was not only the object of such analysis, but also a potential obstruction to it; to accept the idea that Scripture was a privileged source of truth was to undermine rational analysis from the start. Stillingfleet held the more traditional view, that revelation and reason went hand in hand, and that God's twofold gift of reason and revelation must never be conceived to conflict. In the late seventeenth century, cracks began to appear in this methodology; compromises such as insisting on the integrity of a text in the face of irrefutable evidence to the contrary began to be made. In 1682/83, Stillingfleet perhaps relied too much on the weight of an establishment theology whose rational analyses of Scripture, enunciated in hundreds of texts, readily accepted different kinds of certainty—not only mathematical—for the intellectual assent on which faith was based. The vocabulary of rationalism is present throughout Stillingfleet's works, but not rigorous Spinozan methodology.

Intertextual analysis of particulars leads to a conclusion of fundamental opposition between Spinoza and Stillingfleet on religion's relationship to reason. The truth of the matter, however, does not rest here. Such analysis misses major points of similarity and major critical suppositions they share. The application of wider frames of reference is needed. By pressing this material from the outside, by means of concepts not strictly inherent in it— and therefore concepts that will always remain suspect—further insight into the manifold nature of these texts is achieved. In this case at least, the deconstruction of textual analysis needs the construction of intellectual history as a dialectical ally in the understanding. From the arsenal of concepts that intellectual history provides to validate an historical Enlightenment, two seem to be of special use for a comparative analysis of Spinoza and Stillingfleet on prophecy: the assumptions that reason, as opposed to imagination and the inner light, is the source of all compelling truth, and that the senses of Scripture need careful discrimination when a catalogue of theological truths is assembled.

Some common agreement about reason is an obvious goal in searching for how the concept of *Enlightenment* might unite two dissimilar modes of argument. Although Spinoza and Stillingfleet clearly mean different things when they invoke reason and rational proof in matters of divinity, both attempt to liberate divinity from superstition and from reliance on inner light as a means of verification. Spinoza explicitly scorns superstition (4–5); less explicit about his presuppositions, owing to the small space of the sermon, Stillingfleet nevertheless contrasts the rationality of Old Testament prophecy to that of Savonarola, classical oracles and sibyls, Montanus and Maximilla—prophets of a doomsday in the second century after Christ—and "other Enthusiasts" (41r). Stillingfleet will only accept prophecy under certain traditional guidelines. Both he and Spinoza assume, in differing degrees, that religious truth grows through rational debate. Both compliment their audiences as special groups, set apart from the masses by their intolerance of the irrational. Both accept the epistemological principle that truth occurs only in concepts, not in the issue of imagination. Spinoza denies the rubric of truth to the prophets because of their imaginative writing; Stillingfleet accepts the incompatibility of truth and imagination and denies, with the witness of prophecies come true, that imagination figures greatly in the essence of prophecy. The epistemological bias remains the same.

Stillingfleet praises the prophets for their "Reason," "the use of their Reason," and "their commanding force of Reason" (41r). He disagrees with much of Spinoza but accepts rational content as the core of true religion. So insistent was he that revelation could be expressed in concepts of at least moral certainty that he and other divines, especially Archbishop Tillotson, frequently were accused of Socinianism. Strictly applied, such a charge meant a denial of the truth of key scriptural doctrines such as the Trinity and the divinity of Christ. In practice, the charge came to mean the vague vice of excessive use of reason in religious matters. The first meaning does not apply to Stillingfleet or Tillotson; the applicability of the second was then and is still a matter of opinion and argument. In controversy, Spinoza had the easier lot, for he could only be attacked by those who would moderate his rationalism in some way. Stillingfleet, a moderate rationalist, was vulnerable on the right and the left, for having gone both too far and not far enough in rational methodology.

Both Spinoza and Stillingfleet had a heightened awareness that the "senses" of Scripture are not easily sorted out and understood. It was common for late-seventeenth-century writers, especially Anglicans, to skirt the problem of the senses of Scripture by referring to its "plain sense," a vague term that often merely hid the problems it attempted to unravel. Late-seventeenth-century controversy shows, in overwhelming detail, that what was plain in Scripture to one writer failed to be so to another. Spinoza and Stillingfleet both realized that, having granted preeminence to rational content as the basis for scriptural doctrine, it was still necessary to ascertain in what sense or senses of Scripture, as they had been traditionally formulated (e.g., literal, typological, tropological), that rational content lay. They agreed that the plain or literal sense, especially in a complex genre such as prophecy, was not an obvious given. Both were hermeneutically aware. Both begin their analyses of prophecy with a discussion of the historical sense—that is, what prophetical passages meant or could have meant to their authors. Both use such historical analyses to further the wider thrusts of their divergent arguments.

Spinoza's analysis has three stages. In the first, he demands that interpreters of Scripture know the language, culture, and historical provenance of each book. He casts his demand for scholarly discipline in revolutionary terms; from at least the 1650s onward, however, Anglican scholars had been attempting corporately to construct what Spinoza calls the "history" of Scripture. Second, Spinoza carefully compares the texts of one book or prophet with another to find discrepancies; he also at times compares the historical sense he has found with what humanity has later learned—in particular, the knowledge of scriptural authors with the knowledge gained by natural philosophy. Here too he finds, of course, discrepancies. Part of Spinoza's rationalism, as we identify it now, consists in the eagerness with which he delights in discrepancy rather than harmony. Third, Spinoza finds again and again that Scripture is often without the scientific merit of natural philosophy. This leads him to deny the title of truth and knowledge to scriptural teaching. Its purpose is only to foster morality; the attitudes of the prophets, not their ideas, are the message. Thus he reduces the content of Scripture to its moral content. The only sense of Scripture that survives rational analysis is, in traditional terminology, its tropological, or moral sense.

For Stillingfleet and some other Anglican theologians of his generation, it was a self-conscious modernity to attempt to write theology that used historical meanings of Scripture as a base. For example, when writing about the Psalms, or using passages from the Psalms in the service of theological exposition, these theologians considered as much as possible the meaning a Psalm had in David's life and avoided as much as possible its typological reference. The Psalms were understood not so much as predictions of the future (e.g., of the life of Christ) as narrative fragments of David's own life that gave ethical models of gratitude in success and strength in adversity. A text that clearly states this interpretative tactic is Clarendon's commentary on the Psalms; but many sermons use the Psalms in this way without explicitly stating their intentions. For political and theological reasons, late-seventeenth-century Anglicans did not like typological interpretation of Scripture.

When Stillingfleet discusses the prophetic books, however, his role as a Christian theologian prevents him from insisting that historical intentionality circumscribes meaning. Because the messianic nature of Jesus' mission was widely proved—as it would be for a long time after—by his fulfillment of Old Testament prophecies, it would have been self-destructive for a Christian theologian to insist that prophecies concern only the historical circumstances of Israel. One way Stillingfleet remains faithful to both traditional and newer thought is to bring messianic prophecy into the discussion but only as part of a series of prophecies that mostly concern secular developments (38r–40r). Moreover, Stillingfleet was not free to resolve the problem by stating that the author's historical intention included a typological sense. Such a claim would involve him in psychological arguments, including discussion of inspiration, that Anglicans of Stillingfleet's political background found fruitless. It was considered a moot point whether or not a prophet knew that his words foretold the nature of Jesus' messiahship; Anglicans regarded this kind of discussion as hopelessly disputable, as wasteful expenses of exegetical energy, doomed to produce not consensus but only more squabbling. Stillingfleet's alternate historical and typological readings—one eye on historical provenance, the other on theological necessity—represent the kind of methodological waffling that distressed the orderly mind of Spinoza.

In spite of his adoption of the typological sense, with its reordering of massive chapters of history according to the scheme of Christian belief—Stillingfleet tries to move through the prophetic books with objectivity. He establishes a chronology of the prophets, aligns sacred prophecy with secular history, and mentions predictions fulfilled by Jesus (39r) in a list of prophecies come true. The argument aims always to prove that, the prophecies being true, the prophets must have had their wits about them. Stillingfleet also writes ethical history: he reads the characters of the prophets from their writings and from the relationships he infers with their audiences. That the prophets at times castigated their audiences shows that they can be depended on not to trim the truth of their revelations in order to gain popularity (42r). Unlike Spinoza, then, Stillingfleet constructs an argument from various senses of Scripture—historical, typological, and tropological—to establish the rationality of the prophets. What most interests about the argument is not that he concludes to traditional meanings (e.g., a typological sense in Isaiah), but that his methodology implies that typology alone is insufficient to merit rational assent.

The Enlightenment does not give birth to critical awareness of the senses of Scripture; the period from 1650 or so on does, however, seem to exhibit an intensified interest in the area. If in nothing else, the period offers an epochal change in the work of Richard Simon, a French Oratorian, on the text of Scripture and, by implication, the senses of Scripture as well. In England, the new critical awareness shows up in sermons and theological books, but in the odd place as well. For example, the contractual theory of government, forwarded by Locke in the early 1680s in his *Two Treatises of Government*, rests on a renewed clarity about what sort of meanings Scripture was permitted to have. Before Locke presented his positive theory in the second treatise, he had to deny, in the first, the validity of extant patriarchal theories of government. This denial involved showing how patriarchal readings of Scripture were not based on clear readings of the texts, especially Genesis. Relying on a curiously rationalistic idea of God then popular, Locke argued that if God were to instruct mankind through Scripture on a matter as significant as polity, and if he expected to be obeyed, he would surely have been so kind as to make his meaning clear by putting it in the clear meaning of the text. New awareness of the senses of Scripture, constitutive or not of the Enlightenment, surely made its presence felt. In this area, in spite of their many differences, Spinoza and Stillingfleet too were Enlightened figures.

Individual styles of analysis, like human beings, have particular vices to which they are prone, and the practice of intellectual history is prone to the vice of false or exaggerated categorization. As John Lough complains, the category of *Enlightenment* has been stretched too far and needs watching. On the other hand, having insisted on the discontinuity between things, one still must search for evidence that thematic as well as temporal continuities exist between texts of the same period. In the matter of Spinoza and Stillingfleet on prophecy, both contrast and comparison, the latter invoking some common features of the Enlightenment, seem to help us to understand the controversy; continuity and discontinuity both exist, and it is necessary to see that they are present. It is possible to stand both too close to and too far from a text.

Deism, Immortality, and the Art of Theological Lying

DAVID BERMAN

1. Introduction: Collins on Immortality

To what extent did the "foremost British deists"[1]—Charles Blount, John Toland, Anthony Collins, Matthew Tindal—practice the art of theological lying? Instead of trying to define theological lying, I shall begin with an example from Collins's *Discourse of Free-Thinking* (1713):

> the true principles, upon which the immortality of the soul depends [Collins asserts] are only to be fetch'd from the New Testament . . . [which] teaches us . . . that God had but one way to put mankind in a capacity of enjoying immortal happiness, viz by sending JESUS CHRIST into the world, who (as *God and man, and God's son, and the same numerical being with that God whose son he was, and yet personally distinct from him*) only could by his sufferings and death (tho God can neither dye nor suffer) give an infinite satisfaction to an infinitely offended and infinitely merciful God, appease his wrath, and thereby save the *elect*. Now I would ask, how any man without revelation could know that *death* signify'd *eternal life in misery*. (COL-1)[2]

Here Collins is openly subscribing to such orthodox Christian doctrines as the belief in immortality based on the Gospel promise and the Athanasian doctrine of the Trinity. Plainly, if Collins meant what he says, then he could not be a deist. For a deist, it is agreed, must, minimally, reject Christian mysteries and the authority of Scripture. Hence those scholars who see Collins as a deist must also accept that he was a liar—that is, he did not mean what he said.[3]

Most of us do not like liars or lying; nor are we inclined to accept conspiracy theories or explanations that postulate secret codes or cabals. These aversions may explain why the art of theological lying has been so generally ignored, even though it was, I maintain, practiced not only by Collins but by Toland, Tindal, and Blount. For the sake of simplicity, I shall be restricting the subject area to the question of immortality. More specifically, I shall be arguing that although these alleged deists say they believe in a future life, their statements constitute a subversion of the belief. Their art raises a fundamental dilemma for the standard view of the British deists and deism. Briefly, if we take Collins, Toland, Tindal, and Blount at their word, then they were really Christian fideists, at least concerning the afterlife; yet if we allow that they lied about immortality, then their other theological assertions must also be considered problematic. In section 8 I briefly discuss the implications of this dilemma for an atheistic interpretation of these (so-called) major English deists.

2. Background: Toland and Shaftesbury on the Art

In trying to uncover the Art I shall be largely using a comparative method: by juxtaposing statements similar to COL-1, above, I hope to reveal the techniques of the Art. Fortunately, we have other sources of information on the Art, since some of the practitioners and their opponents have written about it. The most extensive such examination is Toland's "Clidophorus; or of the Exoteric and Esoteric philosophy," the second essay in his *Tetradymus* (1720). What Toland calls the "exoteric and esoteric distinction" has also been called "double doctrine" by William Warburton, "defensive raillery" by Lord Shaftesbury, "irony" by Collins, "secret insinuation" by Hume, dissembling, dissimulation, and sneering by many.[4] There is no agreed name, which may be no bad thing, since these labels tend to mislead by focusing on only one aspect of a complex phenomenon. Hence I have chosen a new and inclusive name—the art of theological lying.

The background of the Art is a fear or unwillingness to write truthfully about religion. As Blount notes in 1680: "'Tis a thing of most dangerous consequence to oppose any doctrine that is publicly received, how sottish however it be"; for which reason Blount is, as he says, prepared to subscribe to any dogma of the established religion (1680b, preface). That the seventeenth- and eighteenth-century freethinkers could or would not write openly on God, immortality, miracles, the Bible, is evident from their writings as well as from the works of their opponents. Collins's *Discourse of Free-thinking* is a plea not only for freethought, but also for free speaking and free writing. And in his other *Discourse* (1729), on ridicule, Collins says that the freethinker will "sacrifice the privilege of irony" only when there is freedom of expression (24).[5] In "Clidophorus" Toland states that esotericism is "as much in use as ever" (94): "And indeed, considering how dangerous it is made to tell the truth, 'tis difficult to know when any man declares his real opinions" (95). By the 1697 Blasphemy Act—9 and 10 William III, ch. 32—it was an offense to "deny any one of the persons in the holy Trinity to be God . . . or deny the Christian religion to be true, or the holy scriptures of the Old and New Testament to be of divine authority." Nor was this a token act. Thomas Woolston and Peter Annet were imprisoned for their freethinking pamphlets; indeed, Woolston died in prison (Bonner 1943, 34–37). In such a religiously intolerant, persecuting age, the sensible practice for a prudent writer was artful lying. To describe the Art more euphemistically—as prevarication, for example—does justice neither to its practitioners nor to its significance. The unwillingness of most freethinkers to speak their minds is shown in the candid statements of friendly opponents such as James Foster and unfriendly ones like Philip Skelton; in the preface to his *Ophiomaches, or Deism Revealed* (1749) Skelton writes: "they stand miserably in awe of fines; they are afraid to speak out their principles, lest they should shock or alarm" (xvi).[6] Nor did this apply only to radicals like Collins and Toland. Even so moderate a philosopher as Francis Hutcheson had to be guarded about his published statements. In a private letter of 6 September 1727, he writes:

> As to the main point in your letter about our activity, we are very much of the same opinion. But you know how sacred a point human liberty and activity, in the common notions, are to the generality of men, and how prejudicial any singularity on these heads might be to one whose business depends upon a character of orthodoxy. . . . I have some nearer touches at these points in another set of papers [1728], which I shall send over very soon to be joined with the other. But I am still on my guard in them.[7]

Nor was fear the only cause that dictated dissembling and disguise. For Lord Shaftesbury, Hutcheson's philosophical mentor, it was benevolent feeling towards "the generality of men" and the cause of truth that demanded the Art, or "defensive raillery" as he calls it:

> There is indeed a kind of *defensive Raillery* . . . which I am willing enough to allow in Affairs of whatever kind; when the Spirit of Curiosity wou'd force a Discovery of more truth than can conveniently be told. For we can never do more Injury to Truth, than by discovering too much of it on some occasions. 'Tis the same with Understandings as with Eyes: To such a certain Size and Make just so much light is necessary, and no more. Whatever is beyond, brings Darkness and Confusion. 'Tis real Humanity and Kindness to hide strong Truths from tender eyes. (1723, 1:63)

Shaftesbury is opposed, however, to raillery that banters and deceives not only the tender but also the wise and sensible:

> It may be necessary, as well now as heretofore, for wise Men to speak in *Parables*, and with a double Meaning, that the Enemy may be amus'd, and they only *who have Ears to hear may hear*. But 'tis certainly a mean, impotent, and dull sort of Wit, which amuses all alike, and leaves the most sensible Man, and even a Friend, equally in doubt, and at a loss to understand what one's real Mind is, upon any subject. (1:63)

To make things clear to friends and sensible men, while amusing or deceiving the enemy, the foolish, and the tender—that requires art, indeed the Art. This is not to say that the Art was a straightforward artificial code or cypher, with a clear key available to both the senders and receivers. Although certain specific techniques were widely employed—such as using overingratiating pious expressions like "our most holy church," and the first, ultimate, or penultimate paragraphs for sensitive messages—the text itself had to carry the message to those "who have Ears to hear." As Toland put it in "Clidophorus," the "key" to "secret meaning . . . is to be, for the most part, borrow'd by the skilful from the writers themselves" (76). By virtue of having a sensible and skillful eye, one would be able to see what the artful writer was pointing at.

Yet Toland does offer two general principles for determining a writer's true opinions, one of which is:

> *When a man maintains what's commonly believ'd, or professes what's publicly injoin'd, it is not always a sure rule that he speaks what he thinks: but when he seriously maintains the contrary of what's by law established, and openly declares for what most others oppose, then there's a strong presumption that he utters his mind.* (96)

There is, however, a conflict between this interpretative principle and another that Toland had stated earlier in *Vindicius Liberius* (1702), where he says that if there is a conflict or uncertainty in interpreting a text, we should read it in the most unexceptionable, least culpable way:

> We are . . . oblig'd to make the most candid Construction of their [i.e., our theological opponents'] Designs, and if their words admit of a double sense, (which is hard to be always avoided in any Language) we ought to allow the fairest [i.e., least culpable] interpretation of their Meaning. (6)

How is one to resolve the conflict? Toland has provided the means in his other, even more fundamental principle:

> that *the same men do not always seem to say the same things on the same subjects* . . . can only be solv'd by the distinction of the *External* [i.e., exoteric] and *Internal* [esoteric] *Doctrine*." ("Clidophorus" 1720, 85)

Conflict or inconsistency may well indicate the Art, particularly if one side of the conflict articulates "strong Truths," "contrary of what's by law established." Toland's own interpretative conflict is to be resolved, then, by supposing that he spoke exoterically in *Vindicius* and esoterically in "Clidophorus."

3. Blount, Toland, and Gildon's Rule

The specific technique most in evidence in the texts that I shall be examining is described by Toland as "the bounceing compliment . . . [that] saves all" ("Clidophorus" 1720, 68). Here is an example from Blount's work on immortality, *Anima Mundi* (1679):

> Others of later times, not taking the truly wise advice of St. *Paul*, to *beware of vain Philosophy*, have adventur'd to uphold the knowledge of Humane Souls after Death, not by Faith and the Scriptures, whose sacred Authority were the most proper support of that Belief, but . . . by the meer light of Natural Reason; and because this appears not easily intelligible, they endeavour to illustrate it by terms to Nature as unintelligible, telling us of the separate Souls intuitive knowledge, and that without help of the imaginative part, which is acknowledg'd to perish with the Brain, its Seat and Organ. But Divinity is too sublime a thing to be tryed by the Text of our imperfect Reason, for that were to try God by Man, and in these matters may it justly be call'd Folly before God. (BLO)[8]

Like Collins in COL-1, Blount is asserting the very opposite position of deism. He is affirming scriptural immortality and attacking immortality based on reason. Again like COL-1, there is perhaps too much piety. Thus the "truly wise advice" of Saint Paul contrasts with "vain philosophy" and "the meer light of reason." It is not clear how many readers would be taken in by Blount's "bouncing compliment" to revelation. Many, one imagines, would see the sneer. Although Blount *says* he believes in personal immortality, it is clear he does not. Why? Because (as we shall see below) the most powerful principles and arguments in his book are against immortality, although he persistently describes them as "vain" and "ignorant." In short, when we find strong antireligious principles and arguments, and "pious" proreligious affirmations joined with weak arguments, we must suspect that the Art is being practiced. This is the warning offered by Charles Gildon— once a militant freethinker as well as a close friend and editor of Blount—in his *Deist's Manual* (1705), a work published after Gildon's reconversion to Christianity:

> . . . there may be some favourable Expressions of God in Mr *Hobbs* . . . but when the Principles he lays down are destructive of the existence of God, those who are willing to have it so, easily distinguish betwixt formal and empty words, and the force and energy of Argument. (195)

For "God" we can, I suggest, substitute "immortality"; for "Mr Hobbs," "Blount."[9] To Toland's first principle (above) we can add this of Gildon: where there is a conflict, the writer's real meaning is to be gathered not only from what is most daring or unconventional but also from the force or weight of his arguments. This makes sense not only of Blount's *Anima Mundi* but of Toland's own views on immortality as stated in the second of his *Letters to Serena* (1704), the "History of the Soul's immortality among the Heathens." In section 1, Toland writes to Serena (i.e., Queen Sophia of Prussia):

> You have no Doubts, I'm certain, about the Soul's Immortality, and Christianity affords the best, the clearest Demonstration for it, even the revelation of God himself. (TOL-1)

What Toland actually does in his essay, however, is to reveal the naturalistic causes of belief in immortality; he then shows the diversity of philosophical conceptions, then the (nonrational) psychic propensity to believe. The force or weight of his argument is *against* belief in immortality. Yet his avowals—more easily understandable to the vulgar—are *for* immortality. The insinuation, however, is that Gospel immortality is no more rational or credible than the weak pagan conceptions and arguments for immortality. "The vulgar . . . embraced [immortality] . . . (as they do still) upon trust or from Authority" (54). Having elaborated the diverse conceptions of and weak arguments for immortality, Toland returns to his "bounceing compliment" in section 13:

> in my opinion [he asserts] the Moderns have not the same right to examine this matter as the Ancients, but ought humbly to acquiesce in the Authority of our Savior JESUS CHRIST, who brought Life and Immortality to Light. (TOL-2)

An even more extreme, though no less empty, statement is to be found in the preface:

> I told her [Serena] that Divine Authority was the surest Anchor of our Hope, and the best *if not the only Demonstration* of the Soul's Immortality. I added, that it was not strange to find this opinion doubted or deny'd by many of the heathens.(TOL-3) [My emphasis.]

The surface resemblance between these two statements and those from Collins (COL-1) and Blount (BLO) should be clear. They all assert that it is revelation, not reason, which offers the only, or best, ground for our belief in immortality. While Toland is less fideistic than Collins, although more so than Blount, they are all asserting precisely the opposite position of a deist. They are all, I submit, theological liars.

Yet there is an obvious objection to be considered, namely that we are dealing with irony, not lying. Moreover, lying is not merely "saying what you do not mean"; it is also "aiming to deceive by what you say." In short, instead of examples of a hidden art, COL-1, BLO, and TOL-1–3 are, it may be objected, fairly transparent cases of irony. They are not instances of lying, since they were not intended to deceive, nor could any intelligent reader be deceived by them.

There are two difficulties with this not unnatural objection. As stated, it begs the question, anachronistically assuming that contemporary readers of Collins, Toland, and Blount would see their statements as transparently ironic. It assumes that the contemporary reader would know that the authors were deists or critics of Christianity. Further, the quotations and their context conflict with a deist interpretation. For in COL-1 and (to a lesser extent) BLO and TOL-1–3 the writers are asserting, arguing, or suggesting that there are no satisfactory nonscriptural grounds for belief in immortality. But a deist, it is generally agreed, believes in immortality on nonscriptural, rational grounds. Yet Toland and particularly Collins and Blount devote much of their works to undermining the traditional and respected rational justifications for belief in immortality. As far as I can see, Collins offers no arguments—traditional or otherwise—in support of immortality. Blount does offer arguments, but, I would argue, they are intentionally weak. He intends to damn by faint argument. It is difficult to show this in a short space. Nor will everyone regard the statement of a certain argument as intentionally weak. Indeed, this is inevitable, since the Art can only work if some innocent readers failed to recognize it. Yet as Shaftesbury suggests, the sensible and skillful would. A not subtle example of Blount's technique of feeble argumentation occurs in section 28 of *Anima Mundi*, where, among a number of bad arguments against mortalism, there is the following:

> To say that the Soul is mortal, because it acts only by the help of its organs, were to draw a conclusion, from an uncertainty, it being never yet proved, that the Soul cann't act of itself without its organs. (93)

This comes down to an assertion that disembodied existence has not been proved impossible. Yet that hardly affects Blount's four persuasive (but disavowed) Epicurean arguments offered on pages 90–92 for the (disavowed) materialist thesis. Indeed in BLO Blount himself ridicules the notion that "separate Souls [can have] intuitive knowledge . . . without help of the imaginative [or sensory] part." And if this were not clear enough, Blount later, in section 36, explicitly attacks the mode of argumentation based on mere possibility: "he who believes a thing only because it may be true, may as well doubt of it because it may be otherwise" (111–12).

Another, even more crucial conflict is to be found in sections 9 and 29, both of which contain affirmations of immortality—like COL-1, TOL-1–3, and BLO—based on Scripture. In section 29 Blount begins by asserting that "all our knowledge arises out of the Experience which our Senses give us; and therefore a Man born throughly [sic] deaf, can have no apprehension of

Musick." He then, however, seems to qualify this empiricist position: "But the Soul is of a Spiritual nature, and so in it self utterly imperceptible by our Senses; the Soul it self alone can reflect on its own acts and conceptions." He then enters his religious caveat: "'Tis indeed very unsafe, any farther than it can be made appear we are guided by the clue of Divine Revelation, to guess and discourse over boldly concerning the nature of the Soul, or peremptorily to determine of its future condition" (95). Yet in section 9 Blount argues that the soul *cannot* purely reflect on its own acts; and hence is not separable from the body:

> ... if we confidently mark this inward perception of our knowledge, it may perhaps be nothing but the inward experience, which our imagination faculty gives us of what we know; and doth no more evince any separable faculty of the Soul, (as *Lucretius* observes) than the reflex and intrinsick perception of smart, which a Man's Foot gives him in a Fit of the Gout. (32–33)

What the soul reflects on is, ultimately, of a sensory nature; thus there is no justification for supposing that the soul (or its acts) is purely spiritual. Yet if there is no reason to suppose a purely spiritual soul, then there is no reason to believe in disembodied existence, or existence after death.

Throughout *Anima Mundi* Blount abuses the classical mortalists—Epicurus, Lucretius, Pliny; he speaks of their opinions as "absurd and monstrous" (12), "foolish" (33), "erroneous" (70, 106), "wicked" (87), "sinister" (103), "impious" (106), "fallacious" (110). But his favorite term of abuse, following Saint Paul, is that they are "vain." On seven occasions, the arguments of classical authors are called "vain" (13, 58, 71, 87, 91, 92, 105), yet, in fact, he shows these arguments to be formidable.

4. Tindal and Collins

The theme of "vain philosophy" is also in Matthew Tindal's *The Nation Vindicated*, part 2 (1712), one of his more speculative works that briefly but clearly criticizes rational or philosophical immortality while accepting scriptural immortality. Tindal is responding to a number of accusations contained in Francis Atterbury, *A Representation of the Present State of Religion* (1711). One accusation is that infidels have criticized the "natural immortality of the Soul ... as a Vulgar and groundless Error," to which Tindal replies (17–18):

> They indeed may be truly charg'd with Infidelity, who think that God's saying of a thing is not a sufficient Proof of its Truth, except we have recourse to vain Philosophy to help him out.... Is not this highly to weaken the Evidence of all those Matters that depend wholly [!] on the Promises of God.... I think it is highly uncharitable to condemn those of

> Infidelity, who presume not *to be wise above what is written;* and who, because the Scripture affirms, that *Christ hath abolish'd Death, and brought Life and Immortality to Light thro the Gospel,* 2 Tim. 2.6. dare not say in opposition to it, that the Light of Nature, antecedent to Divine Revelation, has brought the natural Immortality of the Soul to Light: especially when they see those who maintain this, divided about the Nature of the Soul, some making it an *extended,* some an *unextended* Being; some saying 'tis in a Place, others in a *Ubi;* some affirming 'tis in a Place *circumscriptive,* others only *definitive:* which is as intelligible as their saying, 'tis *All in All,* and *All in every Part.* (TIN)

As with COL-1, TOL-1–3, and BLO, Tindal here says precisely what a deist should not say, while doing what a covert mortalist would do: he magnifies revelation and faith and plays down reason and the "light of nature." Like his fellow freethinkers, he is a theological liar.

There are, it seems to me, three ways of reacting to my thesis and the evidence so far adduced in its favor. First, one could take Collins, Blount, Toland, and Tindal at their word and suppose that they were fideistic Christians, at least so far as the afterlife was concerned. However, I do not imagine that this will find much scholarly support. The more likely response would be to insist that their statements are so transparently insincere as to be instances of nondeceptive irony. Finally, some critics might agree that they were lying about immortality, yet maintain that it need not qualify or call in question their essential deism. For they could still believe in a transcendent creator of the world who is endowed with intellectual and moral perfections. Although I shall be discussing this last position in section 8 below, my primary concern in this paper is with the second objection.

The Collins text (COL-1) is, I think, the most transparent or nondeceptive of the texts adduced, but I am not sure that all or most contemporary readers would have clearly seen its dissimulation. We are apt to underestimate the gullibility and uncertainty of the average eighteenth-century reader. Thus Percy records a story of "a respectable alderman of Oxford" who believed that *Robinson Crusoe* was fact, rather than fiction. And, as Berkeley puts it in a pamphlet of 1735, "It must be owned, in an age of so much ludicrous humour, it is not everyone can at first sight discern a writer's real design" (1948–57, 4:147). Collins's *Discourse* could not have been transparently ironic, since some of its opponents—Hoadley, for example—felt obliged to reveal some of its techniques.[10] Nor, in any case, was Collins always so obvious. Consider, for example, the last paragraph of his *Letter . . . on . . . the Soul* (1707) against Samuel Clarke:

> I shall now only add, That under the Uncertainty in point of Reason, both of the Soul's Immateriality and Natural Immortality, I am not the less certain of Man's Immortality from the Gospel of Christ. . . . (COL-2)

or the first paragraph of his *Reply to Clark's Defence* (1707), where Collins says that he still thinks Clarke's argument to prove the natural immortality of the soul is "inconclusive"

> and proposes to show its inconclusiveness . . . and thereby contribute towards the Establishment of the Immortality of man on that Evidence only that God has thought fit to afford us of it. (COL-3)

by which Collins is clearly alluding to the often-quoted assertion from 2 Tim. 1:10, which appears (slightly misquoted) on the title page of this pamphlet. There is nothing obviously ironical about either COL-2 or COL-3, unless we anachronistically read them in the light of COL-1. If this is not granted, however, consider this bland statement from Collins's *Scheme of Literal Prophecy* (1727):

> . . . the true *end*, which man ought to have in *view*, is *happiness* during the extent of his being; *happiness* in *this* and *happiness* in a *future state*. (425)

I can see no grounds for interpreting this as ironical. It is either sincere or a case of lying. There is, in short, nothing plainly ironical about Collins's putative immortalism. Indeed, James O'Higgins, in two studies of Collins, is far from dismissing Collins's talk of immortality as ironical. Although he does not explain the theoretical basis of Collins's (supposed) belief, O'Higgins holds that Collins *was* a believer in an afterlife (1970, 230; 1976, 5).

5. Hume and Locke

Another way of showing the difficulty in interpreting our texts as (patently) ironic is by comparing them with statements by Locke and Hume on immortality. Hume's Christian assertions in "Of the Immortality of the Soul" come, predictably, in the first and last paragraphs of his essay:

> By the mere light of reason it seems difficult to prove the Immortality of the Soul. The arguments for it are commonly derived either from *metaphysical* topics, or *moral*, or *physical*. But in reality, it is the gospel, and the gospel alone, that has brought life and immortality to light. (HUM-1)

> Nothing could set in a fuller light the infinite obligation which mankind have to Divine revelation; since we find, that no other medium could ascertain this great and important truth. (HUM-2)

Sandwiched between these two "bounceing" statements are some of the most effective arguments against immortality. Hence it seems, and Toland's and Gildon's principles plainly support it, that Hume must have been insincere and ironic in his claim that "the Gospel alone . . . has brought . . . immortality to light." Having detected a conflict, one can easily see on which side the subversive and argumentative force lies. Yet there is something quite similar in Locke's *Second Reply to Stillingfleet* (1699; 1722, 1:571). There Locke argues that the usual philosophical arguments, taken from Plato and based on the substantiality, immateriality, and indivisibility of the soul, are not certain. Yet like Hume (and Collins) Locke affirms that they do not affect his belief in immortality:

> So unmovable is that Truth deliver'd by the Spirit of Truth, that tho' the Light of Nature gave some obscure Glimmering, some uncertain Hopes of a future State; yet human Reason could attain to no Clearness, no Certainty about it, but that it was JESUS CHRIST alone who had *brought Life and Immortality to Light thro' the Gospel*. (2 Tim. 1.10) Tho' we are now told [by Bishop Stillingfleet], that to own the Inability of Natural Reason to bring *Immortality to Light*, or, which passes for the same, to own Principles upon which the Immateriality of the Soul (and, as 'tis urg'd, consequently its Immortality) cannot be demonstratively prov'd; *does lessen the Belief of* this Article of Revelation, which JESUS CHRIST alone has *brought to Light*, and which consequently the Scripture assures us is establish'd and made certain only by Revelation. (LOC)

There is a clear resemblance between this and our other texts, particularly TIN. It is largely because we believe on external grounds that Locke was a sincere (although not an orthodox) Christian that we are inclined to read LOC straightforwardly. We read LOC as a statement of a sincere conditional immortalism rather than covert mortalism, even though it is wedged between interesting arguments questioning rational or philosophical immortalism. On the other hand, we read HUM-1 and HUM-2 as blatantly ironical, partly because we know—from Boswell, for example—that Hume was a mortalist (1971, 11–13). LOC and HUM-1, 2 may be seen, then, as two extreme ends of a spectrum in which our other texts hold intermediate positions. What this shows is that for a contemporary eighteenth-century reader, coming on the texts with little external knowledge of the authors—Collins's and Tindal's works are anonymous—the texts would not seem plainly ironical.

Another even more instructive way of showing the lack of patent irony in COL-1 and even perhaps in HUM-1, 2 is by comparing them with Philip Skelton's statements on immortality. In Dialogue 3 of *Ophiomaches* Skelton states that "we can have no assurance [of future rewards and punishments], but by revelation" (1:167). He then subjects various respected conceptions of the soul and arguments for immortality to harsh criticism (see 168–85). He concludes that there have been few philosophers outside the Christian tradition who seriously believed in immortality, and even these, he says, "defend it with but nonsense and sophistry" (183). Had one found such expressions in Collins, Blount, Toland, or Tindal, one would have little doubt that they were artful. Yet there is every reason to believe that the Reverend Philip Skelton was a sincere Christian fideist. This shows that Gildon's principle is by no means infallible. Here the extremes of Hume and Skelton meet, to be distinguished, largely, by external evidence.[11] Not everybody would find HUM-1, 2 ironic "at first sight." A fideistic Christian, in the mold of Skelton, might well wonder. Nor is it evident that Hume expected *everyone* to see his ironic intent. Thus in a private letter of 1764, he makes the following comment on theological dissimulation: "It is putting too great a respect on the vulgar, and on their superstitions, to pique one's self on sincerity with regard to them. Did ever one make it a point of honour to speak truth to children or madmen?" (1932, 439).

6. The Art: Protection, Communication, Insinuation

In my account of Collins, Tindal, Toland, Blount, and Hume, I have so far followed Shaftesbury, Toland, and Gildon in seeing two components or purposes in the Art: (1) the literal meaning, used to deceive the vulgar, and protect the writer and "tender" reader—this component might be called "defensive raillery"; and (2) the esoteric message, which was to be communicated to other knowing or sensible freethinkers, but which, perforce, could also be comprehended by knowing orthodox clerical enemies.

There are difficulties with this two-term theory. In particular, it supposes that freethinkers were artfully communicating ideas that were already known and accepted. But why go to so much trouble to preach to the converted? Of course, although the general position or message would be known, new details or arguments could be communicated. Practicing the Art would also have angered the knowing clerics, whose rage would delight the practitioners. Yet even granting this, there would seem to be something vain in the Art if it included only those—friends and foes—who already generally understood it.

I suggest that there is another component or purpose in the artful writings of Collins et al; this is: (3) insinuation, or gently and covertly suggesting the second component (the radical message) to some of those ignorant of it. Such insinuation might be called "offensive raillery." Among those who saw and wrote about it were George Berkeley and Skelton. In *Alciphron* (1732) Berkeley speaks of those freethinkers who "write . . . by insinuation"; he calls them "moles," who work "with much art and industry, and at first with secrecy . . . like moles underground, concealing [their] progress from the public" (Dialogue 2.23, also see 7.26). In his *Theory of Vision Vindicated*, published in the following year, Berkeley says that the "atheist who gilds and insinuates, and, even while he insinuates, disclaims his principles is the likeliest to spread them" (section 3). This fits most of our texts. They claim to be endorsing belief in immortality while insidiously undermining it.

I shall argue that, with the (probable) exception of LOC, all the quotations

I have produced can be read in a threefold way: (1) literally they assert the truth of Gospel immortality in order to deceive the vulgar and protect the writer; (2) yet they assert it in such a way, and in such a context, that fellow freethinkers would recognize that it amounted to an assertion of disbelief in immortality. (3) They insinuate and suggest to some unknowing and unwary readers that immortality (and religion in general) was more questionable and sillier than they had originally thought.

In order to appreciate (3), the insinuation, it is often crucial to see the context in which a "bounceing compliment" is embedded. Consider COL-1; its context is Collins's attempt to show that (the biblical) Solomon was a freethinker. Collins begins by noting that Solomon is described in the Bible, the "*word of God* [,] to be the *wisest of men*" (124); yet Solomon also "argues against a future state . . ." (126). Collins then indirectly, as it appears, embarks on a "vindication" of Solomon, which amounts to showing that other wise ancients also disbelieved in a future state. Collins insinuates that the wise position is in fact unbelief. Then follows his fideistic, Gospel assertion of immortality, which "bounceing compliment," as I have said, is so extreme that it would, at the least for the more intelligent vulgar, engender suspicion, particularly when taken with the accompanying crude trinitarian assertion. There are other insinuating signs as well. If the Bible, "the word of God," states that Solomon was the "wisest" of men, how can he then be wrong or ignorant about so fundamental a truth as immortality? Either he is wisest, and then he is right about mortalism, or he is not wisest, and then the Bible, "the word of God," is not always truthful. But if the Bible is not always truthful then we cannot depend on its assertion that Christ brought immortality. This implication would have been evident to Collins's fellow freethinkers; they would have seen the message. Others, though, the innocent and vulgar, might have been puzzled. The insinuations may have raised questions in some of their minds. Some of Collins's critics, as I have mentioned, saw this danger and pointed out the insinuations, presumably in order to warn the unwary. Yet that strategy also had its danger, since it would reveal a subversive message that were better left disguised. Literally, of course, Collins was asserting a belief in Gospel immortality, as his mentor, Locke, had done some fifteen years earlier.

Insinuation (3) and esoteric communication (2) are difficult, by their natures, to pinpoint or prove. But the way to proceed is by using the clearer cases, comparing them with those less clear. Hume's assertions are most clear. It is significant that they occur in the first and last paragraphs, which, I have suggested, was part of a code that developed in the eighteenth century, a code most blatantly seen in Hume, particularly in his essays on miracles and immortality. There were, in short, certain signs whereby a freethinker could recognize another freethinker's work.

In his discussion of immortality in *Ophiomaches*, Skelton offers details of the way freethinkers use "artful expressions, capable of double meanings, to bear their unwary readers . . . at last, to disbelief of all futurity" (1:168). Here is his analysis of Tindal:

> It is true, he [Tindal] hath here and there dropped a saving expression concerning the happiness and misery to come, in order to prevent the offence, which doing otherwise might have given, and by that means keep his book open to a class of men, who desire extremely to be deceived, yet are so delicate, that if they saw at first he was endeavouring to lead them into Atheism in effect, they would wholly lay him aside. On the other hand, he takes much pains to inculcate such principles, as, if true, would intirely render needless all accounts to be given in another life, of what is done here. (1:169)

For Skelton the "bounceing compliment," or "saving expression"—as he puts it—not only protects the freethinker but helps him to insinuate his message. Skelton's specific examples from *Christianity as Old as Creation* (1730) of mortalistic insinuations are interesting and plausible but not conclusive. They are not as clearly or openly artful as the arguments in Collins, Blount, Toland. Yet surely we must expect something like this. If they were to be successfully insinuating, then they could not be too obvious. Indeed, perhaps one reason for the enormous impact of Tindal's *Christianity as Old as Creation* was its effective use of insinuation. It was more alarming to hostile clerics than more overtly mortalistic work, such as Collins's pamphlets against Clarke, or the even more radical works by Hume and Count Radicati (Berman, 1983).

7. The Art of Insinuation: Its Prevalence

How common was the Art and, specifically, its use of insinuation or offensive raillery? If we suppose that it was widespread, we can resolve a notable puzzle or anomaly that has not, I think, been squarely faced by scholars of eighteenth-century intellectual history. Briefly, one finds numerous eighteenth-century treatises, pamphlets, and sermons arguing for immortality and a future life. Part of the purpose of these works must be, one assumes, to convince opponents, the mortalists; and indeed mortalists are often alluded to in the works of R. Bentley, S. Clarke, W. Sherlock, Berkeley, and, as we have seen, the *Representation* attacked by Tindal. The impression given is that there were dozens, perhaps hundreds of active mortalists. Yet who are the eighteenth-century British mortalists? I claim that there were no such overt British mortalists. No avowed or published statements of mortalism can be found. The earliest published statement of mortalism I have found is that by George Ensor in 1801.[12] Even the first published work of British atheism, issued in 1782, does not contain a clear statement of overt mortalism.[13]

How then, are we to explain this anomaly? Why is so much effort spent in proving something if no one denied it? I suggest that the orthodox were not shadowboxing; they were aware of an enemy. This enemy was covert, but not the less formidable for that. Hence the numerous orthodox treatises aimed at demonstrating immortality argue for the widespread deployment of the freethinking moles—as Berkeley called them—the theological liars and covert mortalists. Their artful books offered the principles, arguments, and hints that, as Berkeley said, could be improved upon in conversation (see *Alciphron*, "Advertisement").

Insinuation, like esoteric communication, can be viewed as a spectrum, and here again Hume occupies one extreme. He is the most obvious insinuator, and he was, I think, aware of this. This comes out in the letter I quoted from above, where he seems to regret not being more covert or hypocritical, and also in the *Treatise of Human Nature* (1739), in book 1, part 3, section 13, "Of Unphilosophical Probability," where he speaks of

> an indirect manner of insinuating praise or blame, which is much less shocking than the open flattery or censure of any person. However he may communicate his sentiments by such secret insinuations, and make them known with equal certainty as by the open discovery of them, 'tis certain that their influence is not equally strong and powerful. One who lashes me with conceal'd strokes of satire, moves not my indignation to such a degree, as if he flatly told me I was a fool and coxcomb; tho' I equally understand his meaning, as if he did.

Hume compares this secret insinuation with sexual mores. Thus when sexual

> violations [are] open and avow'd, the world never excuses, but which it is more apt to overlook, when the appearances are sav'd, and the transgression is secret and conceal'd. Even those, who know with equal certainty, that the fault is committed, pardon it more easily, when the proofs seem in some measure oblique and equivocal, than when they are direct and undeniable.

A socially unacceptable action is less objectionable if it is done covertly, rather than overtly. To illustrate this Hume nicely quotes Cardinal de Retz's observations that

> *there are many things, in which the world wishes to be deceived;* and *that it more easily excuses a person in acting than in talking contrary to the decorum of his profession and character.*

To apply this to our particular topic. Although Hume *says* that he believes in Gospel immortality, he *shows/proves* that the doctrine is groundless. The same can be said of Collins, Toland, and Blount, although their secret insinuations, and intentions, are less obvious than Hume's. With Hume the secret insinuation is "known with equal certainty" as an "open" denial of immortality. Yet because it is not open, it is more tolerable. COL-1 would be closest to Hume in transparency of insinuation; then TOL-1–3, BLO, TIN, and then (perhaps) LOC. The greater the insinuation the more difficult, perhaps, the communication of (2), the esoteric message. Conversely, what a freethinker gained in (2) he would, very likely, lose in (3).

8. Mortalism and Atheism

I have argued above that the immortalist assertions of Collins, Toland, Blount, and Tindal were instances, not of simple irony, but of the Art of theological lying. I have also suggested that this questions the description of them as deists. Yet, as I noted, a possible response to this suggestion is to insulate their theological lying on immortality from their assertions and beliefs concerning God's existence. The deists, according to this view, were (if need be) insincere in their immortalism; but that need not cast doubts on the sincerity of their deism, their belief in God. Yet there is, prima facie, a fatal difficulty with this response. One is reminded of the story (attributed to G. B. Shaw) about a woman who was asked if she would prostitute herself for a million pounds. When she said yes, the questioner asked if she would accept one pound, to which she indignantly retorted: "What sort of woman do you take me for?", to which the propositioner replied: "That, madam, has already been established." The theological lying of Collins, Toland, Blount and Tindal has been established. Hence, no one should be indignant, prima facie, about the possibility that they are also lying about God's existence. The onus of proof now lies with those who claim that they were sincere deists to show that they were.

Let us, however, move somewhat below the surface of this challenge and examine the following statement from Blount's 1680 letter to Lord Rochester, "Concerning the immortality of the soul," first printed in the *Oracles of Reason* (1693). Having presented some difficulties in accepting immortality, Blount indicates his acceptance, particularly on account of "the absolute necessity and convenience that it should be so." Yet Blount ostentatiously repudiates the *anima mundi* notion of immortality, which he associates with Seneca; for such immortality carries no implications for otherworldly rewards and punishments and, hence, social order. Such a notion, Blount says, is "unaccountable or contradictory," although it is clear from his book *Anima Mundi* that he looks favorably on it. His verbal repudiation is linked with the rejection of another nontheistic notion—of God—yet the insinuation is that he favors both, or, more precisely, atheism:

> For, as to suppose a hum-drum Deity chewing his own Nature, a droning God, sit hugging of himself, and hoarding up his Providence from his Creatures, is an Atheism no less irrational, than to deny the very Essence

of a Divine Being; so, in my Opinion, to believe an immortality of the
Soul without its due Rewards and Punishments, is altogether as irrational
and useless as to believe the Soul itself to be mortal; by such a Faith we
rob the Soul of its best Title to immortality: for what need is there of an
Executor where there are no Debts to pay, nor any Estate to inherit? (1695,
126–27)

Here the belief in personal immortalism and a providential God are connected and affirmed. And yet there is reason to believe that both affirmations are insincere and that the connection of theism with immortalism was meant to undermine the latter. "What need *is* there of an Executor where there are no Debts to pay"? In short, theism without immortalism is vain. It is our desire for immortality, as Schopenhauer was later to argue, that prompts us to postulate a God able to superintend the other world. Conversely, once mortalism is accepted, then God is no longer required; for it is immortality (will-to-eternal-life), not theism, that is the primary desideratum.

Indeed, if mortalism is proved or assumed, then one has a plausible *ad hominem* argument for atheism. According to rationalist theologians such as Clarke, immortality and a future life ineluctably follow from (1) God's justice and providence and (2) the fact that the just and unjust do not always get their proper rewards in this world. If one accepts (2) and mortalism, then it will be difficult to resist the conclusion that God cannot be just or providential; yet these were regarded as necessary features of the Christian God. Once mortalism is accepted, atheism seems to follow. Indeed, one can argue historically that it is more likely that a mortalist will be an atheist, than that an atheist will be a mortalist. The first avowed British atheist and the second—Shelley—and McTaggart were militant atheists, yet also immortalists.[14] It is, then, difficult to insulate mortalism from atheism.

There are also more specific reasons for believing that Collins, Toland, Blount, and Tindal were atheists, although I can only briefly allude to them here. I have elsewhere offered internal and external evidence for such an interpretation of Tindal ("Tindal," 1985, 167–68). Blount himself insinuates atheism in the passage I just quoted. Hume, as I have argued, insinuates his atheism by the denial of atheism, and Toland does the same.[15] In any case, Toland's later avowed pantheism is hardly consistent with deism; and his earlier deistic assertions, as in the penultimate section of the *Letters to Serena*, should be read, I have maintained, as theological lying.[16] The so-called major deists were not, I contend, deists at all; they were atheists. Instead of the shallow, superficial deism—as described by Leslie Stephen (1876, III, sect. 74)—we are, I suggest, dealing with deep, covert atheism. Whereas most scholars[17] seem inclined to detach Hume from the so-called major deists—Collins, Toland, Tindal, and Blount—on the grounds that Hume was no deist, I have tried to show, in one area at least, that they all make up a fairly homogeneous group. The history of deism may turn out to be more like the history of covert atheism.

NOTES

1. This is Ernest Mossner's expression; see "Deism," 1967, 2:328. Peter Gay describes Toland, Collins, and Tindal as the "major" English deists (1968, 52).
2. I shall be using the 149-page edition of the *Discourse*, probably published in Holland (127). For convenient reference, I shall also be appending identifying abbreviations to the primary quotations.
3. Nearly all writers on deism—J. Leland, L. Stephen, J. M. Robertson, E. Cassirer, P. Gay, E. Mossner, J. O'Higgins—have taken Collins to be a deist.
4. See Toland, "Clidophorus," 1720, 61; Warburton, 1742, 1:337; Shaftesbury, 1723, 1:62; Collins 1729; Hume, *Treatise*, in 1875, 1:446.
5. 1729, 24. On Collins's authorship of the *Discourse*, see O'Higgins 1970, 196, who is unaware that the *Discourse* was attributed to Collins as early as 1730, in *Free Thoughts* 1730, 3.
6. Also see Foster 1731, preface, who speaks of the "danger of being deceived" by the books of the "opposers of revelation" (v).
7. 1788, 158–60. Hutcheson's "reticence" concerning free will had been noticed by J. Martineau 1901, 563.
8. I shall be using the edition of *Anima Mundi* contained in Blount's *Miscellaneous Works* (1695), 31.
9. Gildon himself applies this principle to William Coward's views on immortality: "if I think his Arguments for that [conditional immortality] weaker, than for the Mortality of the Soul, I must beg his Pardon if I believe one, and not the other" (*Deist's Manual* 180–81). It is not clear to me that Coward was a covert mortalist. Another problematic "deist" is Thomas Chubb. In his *View*, Leland argues that while Chubb says he believes in an afterlife, he also argues against it (1:299–303).
10. In his *Queries* (1713) on Collins's *Discourse*, Hoadley writes:

> ... lest any of [Collins's] less heedful Readers should be led to think [him] too hardly dealt with, in being taxed expressly with such a Design [i.e., writing against "the Belief of Christianity"], they are desired to consider . . . [that] . . . No favourable Word, concerning the Gospel itself, is spoken, which doth not look more like Banter, than the Sense of the Writers. As, our most Holy faith, and the like; when there is least Reason to think them serious. . . . Many sly Insinuations, at the same time, are drop'd against it: even where the Difficulties cannot possibly touch the Foundations upon which that stands. (28–29)

Compare Swift's strategy in *Mr. C——ns's Discourse of Free-Thinking, Put into Plain English* (1713).

11. According to Burdy, Hume was partly responsible for the publication of Skelton's *Ophiomaches*, since he advised his publisher, Andrew Millar, to print it (1914, 100).
12. In *The Principles of Morality* (1801) Ensor writes: "it seems to me the most extreme frenzy, to suppose that man shall survive his mortality on earth, in a conscious independent existence" (182).
13. This is Matthew Turner, *An Answer to Dr. Priestley's Letters to a Philosophical Unbeliever;* See Berman 1978, n. 18.
14. See note 13, above; Shelley 1845, vii–viii; McTaggart 1906, chaps. 3 and 6.
15. See Toland 1695, where he denies being "the least tintur'd with Atheism, a crime charg'd upon many excellent Men. . . . I have Travel'd many Countries, yet could never meet with any Atheists, which are few, if any; all the noise is against Castles in the Air; a sort of War, like that of Don Quixote, with the Windmills" (iv–v). For esoteric meaning of this, see Berman 1983, 375–87.
16. Berman, "Toland," 1985, 669; this is the way Robert Sullivan reads Toland in his useful *John Toland*, chap. 6. J. M. Robertson, on the other hand, takes Toland literally in his *Dynamics of Religion*, 89.
17. Stephen 1876, II, sect. 12; Cassirer 1966, 178–79; Gay 1973, 1:374; Mossner, "Deism" 1967, 2:331. I am grateful to Dr. Ian Ross, Mr. Stephen Lalor, Mr. Ian Tipton, and Dr. Bertil Belfrage for comments on an earlier draft of this essay.

The Amerindian in the Early American Enlightenment: Deistic Satire in Robert Beverley's *History of Virginia* (1705)

J. A. LEO LEMAY

Robert F. Berkhofer's *The White Man's Indian: Images of the American Indian from Columbus to the Present,* published in 1978, synthesizes and summarizes Amerindian scholarship and contains numerous stimulating perceptions based upon Berkhofer's own reading of the primary works. The book generally reflects the state of Amerindian historical and anthropological scholarship to that date. Yet Professor Berkhofer says, "in the English colonies the literary and ideological use of the Noble Savage came on the scene only during the Revolutionary era" (76). He knows that Americans made literary and ideological use of the Noble Savage during the Revolution because he cites Professor Alfred Owen Aldridge's 1950 essay, "Benjamin Franklin's Deistic Indians" (Berkhofer 1978, 218 n. 14). Aldridge showed that Franklin, in essays of 1768 and 1784, used the Indian for deistic propaganda.

Beside the historical and anthropological studies of the Amerindian, another scholarly tradition that bears upon my subject is represented by Henry F. May's study entitled *The Enlightenment in America,* published in 1976. Of the half-dozen books devoted to the intellectual history of eighteenth-century America that appeared from 1975 to 1978 (Cassara, Commager, Meyer, White, and Wills), Professor May's is the most comprehensive, ambitious, and best-received volume (e.g., reviews by Kammen and Segal). He devotes the first hundred pages to what he calls the "Moderate Enlightenment," which he believes existed in America from approximately 1688 to the end of the American Revolution. May's overlapping second division of eighteenth-century American intellectual history is the "Skeptical Enlightenment," which begins, he argues, at about 1750. In May's account, few American skeptics, freethinkers, or deists existed in America before 1750. May several times cites with approval the monograph published by

Herbert M. Morais in 1934, entitled *Deism in Eighteenth-Century America*, which finds little deism in America before the mid-eighteenth century.[1]

But R[ay] W[illiam] Frantz pointed out in *The English Traveller and the Movement of Ideas, 1660–1723* (1934) that the English freethinker John Toland, who died in 1722, wrote a sketch concerning the Indians of Carolina (Toland 1726, 2:423-28). Since Toland never visited America and since he was a notorious freethinker, his "Account of the Indians at Carolina" is clearly recognized as deistic propaganda. Frantz notes that Toland's sketch was inspired by the treatment of the Indians in John Lawson's *A New Voyage to Carolina*, published in 1709 (Frantz 1934, 151). Because of Toland's indebtedness to Lawson, one might well hypothesize that Lawson, in his *New Voyage*, also wrote deistic propaganda. And that was indeed the case. Lawson, in turn, was influenced by Robert Beverley, a native Virginian, whose *History of Virginia* appeared in 1705. It had six early-eighteenth-century editions, four in French and two in English (Clayton-Torrence 1908, nos. 92, 96, 97, 99, 102, and 104). I shall argue in this essay that Beverley uses the Amerindian as a vehicle for his religious satire.

Perhaps Roland Stromberg gives the best definition of deism (the belief that natural religion alone is sufficient for salvation [1954, 55]), but the definition is too narrow to encompass the various seventeenth- and eighteenth-century beliefs that those people held who called themselves deists. And it is certainly too narrow to describe the various beliefs that seventeenth- and eighteenth-century critics of deism referred to under that name. But a term that encompasses too many meanings gradually loses its usefulness in intellectual history. I therefore choose a middle way between Stromberg's rigorous definition and the impressionistic usages of Enlightenment contemporaries. I adopt Leslie Stephen's categories. He divided deism into *critical deism* (writings that satirize the Bible, miracles, superstition, and in general the claims of revealed religion) and *constructive deism* (writings that gather together and define the truths of natural religion).

Actually, although Beverley's ideology clearly derives from his Virginia background and experience, as well as from his reading of John Locke and the early deists, he belongs in a literary tradition that includes Michel de Montaigne (Chinard 1911, 193–218; Fairchild 1928, 15–21; Keen 1971, 156–62; and Scaglione 1976) and John Dryden (see the sources and the scholarship cited for "Religio Laici" and *The Indian Emperour* in 1956–vols. 2 and 9). A large number of writers before Beverley used the Amerindian to embody their relativistic and skeptical viewpoints. No records exist of Beverley's library, but the internal evidence in his writings makes it clear that he collected manuscripts concerning Virginia, Americana in general, and standard works of the Enlightenment. Of course he also had access to the library of his brother-in-law, William Byrd of Westover. Byrd owned a three-volume collection of Montaigne's *Essays* (Bassett 1901, 423) and five sets of Dryden, including a three-volume collection of the *Works* and a three-volume collection of the *Plays* (Basset 1901, 422, 424, and 425). Beverley must have owned the recent work by a French explorer and Indian authority, the Baron de Lahontan, whose popular *New Voyages to North America* appeared in English in 1702 (Greenly 1954 and Hayne 1966–) for he frequently cites it (161, 164, 169, 182, 188, 190–91, 195, 198, 200). Its *Supplement* of 1703 (probably coauthored by Nicholas Gueudeville) contained a series of fictional dialogues between Lahontan and an Indian named Adario. The dialogues portray the Huron as living in a Cartesian and deistic primitivism (P. Adams 1962, 199–200; and Betts 1984, 129–36).[2] Although Lahontan's Adario conversations are frequently mentioned by Enlightenment scholars, they seem not to realize that American contemporaries of the English and French freethinkers wrote similar propaganda. Like many Americans, Beverley was thoroughly immersed in Enlightenment ideology. He praises religious tolerance, ridicules adherence to unexamined tradition and authority, celebrates the experimental method, and uses Lockean epistemology and psychology. Further, like a number of other early Americans, he advocates republicanism in his writings.[3]

Beverley devoted the third part of his *History of Virginia* to the Indians, and here, as throughout the book, his tone is commonsensical and realistic, with touches of satire and irony. In discussing the Virginia Indians' religion, Beverley preserves this plain-dealer persona, and invites the reader's faith by condemning the Baron Lahontan for making the Indians "have such refin'd Notions, as seems almost to confute his own belief of Christianity" (198). And yet, Beverley's Virginia Indians are strangely contradictory. On the one hand, they are superstitious and priestcraft-ridden; and on the other, they believe in the principles of natural religion. The explanation for these contradictions is that Beverley was writing deistic propaganda.

In fact, we can be fairly certain that Beverley (and not the Virginia Indians) is responsible for the religious satire. It has long been known that Beverley borrowed heavily from Captain John Smith (of course Byrd owned Smith's folio *History of Virginia* [Bassett 1901, 416]) and other early Virginia authors, and that he had Theodore De Bry's engravings for Thomas Hariot's *Brief and True Report of Virginia* (1590) reengraved by Simon Gribelin (with minor additions and changes) for his own *History* (Winsor 1889, 3:164). Although scholars have repeatedly used Beverley's information about Virginia Indians, they have also caught him in some questionable statements and some surprising errors. John R. Swanton found that Beverley generalized from a single statement in the earlier literature (1946, 645; Beverley 1705, 174) and caught him in one obvious mistake (Swanton 1946, 483). Swanton also cast doubt upon Beverley's originality and accuracy by pointing out that he slavishly followed De Bry's engravings and Thomas Hariot's notes (Swanton 1946, 438, 478, 503, and 745). William C. Sturtevant noted that he falsified some information (Hulton and Quinn 1964, 1:101). Joseph and Nesta Ewan discovered that Beverley plagiarized extensively from the manuscripts of a seventeenth-century Virginia scientist, John Banister. And Judy Jo Small observed one instance of Beverley's plagiarizing Lahontan (1983, 536).

Beverley used John Banister not only in the second part of his *History of Virginia*, devoted to natural history, but also in the third part, on Virginia's Indians. Although Beverley rearranged Banister's information into a more logical order, he often borrows Banister's facts, references, diction, and phrases. His changes and interpolations can be especially revealing. Robert D. Arner commented that Beverley reflected Lockean notions of "figure and substance" when he discussed the Indians' setting up "Pyramidical Stones and Pillars" (Arner 1976, 87). Arner did not know that Beverley took most of the passage from Banister (Ewan and Ewan 1970, 377–78), but Arner's point is even more convincing when one realizes that Beverley interpolated the Lockean ideology into Banister's straightforward description. Occasionally, Beverley lifts whole paragraphs from Banister with minimal revisions (e.g., Beverley 1705, 137, cf. Ewan and Ewan 1970, 375–76; Beverley 141, cf. Ewan and Ewan 359; Beverley 142, cf. Ewan and Ewan 359; Beverley 144, cf. Ewan and Ewan 358–59). And we cannot be certain of the entire extent of Beverley's plagiarism, for not all of Banister's manuscripts are extant, and portions are missing from those we have.,

Beverley devotes the third book of his *History of Virginia* to the Indian. By far the longest chapter in the third book concerns the Indians' religion. Beverley claims that the Indian priests and conjurors keep their religion a secret and that they teach the common Indians that it is a "Sacriledge, to divulge the Principles of their Religion." Nevertheless he managed to learn their greatest mystery. "As I was ranging the Woods, with some other Friends, we fell upon their *Quioccosan* (which is their House of Religious Worship) at a time, when the whole Town were gathered together in another place" (195). Beverley says that the temple was eighteen feet wide and thirty feet long. To illustrate his adventure, he prints an engraving of an "Idol in Its Tabernacle" as his plate 11 (199). Here, as in his other illustrations, Beverley had Simon Gribelin copy the engravings published in De Bry. In most of Beverley's engravings, De Bry's originals have been slightly changed, usually by adding some features that occur in Beverley's descriptions (Swanton 1946, 519). But Beverley adds nothing to De Bry's picture of the idol, except for placing it within a large Indian house of worship similar to that shown in another De Bry engraving, one that Beverley also reproduced in his *History*. Beverley's engraving of the "Idol call'd OKEE, QUIOCCOS, or KIWASA" merely combines two of De Bry's illustrations. In the caption accompanying De Bry's sixteenth-century engraving of "Ther Idol Kiwasa," Thomas Hariot had written that the idols are placed "in a darke corner where they shew terrible" (Hariot 1590, 71). I believe that Beverley builds upon this hint and adds suspense by telling of his emotions while supposedly exploring the Indian temple.

Beverley says that he and his friend removed the fourteen logs barricading the quioccosan and entered it:

> We did not observe any Window, or passage for the Light, except the Door, and the vent of the Chimney. At last, we observ'd, that at the farther end, about ten foot of the Room, was cut off by a Partition of very close Mats; and it was dismal dark behind that Partition. We were at first scrupulous to enter this obscure place, but at last we ventur'd and groping about, we felt some posts in the middle; then reaching our hands up those Posts, we found large Shelves, and upon these Shelves three Mats, each of which was roll'd up and sow'd fast. These we handed down to the light, and to save time in unlacing the Seams, we made use of a Knife, and ripp'd them without doing any damage to the Mats. (196)

Within one mat, Beverley supposedly discovers the basic materials from which the idol is assembled. He describes the parts exactly:

> The pieces were these, first a Board three foot and a half long, with one indenture at the upper end, like a Fork, to fasten the Head upon, from thence half way down, were Half hoops nail'd to the edges of the Board, at about four Inches distance, which were bow'd out, to represent the Breast and Belly; on the lower half was another Board of half the length of the other, fasten'd to it by Joynts or pieces of Wood, which being set on each side, stood out about 14 inches from the Body, and half as high; we suppos'd the use of these to be for the bowing out of the Knees, when the Image was set up. (197)

When assembled, Beverley's idol would be constructed exactly like the one portrayed by De Bry in Hariot's *Virginia*. Beverley emphasizes the similarity (and supposedly reinforces his own truthfulness) by presenting an engraving of the idol kiwasa set up in a situation such as he described in the back of the quioccosan.

Beverley goes on to tell how the idol is displayed, emphasizing the imposture that he supposes the Indian medicine men employed in order to awe the people:

> This Image when drest up, might look very venerable in that dark place; where 'tis not possible to see it, but by the glimmering light, that is let in, by lifting up a piece of the Matting, which we observ'd to be conveniently hung for that purpose; for when the light of the Door and Chimney, glance in several directions, upon the Image thro that little passage, it must needs make a strange representation, which those poor people are taught to worship with a devout Ignorance. (197–98)

Although Beverley repeatedly stresses that the Indians will not talk about their religion and will not allow a nonbeliever to see inside their temple, he nevertheless progresses from describing the quioccosan to telling what the ceremony must be like. And then he even describes the ceremony itself:

> There are other things that contribute towards carrying on this Imposture; first the chief Conjurer enters within the Partition in the dark, and may undiscern'd move the Image as he pleases: Secondly, a Priest of Authority stands in the room with the people, to keep them from being too inquisitive, under the penalty of the Deity's displeasure, and his own censure.(198)

How does Beverley know the motivations and actions of the medicine men while they are conducting their religious rituals? Clearly Beverley has not seen the rituals. He *must* have invented the actions and the motivations. The idea of religion as imposture characterized critical deism (e.g., Betts 1984, index, s. v. "imposture"). What Beverley does is to provide an example of the kind of imposture that John Toland described in *Christianity Not Mysterious* (1696), especially in the chapter entitled "The History and Significance of Mystery in the Writings of the Gentiles." Beverley's account supposedly proves Toland's theories.

Any careful reader should realize that Beverley cannot know what actually happens during the Indians' religious ritual. Beverley's description of the actions and motivations of the Indian shamen during a religious ceremony must be his own creation. His description of the ritual is clearly a fiction. One may nevertheless believe that Beverley actually did explore an Indian house of worship. Although John R. Swanton acknowledges that Beverley follows De Bry's engravings and Hariot's notes, he comments that the text "represents apparently direct observation" (1946, 745). And Glyndwr Williams says, "Beverley was one of the few Englishmen who had ventured inside an Indian ceremonial place of worship—an exploit which he considered might have cost him his life" (Marshall and Williams 1982, 194). But I suspect that the entire episode is Beverley's creation. When he began to write his chapter "Concerning the Religion, and Worship of the Indians," Beverley evidently felt that he had practically nothing to say about the "mysteries of the Indian Religion." (Incidentally, the use of the words *imposture* and *mysteries* in connection with religion in 1705 would alert any contemporary reader to Beverley's involvement with the deistic controversies.) Beverley added, "because my rule is to say nothing but the naked Truth, I intend to be very brief upon this Head" (195). But Beverley's chapter on the Indians' religion is the third longest in the entire four books of the *History*. Either Beverley initially misled the reader about his knowledge of the Indian religion or he hoodwinked the audience when he described his exploration of the quioccosan.

Consider his description. He approximates the measurements of the house but gives exact ones for the various parts of the idol. After all, he said that he *chanced* across the vacant temple while ranging the woods (hunting, one naturally assumes) with some friends. Are we to presume he carried a ruler with him? And remember that Beverley, to build up the suspense, emphasizes that he and his companions rushed while inside the quioccosan, fearful lest the Indians return and discover them. Thus, rather than take the time to untie the strings holding the mats containing the idol, they hurriedly cut them. Would they then have carefully measured the idol's dimensions? If so, they must have carried it outside, for Beverley dwells upon the darkness and gloom inside. Furthermore, if Beverley did measure the pieces of wood, did he have these notes with him in London where he wrote, supposedly on the spur of the moment, his *History of Virginia?* Common sense tells us that if he actually entered a vacant Indian temple and examined some objects rolled up in mats within it, he did not measure them and took no notes on them. At best, he makes up the probable dimensions; and we must suspect that he creates a description that he thinks would result in a form resembling the idol Kiwasa as portrayed in De Bry's engraving and copied by Simon Gribelin.

Although a close reading strongly suggests that Beverley makes up the entire episode, perhaps the best reason for doubting that it happened at all is Beverley's use of De Bry's engraving of the idol Kiwasa. Beverley had the bad luck to use the one engraving in Hariot's *Brief and True Report* that does not seem to be authentic. All other Virginia engravings in De Bry's edition of Hariot are taken from John White's drawings made in North Carolina in 1585–86. But De Bry himself evidently added the picture of "Ther Idol Kiwasa" to the printed volume. No such drawing by White exists. William C. Sturtevant, the anthropologist who examined the ethnological details in John White's drawings and De Bry's engravings, has pointed out that the picture of "Ther Idol Kiwasa" is "much too naturalistic in the European manner, bearing no resemblance to any eastern North American (or other Indian) art style." He found "the character of the headdress and the costume" unlike any known Amerindian examples, and further stated that "the very high decorated tops on the mocassins, the beads around the thighs, and the neatly tailored jacket are all unparalleled in this region." Although Sturtevant did not draw the conclusion, he suggested that the engraving represents some artist's imaginative creation— not the reality. Sturtevant also quoted Beverley's account of the disassembled idol and then wrote: "One wonders whether this was really an 'idol.' Beverley's interpretation (and his memory of what he saw) may have been influenced by De Bry's engraving, which he reproduced. Can it have been a medicine bundle?" (Hulton and Quinn 1964, 1:93).

Sturtevant made his observations in the early 1960s. In 1970 Joseph and Nesta Ewan discovered that Robert Beverley copied extensively from John Banister's notes on natural history and on the Virginia Indians. Although

Beverley plagiarizes, he almost always makes the borrowed material more interesting. He occasionally lifts whole sentences from Banister, but he usually rearranges Banister's materials into better order and he often dramatizes them. He characteristically transforms Banister's simple descriptions into rhetorically artful prose by making it more personal and more active, by speculating on the Indians' motives, and by setting the data in the context of contemporary philosophical opinion. In describing the Indian initiation ceremony of huskanawing, John Banister wrote that the youths who were initiated "forget all manner of commerce and conversation they have formerly had in the world; they know neither friends nor relations (at least wise they are forced to pretend so) nor must they claim any property of what they formerly enjoyed" (Ewan and Ewan 1970, 381). Beverley thus revised Banister: "Those which I ever observ'd to have been *Huskanawed*, were lively handsome well timber'd young men, from fifteen to twenty years of age or upward, and such as were generally reputed rich" (209). Notice that Beverley has added a personal element and specific details to Banister's information, as well as an interesting generalization. But, of course, the generalization is wrong, for all Indian adolescent males were initiated. Then Beverley attempted to explain the underlying reason for the initiation ritual: "I confess, I judged it at first sight to be only an Invention of the Seniors, to engross the young mens Riches to themselves; for, after suffering this operation, they never pretended to call to mind any thing of their former property." But Beverley rejected that explanation, since "their Goods were either shared among the old men, or brought to some publick use" (209).

Beverley then changes from an economic to an educational and philosophical explanation of the ritual:

> They hope by this proceeding, to root out all the prepossessions and unreasonable prejudices which are fixt in the minds of Children. So that, when the Young men come to themselves again, their Reason may act freely, without being byass'd by the Cheats of Custom and Education. Thus also they become discharg'd from the remembrance of any tyes by Blood, and are establisht in a state of equality and perfect freedom, to order their actions, and dispose of their persons, as they think fit, without any other Controul, than that of the Law of Nature. (209)

The thoughts and diction of this passage are typical Enlightenment propaganda, reflecting John Locke's writings on the association of ideas in his *Essay Concerning Human Understanding* and reflecting the critical deistic attitudes summarized by Charles Blount in a quatrain published in his *Oracles of Reason:*

> By education most have been misled,
> So they believe, because they were so bred;

The priest continues what the nurse began,
And thus the child imposes on the man.

(150)

Just as Beverley revised and dramatized the writings of John Banister, he seems to have used other sources similarly. Like Swanton, the Ewans observe that in several passages Beverley seems to write imaginative recreations of the scenes in De Bry's engravings (122). Sturtevant too warned, "Beverley's comments on his illustrations are useful, provided it is realized that in them he may be too greatly dependent on De Bry's engravings and on Hariot's captions rather than relying on his own, probably superficial observations in Virginia" (Hulton and Quinn 1964, 1:41n). Sturtevant also found a beautiful example of Beverley's untrustworthiness. The ethnologist points out that in one watercolor, John White accurately showed the Indians sitting in a crouched position. But since the position is "uncommon and awkward" for Europeans, De Bry changed it "by stretching out the legs converting the posture into an ordinary one for Europeans." Sturtevant then observed: "An indication of the extent to which Beverley's reports on the Virginia Algonkians are based on these engravings rather than his personal observations is his remark, accompanying his version of this illustration, that the Indians sat to eat 'with their Legs lying out at length before them, and the Dish between their Legs'" (Hulton and Quinn 1964, 1:101; Beverley 182). Like Beverley's comments on the Amerindians' posture while eating, his entire description of the exploration of the Quioccosan seems to me a fiction, in this case inspired by De Bry's engraving of the idol Kiwasa, by Thomas Hariot's note accompanying the plate, and especially by Beverley's own freethought.

I have focused upon Beverley's account of his exploration of the quioccosan because scholars generally (e.g., Swanton 1946, 745; Feest 1978, 270; Davis 1978, 88–89; Marshall and Williams 1982, 194; and Sheehan 1980, 182) regard it and his writings about the Indians' religion as notable contributions to Amerindian studies. But other passages in the same chapter and in the book are also deistic satire. That common earmark of critical deism—anticlericism—is found throughout Beverley's *History*.[4] Beverley relates a conversation with an Indian "of whom an extraordinary Character had been given me, for his Ingenuity and Understanding" (200). Beverley tells how he set up the Indian: "When I see he had no other *Indian* with him I thought I might be the more free; and therefore I made much of him, seating him close by a large Fire, and giving him plenty of strong Cyder, which I hop'd wou'd make him good Company, and open-hearted." Beverley then introduced the subject of religion. He tells the Indian that his idol was nothing more than "a dead insensible Log, equipt with a bundle of Clouts, a meer helpless thing made by Men, that could neither hear, see, nor speak; and that such a stupid thing could no ways hurt, or help them" (201). (Incidentally, Beverley's reference to the idol as a "dead insensible Log" recalls Aesop's popular—but irreverent—fable of the frogs who asked Jupiter for a God and were given a log [Aesop 31–32].) According to Beverley, the Indian replies: *"It is the Priests—they make the people believe, and*———Here he paus'd a little, and then repeated to me, that *it was the priests*———and then gave me hopes that he wou'd have said something more, but a qualm crost his Conscience, and hinder'd him from making any farther Confession" (201). This scene clearly reflects the standard critical deistic satire of religion as imposture.

Furthermore, Beverley's next paragraph begins in a way that leads his readers at first to believe that he is generalizing about all peoples and cultures—as, I suspect, he really was:

> The Priests and Conjurers have a great sway in every Nation. Their words are looked upon as Oracles, and consequently are of great weight among the common people. They perform their Adorations and Conjurations, in . . . [a secret language], as the Catholicks of all Nations do their Mass in the *Latin*. They teach, that the Souls of Men survive their Bodies, and that those who have done well here, enjoy most transporting Pleasures in their *Elizium* hereafter; that this *Elizium* is stor'd with the highest perfection of all their Earthly Pleasures; namely, with plenty of all sorts of Game, for Hunting, Fishing and Fowling; that it is blest with the most charming Women, which enjoy an eternal bloom, and have an Universal desire to please. That it is deliver'd from excesses of Cold or Heat, and flourishes with an everlasting Spring. But that, on the contrary, those who are wicked, and live scandalously here, are condemn'd to a filthy stinking Lake after Death, that continually burns with Flames, that never extinguish; where they are persecuted and tormented day and night, with Furies in the Shape of Old Women. (201–2)

Just as a favorite subject for ridicule in the deists' criticism was the sensuous ideas of heaven and hell of the Mohamedans (and of some Christians [cf. Locke 1689, 94]), so too, I think, Beverley means for his audience to be amused at the Indians' sensual views of the afterlife—and, by implication, of some traditional Christian ideas of heaven and hell.

At one point, Beverley considers the theoretical problem posed by the fact that the Indians' religion was not a perfect, natural religion. Beverley writes:

> In this state of Nature, one would think they should be as pure from Superstition, and overdoing matters in Religion, as they are in other things: but I find it is quite the contrary; for this Simplicity gives the cunning Priest a greater advantage over them, according to the *Romish* Maxim, *Ignorance is the Mother of Devotion* [cf. Mencken 1976, 570]. For, no bigotted Pilgrim appears more zealous, or strains his Devotion more at the Shrine, than these believing Indians do, in their Idolatrous Adorations. (211)

Elsewhere he tells us that the Indian priests and conjurers "riot in the fat of the Land, and grow rich upon the soils of their ignorant Country-men" (226).

Although Beverley feels free to scoff openly at the religion of the American Indians and of the classical Greeks and Romans, he is, of course, circumspect regarding his countrymen's Christianity. Nevertheless, he covertly satirizes the biblical account of the fall of man (17); and, in telling of the Indian Chief Nemmattanow (who convinced his followers that he was "invulnerable and immortal" [52–53] and who may have been primarily responsible for the Indians' massacre of the whites in 1622), the Virginian even seems to advance a personal theory of the origins of gods.

In addition to the critical deism that is found repeatedly in the book and that occupies most of his chapter on the Indians' religion, Beverley at one point writes a relatively straightforward bit of constructive deism. In contrast to his frequent condemnation of Indian superstition and priestcraft, Beverley finds that the fundamentals of Indian religion are the same as those of all religions. According to the Indian who had "an extraordinary Character . . . for his Ingenuity and Understanding" (200), there are five fundamental points in the Indians' religion (the numbering is my own):

1. God was universally beneficent, that his Dwelling was in the Heavens above, and that the influences of his Goodness reach'd to the Earth beneath.
2. That he was incomprehensible in his Excellence, and enjoy'd all possible Felicity:
3. That his Duration was Eternal, his Perfection boundless, and that he possesses everlasting Indolence and Ease. . . .
4. God do's not trouble himself, with the impertinent affairs of Men, nor is concern'd at what they do: but leaves them to make the most of their Free Will, and to secure as many as they can, of the good things that flow from him.
5. That therefore it was to no, purpose either to fear, or Worship him. (200–201)

Although some passages in this creed may reflect the Indians' religion, most of it, as the diction itself testifies, is Beverley's constructive deistic propaganda. Indeed, the fifth point contradicts what we know of Algonkian religion (Flannery 1939, 162–63), and the fourth justifies Beverley's hedonistic and acquisitive materialism.

Beverley's supposedly empirical proof of critical deistic theories advances the deistic argument. Beverley's proof depends upon the comparative method, the theory whereby, to use John Locke's words, the Indian was regarded as "a pattern of the first Ages in *Asia* and *Europe*" (1690, 357). John

Toland, like most early deists, ostensibly directed his satire of priestcraft at the Catholic church, for it was illegal to criticize Protestantism in England. The effect of Toland's and Chubb's deistic satires was to say that since the time of Christ, the Roman Catholic church had faked miracles and mysteries. One could, therefore, think with John Dryden in "Absalom and Achitophel" that there had existed, before the establishment of the Catholic church, "pious times ere priestcraft did begin" (line 1). But, using the comparative method and stage theory of civilization (see Lemay 1979), Beverley implied that the cheat of religion began with religion itself. In effect, Beverley claims that religion and religious imposture arose together. They are inseparable and synonymous. Beverley, then, actually used the deistic traditions to advance a covert atheism. As David Berman has shown in his essay in this volume, Beverley's strategy was not unusual for the ostensibly "deistic" writers of the period.

Besides proving that Beverley uses the Amerindian as a fictional abstraction to advance his own literary and ideological purposes, I want to point out that he was only one of a number of American deists to do so.[5] The noble savages in John Lawson's *New Voyage* (see Diket 1966) are another example. And evidently the second most popular single piece of American deistic propaganda—surpassed only Franklin's 1747 "Speech of Miss Polly Baker" (Hall 1960; Aldridge 1972; Lemay 1976)—was a version of an actual Indian speech delivered in Delaware in reply to the sermon of a Swedish missionary in 1700. Tobias Eric Bjorck published it in his *Dissertatio Gradualis, de plantatione ecclesiae svecanae* (Upsaliae, 1731). Then, in an English version that strengthened the deistic satire, the Philadelphian John Webbe printed it in the *American Magazine* for March 1741. Since this is the earliest dated deistic version of the speech, Webbe himself may first have made the translation and transformed it into a deistic satire. When Benjamin Franklin's friend James Parker printed it in the *New York Gazette* for 27 April 1752, the New York authorities prosecuted him. In a letter of 14 May 1752, Franklin interceded for Parker with New York's Lieutenant Governor Cadwallader Colden. Franklin said that it was "an old Thing, [and] has been printed before both in England and by Andrew Bradford [in Webbe's *American Magazine*] here." Despite Franklin's assurance, the speech was evidently not well known in England before 1760 (there was, however, a 1758 London printing in pamphlet form), for it caused a stir upon its publication in the *London Magazine* for 1760, Appendix, 694–96. (Both the speech and the subsequent articles concerning it in the *London Magazine* for 1761 [92–93, 407–9, and 635–37] were reprinted in the *Scots Magazine* for 1761.) Printed and reprinted as a broadside, the speech also appeared repeatedly in English and American newspapers, magazines, and books throughout the late eighteenth and early nineteenth centuries. Other supposed Indian speeches and anecdotes advancing a deistic viewpoint turn up in the periodicals and in such miscellaneous repositories of eighteenth-century thought as Horace Walpole's correspondence (17:477). As Alfred Owen Aldridge (1950) has pointed out, Benjamin Franklin used the tradition in his hoax "The Captivity of William Henry" (1760) and in his essay "Remarks Concerning the Savages of North America" (1782). And of course Joel Barlow continued it in his *Vision of Columbus* and the *Columbiad* (Ball 1967; Christensen 1956; Lemay 1982).

As scholars have long known, deism flourished in America during the late eighteenth century,[6] but there also existed a strong deistic tradition in early-eighteenth-century America, and Robert Beverley helped create a minor but significant literary tradition of deistic American Indians.[7]

NOTES

1. Because of Morais, scholars of the American Enlightenment have been reluctant to find open deism in America before 1750. After Alfred Owen Aldridge pointed out that deism existed in the 1730s in the *Maryland Gazette* and in the *Pennsylvania Gazette* ("Benjamin Franklin and the *Maryland Gazette*"), Nicholas Joost attempted to refute Aldridge's evidence in two essays. Although Joost notes (1952, 7) that Franklin reprints "Copy of Part of Sir John Randolph's Will," he does not comment on the reason for the will's notoriety—it was deistic. Like Franklin's patron Andrew Hamilton (d. 1741), Sir John Randolph (ca. 1693–1736/7) was not only widely known as a deist but was also the dominant political leader of his colony. Their political enemies attempted to use their deistic beliefs against both men, but the charges obviously did not influence the majority of their supporters. One must conclude that early-eighteenth-century Virginians and Pennsylvanians did not find deism as unusual or as reprehensible as do some modern scholars.

2. Gilbert Chinard (1931, 59) noted that Beverley cited Lahontan, but Chinard did not comment on Beverley's deistic satire.

3. Although I believe that J. R. Pole correctly argues that Enlightenment doctrines of politics did not create American political ideology but only confirmed the "long established and deeply valued" traditions of American self-government (1981, 195—a point made earlier but more briefly by Hornberger and other scholars), I nevertheless suspect that Beverley and other early eighteenth-century American intellectuals knew Locke's political writings. John Dunn has argued that Locke's *Two Treatises of Government* (1690) was practically unknown in America before the Revolutionary period (Dunn 1969, passim, esp. 69–74), but he overlooks the ample citations of and allusions to *Two Treatises* in the newspapers and magazines of pre-Revolutionary America. Indeed, John Webbe, who published a series of essays on government in Franklins' *Pennsylvania Gazette* from 1 April to 10 June 1736, was satirized by his Pennsylvania contemporaries for too frequently echoing Locke's *Two Treatises*. (Since Webbe's essays on government were formerly attributed to Franklin, two of them are conveniently available in Sparks [1836–40, 2:278–84]and Bigelow [1887–88, 1:425–31].)

4. The anticlericism of the *History* strengthens Parke Rouse's attribution to Beverley of a savage verse satire on seventeen Virginia ministers (Rouse 1971, 164–66; followed by Davis 1978, 1356–57) *A Ballad Addres'd to the Reverend Members of the Convocation held at Man's Ordinary at Williamsburg . . . To Defend G[overno]r N[icholso]n, And Form an Accusation Against C[ommissary] B[lair]* (London, 1704).

5. It is not my purpose here to survey literary and ideological uses of the Amerindian by early Americans other than the deists. Numerous promotion writers used the Amerindian to satirize the ills of English society—thereby emphasizing the

attraction of America. (See, for example, Lemay 1972, 62–65). And Thomas Hahn has shown how seventeenth- and eighteenth-century Friends used the Amerindian to propagate the existence of the Inward Light. But these traditions are outside the boundaries of my subject.

6. Recently David Lundberg and Henry F. May have reaffirmed the position of Morais by searching early American book lists and catalogues. But Arthur H. Scouten, after examining the actual copies of the books in the Library Company of Philadelphia, has concluded that "a considerable number of early deist pamphlets found their way from London into the hands of colonial readers" (1978, 225). Scouten makes the point that, in addition to examining the book lists of early America (and the lists in periodicals are only now being brought under bibliographical control by Robert Winans), a scholar who intends to generalize about colonial American reading must also examine the surviving books in at least select libraries.

7. Beverley probably influenced Franklin. He evidently thought highly of the *History of Virginia*, for he reprinted selections from it in his *General Magazine* for February, March, and April 1741, 83–88, 147–53 and 217–28.

Defoe, the Occult, and the Deist Offensive during the Reign of George I

MAXIMILLIAN E. NOVAK

Between 1726 and 1727 Daniel Defoe published a number of works dealing with magic and the occult, the best known of which are *The Political History of the Devil* (1726), *A System of Magick* (1726), and *An Essay on the History and Reality of Apparitions* (1727). At a time when Defoe was deeply immersed in writing on worldly problems—the economy of the nation, the education of tradesmen and gentlemen, economic geography, politics, piracy, and social projects—these books seem oddly out of place. James Sutherland considered them as the product of an interest that Defoe held for many years, but he also thought that Defoe was mainly turning out trash for what was, at the time, a mass reading audience. "He was making some money out of the Devil and the world of evil spirits," Sutherland commented, "and once more it was the readers of *Mist's* and of *Applebee's* that he had in mind" (1950, 264). Sutherland judged *The History and Reality of Apparitions* as the most serious of these studies but thought that Defoe knew well enough that his personal belief in a spirit world would fascinate readers who would match Defoe's accounts of premonitions that came true with their similar experiences. Rodney Baine's study, *Defoe and the Supernatural,* while devoted partly to matters of bibliography and the canon of Defoe's writings, avoided the notion that Defoe might have been trying to increase his income and stressed instead the continuity that might be found between Defoe's most famous ghost story, *The Apparition of Mrs. Veal,* written in 1706, and these later works.

Much truth may be discovered in both viewpoints. Defoe knew that such books would be popular enough to go into many editions. A 1965 paperback edition of *The Political History of the Devil* advertises the work as "a spine-chilling expose of Evil Incarnate." On the cover is a lustful-looking devil holding a scantily draped woman. Although the flames of Hell roar beneath her body, her face reveals a distinct smile, reflecting her expectation of some form of pleasure. As Sutherland suggested, it is still possible to make money out of Defoe's Prince of the Air. Yet Baine was certainly correct in urging how much Defoe was attracted to the occult. The problem with his approach is that Defoe was the kind of writer who responded to contemporary events. His earliest writings reveal how much he was intrigued by the plague of 1665, but he did not write *A Journal of the Plague Year* until 1722, when the plague in the south of France posed a threat to the citizens of Great Britain.

I want to suggest that the same is true of the three works on the occult, and I will try to demonstrate how these works, if juxtaposed against three other treatises that Defoe published during these years, will reveal that he was responding mainly to a group of writers on religious subjects who, starting with John Toland's *Nazarenus* in 1718 and ending with Anthony Collins's *The Scheme of Literal Prophecy Considered*, in 1727, raised questions about the origins of Christianity and the doctrines associated with the teachings of Christ. These writers had vastly different motives and beliefs, but many of them fit the pattern of the deist as outlined by Alfred Owen Aldridge in *Shaftesbury and the Deist Manifesto*. Some, like William Whiston, were Arians, but as a group, they put forward a challenge to orthodox Christianity that a religious controversialist such as Defoe would have found difficult to ignore.

That Defoe should appoint himself a defender of what he considered to be orthodox Christianity during the reign of George I is hardly surprising. In his early works, he seldom missed an opportunity of attacking John Toland's unmysterious Christianity, and he devoted a number of pamphlets as well as a large section of his lengthy *Consolidator* (1705) to assaults upon both the deists and those whose principles seemed to smack of one heresy or another. After Collins published his *Discourse of Free-Thinking* in 1713, Defoe frequently expressed his distaste for what he believed lay behind this plea for freedom of thought, and he seemed convinced that all of William Whiston's abilities lay in the area of astronomy and mathematics rather than theology. It is doubtful that Defoe ever seriously contemplated a career as a dissenting clergyman, but his pronouncements on the decline of the clergy and of preaching in *The Present State of the Parties in Great Britain* (1712) show that he regarded himself as something of an expert on both the form and substance of religion.[1]

Before the great deistic offensive of the 1720s, two important controversies (scandals might be the better word) attracted Defoe's attention, one within the Church of England and the other among the ranks of the Dissenters. In 1716, Benjamin Hoadly, bishop of Bangor, began a series of disputes that lasted in one form or another until 1721 and resulted in a very real diminution of the political power of the Church, along with a temporary loss of credibility as a religious institution. Even before he preached his sermon *A*

Preservative against the Principles and Practices of the Nonjurors Both in Church and State in 1716, Hoadly was ranked with Thomas Hobbes by members of the High Church for his Whiggish politics, but his statements in this sermon about the power of the state over religious institutions and certain remarks about the "sincerity" of most men in their beliefs led eventually to his censure by the Lower House of Convocation and, by way of response, to the king's effective elimination of that body.

In the following year, while controversy still raged, Hoadly preached another sermon, *The Nature of the Kingdom, or Church, of Christ*, in which he argued that no earthly body could set themselves up as a judge of anyone's conscience. The peace of Christ's kingdom, he argued, is built upon toleration. No earthly body, no earthly church, should have the right to determine what a person should or should not believe. Since a large part of the Anglican establishment thought that the course of action denounced by Hoadly was precisely the one that they ought to follow, the violent pamphlet war that followed was hardly surprising. William Law and Henry Stebbing accused Hoadly of presenting a defense for any religious belief and of making the salvation of sincere Jews and pagans a distinct possibility. Law also suggested that there "is not a Libertine, or Loose-Thinker in *England*, but he imagines you intend to dissolve the Church as a *Society*" (1753, 1). Such views were echoed by the report of the Lower House of Convocation.

Even more spectacular than these events was a name-calling contest that developed a few years later between Hoadly and a number of bishops and deans of the Anglican church. This dispute, played out in the popular press, suggested that despite all their professions of honesty and sincerity, several of these clergymen were liars. Defoe participated in these controversies mainly in an ironic, mocking role. Although he mainly agreed with Hoadly and defended him, he also noted that the Dissenters had held similar ideas about sincerity for decades. Assuming the voice of a Quaker, he cheekily invited Hoadly to join a religious group that would appreciate his ideas. And in a less playful manner, he defended Hoadly's position on sincerity in relation to the last words of Jacobites before their executions, arguing that their sincerity was real enough but that such conviction did not make their actions any less heinous.[2] What pleased him less, however, was the way in which Hoadly's arguments opened up the possibility for the sincere deist, Arian, or Socinian to argue their positions with fervor. A defender of Hoadly like John Balguy seemed to invite toleration and even approval of anyone who might claim to be a sincere lover of truth.

While these debates were still raging, the Dissenters managed to shoot themselves in their collective feet in a dispute over the Trinity. Meeting at Salters Hall in 1719 to resolve their disagreement, they split over a demand by one group that everyone present sign an affirmation of his belief in the Trinity. Some of those present viewed the document as a kind of "test" and refused to sign on procedural grounds, but clearly there was a large body present who had moved far in the direction of Arianism and Socinianism.

Since the congregation at Defoe's town, Stoke Newington, was deeply involved in this controversy, it is almost certain that Defoe should have written something on this event. He probably would have wished the controversy away if he could have managed it. The unity of the Dissenters as a political body was one of his fondest dreams. But in a pamphlet that is almost certainly his, *Some Remarks upon the Late Differences among the Dissenting Ministers and Preachers* (1719), Defoe sided with the signers against Peirce and the majority who refused to sign.[3] Since "Sincerity" was the real key to belief, those who refused to sign had to be viewed as weak in both conviction and honesty, Defoe argued. Instead of affirming their true beliefs, those who refused to sign appeared to be using various subterfuges. That it was the majority who refused to sign would not have made Defoe very happy, but he was accustomed enough to such events.[4]

Although Defoe's personal beliefs were unlikely to have been changed by the chaos that ensued in the ranks of the Dissenters after the meeting at Salters Hall, he may have lost much of his respect for the Dissenting clergy. During the last decade of his life, he presented a number of dramatic situations in which the natural religion of savages, particularly sun worship, is presented as a rational form of belief in the absence of revelation and others in which deism is offered as an understandable alternative to the corruptions of Catholicism. I will discuss this problem later in this essay, but despite his willingness to play with such notions, Defoe set himself firmly against the powerful attacks upon the literal reading of the Old and New Testaments by those who seemed heartened by the Bangorian Controversy and by the events at Salters Hall. What Alfred Owen Aldridge called the "Deist Manifesto" was even more powerfully stated in these years than during the time that the third earl of Shaftesbury was publishing the essays that make up the *Characteristics*.

Defoe's objection to these writers may have been more a matter of morality than of specific religious principle. He was one of these who held the not-uncommon belief that morality could not be separated from religion. Writing under the name "Orthodox" in *Applebee's Journal* of 18 March 1721, he argued: "Freethinkers are profane, and *Free-Actors* also; for,—erasing the Awe of God in their Hearts, they plead immediately, and of Course, for a Freedom in all Manner of Vice,—using the Pretence of Liberty for a Justification of Crime, as if the Liberty God gave to Man of being a free Agent, disengaged him entirely from all the restraint of Laws, whether Human or Divine" (Lee, 1869, 2:353). An active advocate for the Societies for Reformation of Manners from their inception, Defoe viewed the civilizing of English behaviour during the transition from the Restoration to the eighteenth century as the product of a moral code enforced by religious sanctions. Writers such as Toland and Collins regarded themselves as soldiers in the cause of Enlightenment, but to a thinker like Defoe, they seemed enemies to the progress of both manners and morals.[5]

Defoe's first full-length attack upon the position of the deists appears to have been *An Essay on the Original of Literature*, which, according to John Robert Moore, appeared early in 1726. Although it has a title that has attracted literary critics, those who have hoped to find clues to Defoe's methods as a writer or to his literary taste have been disappointed. So far from being a pronouncement about *belles lettres*, it is a discussion of what we would now call the semiotics of writing. Asserting that God communicated writing to mankind at Sinai with the Ten Commandments, Defoe urges the miraculous nature of such an invention:

> Mankind had no idea of such a thing among them, it was not in them to make a piece of Paper speak, and to stamp a Voice and Words, which were neither more or less than meer Sounds to stamp them on a Paper and empower other People to speak over again by the help of those dumb Figures, the same Word that the first Person had uttered at a hundred or a thousand Miles distance; no Man could imagin such a thing feasible (16).

It was a miraculous gift that gave the possibility of communicating knowledge not merely over distance but over time as well. Through writing it became possible to stand "upon the Shoulders of our Fore-fathers Learning," and man quickly "improv'd upon their invention; carry'd on progressive Knowledge, upon the foot of their Discoveries, and brought experimental Knowledge both in Arts and in Nature to that Prodigy of Perfection to which it is now arriv'd" (2). Although he sometimes longed for the power of hieroghyphics to communicate directly through the combination of picture and word, here he speculated on the awkwardness of the Egyptian system for communicating complex ideas.[6] Ultimately they were "lame, unintelligible, aenigmatick" (29).

Defoe raised many questions in this work; more than he answered. He speculated on writing as a profession and upon what would have happened to the production of books if printing had not been invented. He wondered at the numbers who would have been employed in an age of so much book production and asked his readers to marvel at the number of manuscripts that might have been saved had printing been invented in an earlier age. But he also established what he considered to be an orthodox chronology for the events recorded in the Old Testament at a time when the chronology of Newton and Fréret's reply to it were creating doubts about the accuracy of previous calculations. Throwing doubt upon the historicity of the Bible was one of the main weapons of the deists. In response, Defoe affirms the coming of letters in 2415 B.C. and makes God the "first Writing Master in the World" (62).

Although *An Essay on the Original of Literature* contains many of Defoe's favorite ideas about writing as a form of industry and about the decline of education in contemporary England, it is unique in being a tribute to the variety of mediums involved in writing, from shorthand, at which he had considerable skill, to cyphers of several kinds, a medium that he used when acting as a spy for Robert Harley. But the most significant contribution of writing has been to spread truth throughout the world:

> How little a Way wou'd the Fame of the greatest Heroe have reach'd? The Noise of a Victory would have scarce been heard farther than the Noise of the Cannon: much less could Things have continued in Time longer than the Memory of the Persons concern'd wou'd preserve them, of which already we see so many fatal Effects, and by which Things of the greatest Moment done as it were but Yesterday, that is to say, within the Compass of two or three Ages, turn into Fable and Romance; Scoundrels are made Heroes, and Heroes are made Gods (114).

Defoe was skeptical enough of the ways in which history was transmitted even with books and printing.[7] Without them, almost nothing in the past could be reported accurately. But it was God himself who gave mankind the means by which his message could be preserved for all to know the truth.

In July of the same year, Defoe published *Mere Nature Delineated*, a work that took direct issue with what he considered an un-Christian way of perceiving man's relationship to nature. If he had answered the efforts of Toland and Collins to suggest that the Jews had received their learning through the Chaldeans and the Egyptians in his study of writing, he was now ready to confront writers such as Shaftesbury and, as the title of the work suggests, William Wollaston, whose *The Religion of Nature Delineated* had created a philosophy of nature in which notions such as original sin and a fallen world had almost no role at all. Nominally about the discovery of Peter the Wild Boy in the woods of Germany in 1725, Defoe's digressive essays permitted him room to speculate about the entire range of ideas that had clustered about the concept of natural man—his possible freedom from sin, his language, his relation to civilization, his education, and his condition as a product of nature. Although Defoe could hardly resist writing on subjects such as these—subjects that had always appealed to him—the wry, half-playful manner of the reply may have been dictated by the graceful style of Shaftesbury and, more particularly, Collins, whose extraordinarily effective irony was disguised behind a pose of openness and a seemingly innocent quest after knowledge. To make his reply more cogent as satire, Defoe pretends for a time to accept what he never actually believes: that Peter is a true natural man who, after some education, would be capable of taking his place in society.

But after jesting over the idea of Peter among the beaux, wits, and court ladies, Defoe gets down to his main subject—the problem of natural good and evil. The example of Peter shows that virtue does not come through contact with nature: "Let those who deny original Depravity, answer this for me, if they think they can; for my Part, I acknowledge it to be out of my Reach, upon any other Foot" (44). Peter may be mentally retarded (a "natural"), but he is a good example of what nature will do to a person who has been deprived of the benefits of society and education. "Such a plain coarse Piece of Work is a Man in the mere Condition he is born in," writes Defoe, "just coming out of Nature's Hand: and by Consequence, the Improvement of the Soul by Instruction which we call Educating, is of the highest Importance" (68). Behind all the playfulness lies the impression that subjects of this kind are of the utmost seriousness.

Both the *Essay on Literature* and *Mere Nature Delineated* are concerned with the nature of language and of learning. Both assert the miraculous gift of writing at Sinai, but only in the latter does Defoe consider the ways in which language is transmitted. In examining the kind of control over learning that can be exerted in teaching the deaf to understand their world, he contemplates what would be necessary to turn Peter into a Christian: "As for that trifle called Religion, I reckon no Time at all to that part, in which I know I please many of my Sceptical, Deistical, Ante-Enthusiastick Readers. I call them Ante-Enthusiasts, because they place so little Weight upon Religion in general, that they never are at Pains to make Pretensions to Inspirations or Revelations of any kind whatsoever" (83). Although he says that he will avoid the subject of religion, he adds that he expects that religion will be inculcated along with other subjects as Peter's instructions proceed.

Defoe abandoned this kind of indirection in the following year. His *New Family Instructor* went directly to what he considered the heart of the matter—the attack upon traditional Christian values by the deists. One of the oddities of this work, however, is the attack upon the concept of miracles. Because Catholicism believed in the continuation of miracles, it had to be considered a "Romantick" religion (57). Even the most outrageous of the Protestant sects had to be considered closer to true Christian belief in this respect than the Catholic Church.

Although Defoe considered his own orthodoxy beyond suspicion, like so many of his contemporaries he had amplified his religious ideas with concepts drawn from the philosophy of Locke and the science of Newton, particularly from Newton's God of infinite space. "The utmost Perfection of Human Knowledge that can be attained to by us, and the best Use that Knowledge can be put to in this World," he wrote, "is to lead our Thoughts into Extasies of Admiration, Wonder, and Astonishment, at The Wisdom and Power of the great Author of Nature, who has made all these glorious Bodies, and directs all their Motions" (251). He gives over one of his dialogues to a character who has some of the qualities of Anthony Collins, but who is misled, despite his "Knowledge and Wit . . . with the new Errors as to the Trinity; and withal a little of a Deist, or Sceptick, or Free-Thinker call them what you will" (253). This new type of thinker looks at the same world as the believer but fails to read correctly what, at the time, was called the "probable signs."[8] He refuses to see the pattern of divine retribution, "covering Things with Words, and amusing us with being quite wrong, as they call it, about Hell, and a Future State of Perdition, which they make a jest of" (255). As we will see, Defoe had moved far from the notion of a horned and cloven-footed devil, but he never abandoned the idea of punishment for sin.[9]

The Bible, which was under attack by Whiston for its inclusion of an immoral piece like the *Song of Songs* and which appeared to Toland as the product of Jewish fanaticism and ignorance, was divine in every part. Defoe argued that these thinkers were simply trying to manufacture a God after their notion of what a God ought to be:

> The problem is that the Deists want a God who is limited in his power: a God without a Devil, according to Epicurus; a God Wise and Powerful, but not infinitely so, not Omnipotent, not Self-sufficient, and All-sufficient; a God that having created the World (and 'tis with some difficulty they go so far) has not power to guide it, but has abandoned it to the Government of it self; to that foolish *Nothing*, that unexisting piece of Nonsense, call'd Chance; or like the Followers of Zeno, that Deist Philosopher, a God depending upon (they know not what, of a) blind Destiny; a God who not being able to break the Chain of second Causes, is carry'd away with them himself, being obliged to act by the Course of natural Consequences, even whether he will or no. (263)

Having established the antideistical thrust of the three works discussed above, I want now to turn to Defoe's explorations of the occult where the comments on deism are less direct but equally important. *The Political History of the Devil* shares with *Mere Nature Delineated* a mocking style intended to meet the irony of Collins on equal ground. Although Defoe boasted of the popularity of his work in the preface to the second edition, he noted the disapproval expressed by one *"Reverend Gentleman,"* (1727b, A2v) over the lack of gravity. But he raises this objection only to dismiss it. Defoe's devil has certain comic elements, but for the most part he is used as a fictional angle of vision to contemplate the follies of mankind, follies extended to include the theological wars of the time. Behind the often deliberate buffoonery, there is a serious purpose, for just as the man who believes in a world of spirits is likely to believe in a God, the same might be said about the belief in the devil. From this standpoint, Defoe's aim is not very different from that of Richard Baxter in his entirely humorless treatise on apparitions.

But Defoe's devil is a far cry from the dragon-winged fiend embodied in Bunyan's Apollyon. He is a spirit who lives in continual envy of man, or rather of those elect humans who will find eternal life through grace. His only major role in human history was the temptation of Eve. After that event and the subsequent taint that dwells with humanity in the world, he functioned mainly as a regulator of evil that would remain on earth forever. Occasionally he would extend that taint of evil into such a major horror as warfare, and he might dwell constantly with someone like Richelieu; but mostly he was simply an observer. The evil in humankind was such that he often would find himself astonished by the invention of new sins.

Defoe's devil is the spirit of negativity and destruction. His dwelling place is not some local hell filled with fire and the varied places set aside for select torture. He dwells with humanity itself and is present whenever human passion drives a soul to commit an evil action:

> Pride swells the Passions; Avarice moves the Affections; and what is Pride, and what is Avarice, but the *Devil* Inside of the Man? ay, as personally, and really as ever he was in the Herd of Swine. . . . In like Manner Avarice leads him to rob, plunder and destroy for Money, and to commit sometimes the worst of Violences to obtain the wicked Reward. How many have had their Throats cut for their Money, have been murther'd on the High-Way, or in their Beds, for the Desire of what they had? It is the same Thing in other Articles, every vice is the Devil in a Man. (403)

Whatever the past may have been, Defoe notes, the present suggests a world in which human ingenuity in the invention of evil has surpassed anything the devil might have imagined.

One of the oddities of this book is Defoe's attack upon Milton, whose poetry, as might be suggested from the extraordinary compliments he lavished on it in *A New Family Instructor* (368), was never more in Defoe's mind and heart. But in the context of the religious controversies of the 1720s, Milton might be seen as an intriguing target. If Milton's greatness had ever been in doubt, Addison's papers on *Paradise Lost* in *The Spectator* would have firmly established his eminence as an epic poet. Under Milton's influence, the turn of English poetry toward blank verse was given a major impetus in the very year of Defoe's book with the publication of James Thomson's *Winter*. And even Defoe was to imitate what he thought to be Miltonic blank verse in 1727.

However much he admired Milton as both a poet and thinker, Defoe knew that Milton took poetic liberties with the Bible. Defoe's devil may seem to be a very modern spirit compared with Milton's Satan, but he was also free from some of Milton's imaginative embellishments. Defoe had no real objections to Milton's poetic fictions, but at a time when the text of the Bible was being probed for errors and ambiguities, at a time when Collins was insisting that only by an allegorical reading could Old Testament types be made the foundation of New Testament antitypes, Defoe was reminding his readers that Milton's brilliant epic was not equivalent to a biblical text.

Having taken the high ground in freeing his devil from the form that medieval iconography would have imposed upon him, and having admitted that most cases of witchcraft were nothing more than the persecution of poor old women, Defoe could turn to the subject of Milton's adherence to "the corrupt Doctrine of *Arius* (75). Focusing on Milton's scene in which God summons the angels to pay homage to Christ, Defoe objects to what seems to be the creation of Christ as a kind of afterthought:

> This is, indeed, too gross; at his meeting he makes God declare the son to be *that day begotten* as before; had he made him not begotten that day, but declared General that day, it would be reconcilable with Scripture and with sense; for either the beginning is meant of ordaining to an office, or else the eternal Generation falls to the ground. . . . And *Milton* can have no authority to tell us there was any Declaration of it in Heaven before this, except it be that dull authority called Poetic Licence, which will not pass in so solemn an affair as that.
>
> But the thing was necessary to *Milton*, who wanted to assign some cause or original of the *Devil's* rebellion; and so, *as I said above*, the design is well laid, it only wants two trifles called *Truth* and History; so I leave it to struggle for itself. (74)

In revealing that he considered one of his favorite poets an Arian, Defoe must have experienced some ambiguity. He praised Milton's powers of invention and argued that the imagery was "exceeding magnificent, the Thought rich and bright, and in some respects truly sublime" (73). He must have considered Milton's reputation strong enough to survive, and no one served so well as a stick to belabor his real opponents.

The Arians he set out to attack were the new objectors to the concept of the Trinity, whether someone like Whiston, whose explorations of the documents of the early church convinced him that the notion of the Trinity was not grounded on the firmest historical evidence, or those among the Dissenters, such as Martin Tompkins or Thomas Emlyn, whose opinions eventually created such discord at the Salters Hall conference. As I suggested previously, Defoe was writing at a time when the Dissenters, particularly the Presbyterians, were still in disarray from the refusal of so many to sign the agreement over a fundamental belief in the Trinity. From Defoe's standpoint, those who did not sign were, as Blake might have put it, of the devil's party without knowing it.

Before the end of 1726, Defoe had produced another work in his fight against the heresies of the time, *A System of Magick*. Since this work reflects the same research as was required for his study of the devil, his productivity is hardly so surprising. Though less satiric than the former work, Defoe continues to preserve a certain sketpicism toward accounts of the supernatural, especially toward stories of apparitions and accounts of miracles. He depicted the prophets of the past as the equivalent of the contemporary scientist—Newton, Halley, and Whiston—and suggested that those who possessed some knowledge of science had to disguise it under a form of magic that would please the ignorant. From this account of true prophets forced to hide their knowledge, Defoe moves on to his main point—the evils done by the deists and Arians of his time.

After remarking on the ways in which the princes of the East were accustomed to punish false prophets, Defoe contemplates the possibility of using such methods with "the Broachers of Atheistical, Deistical, and Enthusiastic Whymsies in our Age" (124). In a manner not very distant from that of Swift, he concludes, with regret, that considering the numbers of these heretics, such severe penalties could not be practical, since they might have the effect of depopulating the world:

> But I am loth to seem vindictive in my Notion, nor would I set up Fire and Faggot; no, not against the *Devil* and his Agents; they may have enough of that hereafter . . . And besides, such a Persecution must necessarily at this time be so bloody, that I know not what City, or Town, Inns of Court, Palace, College or University, *(our own excepted)* which it would not almost lay waste, desolate, and make void of Inhabitants. Mercy on us! persecute and punish Men for being Atheists, and Deists; for dividing the Trinity and unsanctifying the Holy Ghost, who is the Sanctifier of the World, and such difficult Trifles as these? where would it end! and what would become of all the religious Part of the World! what a Schism, in the most literal Sense, would this make among us? and where is there a Church, Chappel, Meeting-house or Congregation, that would not be divided against it self, and set up a new Body of Dissenters? Truly so, as dissenting not from this, or that Opinion of Religion, but from all Religion, and all Opinions in Religion whatsoever. (124)

Although Defoe expresses mock "fear of laying waste the Globe" (125) by such measures, one feels that, as Swift said of his enemies, he "would hang them if he could."

As in his *Essay on Literature*, Defoe defends the authenticity of the *Scriptures*, calling it with deliberate understatement, "a tolerable good history" (185). Relying upon the chronology in Raleigh's *History of the World*, he shows how Moses would have had access to the traditions of Noah and the Creation. And after all, Moses had direct inspiration from God, whereas those, like Whiston, who were ready to question the propriety of sections of the Old Testament, were merely relying upon their reason.

As for writers such as Collins, who wanted every aspect of religion subjected to the ideals of "criticism," or open discussion, they too suffered from an excessive dependence on reason. Defoe wrote that these men believe that "humane Judgement is in its self infallible, and therefore in some manner equal to the divine Being; a Light issued from Heaven, and darted by Emananation into the Souls of Men; which, if rightly cultivated and improv'd, and especially if sincerely follow'd, adher'd to, and obey'd, guides the Soul to understanding things in a superior way" (196). The new deists tend to treat reason as a magical faculty, but reason failed mankind in the Garden of Eden and will always fail when too much is expected of it.

Later in this work, following an attack upon contemporary atheism, Defoe develops his notion of the ways in which reason has functioned as a replacement for a faith in magic:

> It may be ask'd of me, why I will Insist upon this matter in a Treatise of Magick; that this relates to the Atheists, not to *Magicians*, and that by the same Rule, all Enthusiasm, Heresies and mysterious things in Religion, as well as in Science, may be rated in the same Class, and be call'd by the same Name, and so we shall make a Magick of Religion at last.
>
> But let a short Answer suffice to this weak Objection; All Errors in Religion are not equally Diabolic, no, nor equally mischievous; and as I have said above, that this seems to be of an Original deeper than Hell, and out of the Reach of the *Devil;* so as far as it is a Crime which derives from the Man as Independent, and acting the *Devil* by himself, I think it must have the Height of human Imagination and Invention in it, and so may be call'd Magical, as Magick is a Science or Art of doing superlative Evil. (72)

Although Defoe throws doubts on the motives of these new heretics, he never questions their ingenuity.

The purpose of these studies of the occult is even more obvious in the last of the group, *An Essay on the History and Reality of Apparitions*, published in March 1727. In his preface, Defoe tries to steer a middle course between gullibility and complete skepticism. Having asserted that everyone feels impulses and apprehensions that seem to come from outside, he suggests that the spirits reponsible for these warnings should be capable of assuming the form of an apparition, while stating, "I affirm nothing that will bear a Proof." Once again Defoe expresses his disdain for pictures of the devil "with a Cock's Bill, Ass's Ears, Goats's Horns, glaring Eyes, Bat's Wings, cloven Foot, and Dragon's Tail," but he maintains that the existence of spirit itself is so evident as to make debate on this issue unnecessary.

Having made this assertion at the beginning of his book, Defoe allows himself to express doubts about various stories of ghosts that have been accepted by the gullible John Aubrey and scorn for the accounts of apparitions in Homer. After telling the story of a student at Cambridge who heard a voice warning him that his atheism was folly, Defoe hints that the entire story might have been the effect of the student's imagination. He ends his work with the judgment that the British seem to delight in ghost stories: "our Hypochondriack People see more *Devils* at noon-day than *Gallilaeus* did Stars, and more by many than ever really appear'd" (394). Yet he affirms his belief in the reality of apparitions in the midst of all this skepticism about various reports.

In the midst of his accounts of those dreams and impulses that seem to be genuine monitions from a world of spirits, Defoe attacks a variety of modern heresies and their proponents from those who, like Thomas Burnet, believed that the soul experienced a form of sleep after death, to the Boyle Lecturers, who emphasized the littleness of earth in the entire universe and the unlikelihood that there could be a special dispensation for "this despicable Species called Man" (56) that would not be extended to beings on other planets. While allowing for the possibility of beings on other planets, Defoe indulges in considerable play over the beings on Saturn without eyes and those on Jupiter who would be capable of living in freezing temperatures.

In arguing that Defoe's main intent was to attack modern heresies rather than to express his interest in the occult, I do not want to suggest that Defoe did not enjoy writing on subjects of this kind. But he may have felt some genuine irritation at having to please as well as educate a naive audience:

> But hold! wither am I going? This looks like Religion, and we must not talk a Word of that, if we expect to be agreeable. Unhappy Times! where to be serious, is to be dull and grave, and consequently to write without Spirit. We must talk politely, not religiously; we may show the Scholar, but must not show a Word of the Christian; so we may quote profane History, but not sacred; and a story out of *Lucan* or *Plutarch, Tully* or *Virgil* will go down, but not a Word out of *Moses* or *Joshua*.
>
> Well, we must comply however; the Humour of the Day must prevail; and as there is no instructing you without pleasing you, and no pleasing you but in your own way, we must go on in that way; the Understanding must be refin'd by Allegory and Enigma; you must see the Sun through the Cloud, and relish Light by the help of Darkness; the Taste must be rectify'd by Salts, the Appetite whetted by Bitters; in a word, the Manners must be reform'd in Masquerade, Devotion quicken'd by the Stage not the Pulpit, and Wit be brighten'd by Satyrs upon Sense. (42)

Perhaps Defoe did tire of the method of these attacks against modern heresies. What is more likely, however, is that he used this despair at having to titillate his audience as a reminder that they should not ignore the attacks while enjoying the stories. *The History of Apparitions* is in some ways the most personal of these works, with several stories drawn from what would appear to be his own experiences. And in this work, as in *The New Family Instructor*, he defended his fictions as being of the same kind used by Christ: "the most perfect Representations and Illustrations of the things which they were brought to set forth" (51).

"I am Orthodox in my Notions" (44), Defoe asserted, but he obviously had a different concept of the uses of fictions than most of his contemporaries. He accepted the notion that many sections of *Scriptures* were allegories and parables. He clearly did not appreciate the irony with which Collins approached biblical narrative in *A Discourse of the Grounds and Reasons of the Christian Religion* or his assertion that Christianity was mainly a form of mystical Judaism, but he would probably have been less shocked by Collins's allegorical approach than some of the distinguished Anglican clerics who attempted to answer their mocking opponent.

Despite his claim to orthodoxy, Defoe was far from being unsophisticated in his approach to religion. His *Essay on Literature* reveals that he had read Theophilus Gale's *The Court of the Gentiles* and Edward Stillingfleet's *Origines Sacrae*. His first reaction to Addison's essays on *Paradise Lost* was to contemplate what Milton would have made of an apocryphal version of the Genesis story in which Eve separated from Adam after the Fall (1938, 7:637–49). What we would now consider "comparative religion" captured his imagination because it offered alternate fables to what he had learned in his early religious studies. And when he came to answer the heretics of his time, it is hardly surprising that he approached his subject first through the analysis of the mechanics of language and then through the power of illustrative fictions.

The writer of fiction has a certain freedom inherent in his form that the writer of the most illustrative didactic thesis lacks. The Defoe who has appeared in this essay is explorative and lively, but he is also a writer who would seem an unlikely author of novels such as *Moll Flanders* and *Roxana*. And to explain how he could have written passages appearing to praise natural religion and a form of deism in *A New Voyage round the World* and *The History of the Pirates* might appear impossible. Even more difficult to understand would be the outright deism of *Robert Drury's Journal*, a work in which he seems to have participated as a ghost writer. Such an undertaking would require a separate essay, but I want to suggest the directions in which such an essay might move by way of understanding Defoe's full reaction to the radical religious thought of his day.

The freedom that fiction gave Defoe is apparent enough in *The Farther Adventures of Robinson Crusoe* in which Crusoe permits a Catholic priest with ecumenical attitudes toward Christianity to assume the religious duties of his island. Curiously enough, Defoe was writing anti-Catholic propaganda at much the same time. He could create a sympathetic Jacobite hero in the narrator of *Colonel Jack* during a period when his hatred for the Jacobites was unabated.[10] As Captain Johnson, he could find something noble in Captain Misson's rejection of a corrupt Catholicism for a rational deism, and through another sea captain he could represent the worship of some invisible power by the natives of the South Seas as far better than a reverence for idols: "But these people seem to act upon a more solid foundation, paying their reverence in a manner much more rational, and to something which it was much more reasonable to worship" (1895, 148).

What this suggests is that Defoe could see the attraction of deism and that, at times, he considered it superior to the corruptions of the Catholic church. But if he considered atheism and idol worship the worst religious developments, he also fought battles on smaller points of faith throughout his life. He could, on the one hand, accept the Quakers as a true branch of Christian Dissent at a time when many of his fellow Nonconformists thought otherwise, and on the other, he could oppose the majority of his fellow Presbyterians in arguing the wickedness of occasional conformity with the Church of England. He thought he recognized wrong religious thought when he saw it, but he permitted himself all kinds of freedom to explore interesting possibilities when he was writing fiction. Such contradictions should tell us something about the complexity of Defoe, but it should also warn us against oversimplifying the religious thought of the age in which he lived.

NOTES

1. Defoe seems to have contemplated becoming a clergyman for some indefinite period before the age of twenty-one, but his remarks on the abilities of various preachers appear to place more emphasis on their power to move their audiences than on their holiness or religious convictions. Frank Ellis has raised the question of whether Defoe did some preaching himself, but the report of one such an occasion, which he quotes, suggests, on careful reading, that Defoe was listening to the Scottish preacher Robert M'cala and commenting on his poetic style rather than preaching himself (Ellis 1985, 350; Wodrow 1842–43, 2:305).

2. For a discussion of Defoe's attacks upon the value of confessions coming from political prisoners at the gallows, see Novak 1982a, 94–97.

3. Although I do not have space here to argue Defoe's authorship of *Some Remarks upon the Late Differences among the Dissenting Ministers and Preachers*, both internal and external evidence supports such an ascription. It was published by Boreham, who may be described as *the* publisher for Defoe during 1718, and bears all the marks of Defoe's style.

4. In his *Enquiry into Occasional Conformity* (1702), Defoe remarked in a memorable passage, "he that has that Truth on his Side, is a Fool, as well as a Coward, if he is afraid to own it, because of the Currency or Multitude of other Men's Opinions: So to me 'tis every jot as wonderful to find no Body of my Mind, and yet be Positively assured that I am in the Right. . . . 'Tis hard for a Man to say, all the World is mistaken but himself; but if it be so, who can help it" (1:380).

5. Both Defoe and Swift shared the common contemporary notion that an outward show of manners, even where not accompanied by any sincere moral reform, was good for what they considered a somewhat barbarous society. This has led to the charge that Swift's *A Project for the Advancement of Religion and the Reformation of Manners* had to be either ironic or hypocritical, but as Irvin Ehrenpreis remarked, the central idea was to propose something "immediately efficacious" (1962–82, 1:289) and more practical than the hope for sudden moral reform.

6. Reversing the deist's attack on the Jews as a barbarous people who borrowed all

their ideas from the Egyptians and the Chaldeans, Defoe tries to show that the admired hieroglyphics were less effective than words for communication. For Defoe's ideas on language, see Novak 1982b.

7. See Novak 1983, 47–70, for Defoe's attitudes toward recording events through the writing of history.

8. Douglas Patey's *Probability and Literary Form* has demonstrated how important this concept was for the Restoration and eighteenth century. Defoe's ideas on this subject were not unlike those of fellow novelists such as Richardson and Fielding.

9. D. P. Walker has shown that while most religious thinkers of the time had come to consider the standard iconography of hell childish, they were divided on the question of eternal punishment, some suggesting that the translation of the words describing the length of torment meant something less than an eternity.

10. One explanation for the diversity in Defoe's thinking is his tendency to compartmentalize his approach to any subject along separate political and religious grounds. It might be argued that Defoe's Whiggish politics were considerably more "radical" than those of the "classical republicans," who generally held the extreme left among the Whigs. Yet when the *True Born Englishman* was published in 1701, Robert Wodrow and one of his friends (1:7) ascribed it to John Toland, a deist whom Defoe detested. What this demonstrates is the complexity of contemporary politics and the odd mixture of groups enlisted under the Whig banner. J. G. A. Pocock has recently attempted to describe these groups, but he has urged caution. "The field of debate was not simple," he observes, "and we should not hasten to resolve it" (232).

Clio Mocks the Masons
Joseph Green's Anti-Masonic Satires

DAVID S. SHIELDS

On 24 June 1737 (Saint John the Baptist's day) Boston's lodge of Freemasons first took to the streets in public procession.[1] Benjamin Walker, a sugar-baker who kept a copious record of gossip and public affairs, preserved the event in his journal. The parade commenced at the quarters of Grand Master Robert Tomlinson on Wing Street. With "2 trumpeters & 2 haut boys sounding and playing," a company of thirty Freemasons marched through Hanover Street into Queen, from Queen to Tremont, down School Street, and over to Newbury. After traversing most of the town center, they proceeded to Province House, the dwelling of Governor Jonathan Belcher. The governor (who held the distinction of being the first Freemason resident in the Western Hemisphere) joined the procession, taking his place behind the musicians and a sword-bearer and to the right of Grand Master Tomlinson. The Grand Master went hatless and carried a wand, and Governor Belcher wore an apron and badge, as did the members of the fraternity who formed the column behind. With great pomp and noise the procession turned into King Street, where the Royal Exchange Tavern stood. Proprietor Luke Vardy was a member of the brotherhood, so the Royal Exchange served as the lodge's domicile. "Great Numbers of People of all sexes & sizes [assembled] to see them walk thro the streets," observed Walker. "A New Show amongst us" (Walker, 24 June 1737).

Curious to learn more of the lodge's proceedings, Walker later in the evening spied on the society through the tavern window. He discovered nothing untoward except the profligate use of candles.

Benjamin Walker's account conveys something of Boston's fascination with the Honourable Society of Free and Accepted Masons. It expresses a common man's curiosity, and more significantly, his bemusement at an association that cloaks its reason for being in mystery, yet indulges in ceremonies of self-gratulation on the public streets. Walker's careful notation of the symbolic regalia of the procession—the aprons, wands, badges, sword, and ceremonial book—bespeaks a desire to render obscure matters clear; his spying, a zeal to render what is private, public. Walker's efforts went for naught. Expounding the Masonic mysteries demanded an acuter intelligence: that of Joseph Green, the foremost wit in Boston. In a series of verse satires Green supplied Boston with humorous elucidations of Masonic doctrine and practice from 1739 to 1755. He commented on the society's love of show, its exclusivity, its "philanthropy," its mythical origin, and its fashionability among the powerful. The four principal verses constitute the most elaborate reflection on a cultural institution in British America. The second of Green's poems, *An Entertainment for a Winter's Evening*, was the most popular verse satire published in America prior to Trumbull's *M'Fingal* and Barlow's "The Hasty Pudding" (Stoddard 1982, 315). Yet like all satires grounded in occasions, Green's verses dulled as memory of their circumstances faded. By recovering the circumstances we should be able to enjoy Green's entertainment; by reflecting on the issues that made the Masons objects worthy of satire we should be instructed in several mysteries of mid-eighteenth-century New England.

News served as the premise of many of Joseph Green's early satires, for after the demise of the *New England Courant* in 1727 news did not stray far from the official view of affairs taken by the Massachusetts authorities. If a matter appeared in print it carried a presumption of significance, if not official sanction. Newspaper transcripts of Governor Belcher's speeches inspired Green to fashion pastiches for manuscript circulation in which the cant was stripped and the governor exposed as the man who sold the interest of the province for office.[2] When the *Boston Gazeete* of 2 July 1739 printed a description of the third annual procession of "His Excellency" and the Masonic brotherhood, Green marshaled all his burlesque grandiloquence to supply, "A true and exact account of the celebration of the Festival of St. John the Baptist, by the Ancient and Honourable Society of Free and Accepted Masons, at Boston in New-England, on June the 26th, 1739 . . . and rendered into Metre, that children may commit it to, and retain it in their memory." Green's tongue-in-cheek rationale for versification allied his work with those species of poetry conventionally deemed public in New England: versified confessions of condemned criminals and the memorial elegies to the fallen mighty.[3] Throughout his career Green would parody New England's instructive genres—in this case to raise suspicions concerning the noteworthiness of Freemasonic actions. By dressing the proceedings in doggerel, the poet cast ludicrous light on the company as it

> Proceeded onward through the street,
> Unto his Excellency's seat;
> For as *this* Waghorn was a Brother
> His Excellency was *another.*

> Unlucky *name* it grieves full sore,
> Waghorn and Belcher—but no more.—
> Here, having drank and giv'n the *sign*,
> By which he was oblig'd to join,
> From hence in *leather apron* drest
> With tinsel *ribbons* on their breast,
> In pompous order march'd the *train*,
> First *two*, then *three*, then *two* again;
> As thro' the street they pass'd along,
> All kinds of *music* led the throng;
> Trumpets and kettle drums were there,
> And *horns too in the front*, appear.
>
> (*American Apollo* 1, 2 [1792])[4]

Green's dogtrot march took the Freemasons to Luke Vardy's, where the brotherhood enjoyed "pretty pickings"—tongues, hams, green peas, and lambs. The reader sympathizes with the gaping crowd of onlookers who "if from *laughing* we guess right, / They were much pleased with the sight." The mirth attains a crescendo when a ship built by brother Benjamin Hallowell broaches the waters of Boston harbor, turns and reveals a leather apron fluttering atop the mizzen where the British cross should wave. Green did not need to proclaim that proper sovereignty had been usurped on the vessel; that it had become the ship of fools. His mockery permitted matters to speak for themselves. To depart too greatly from the portentous factuality of the news story would disturb the artistry of the performance. Doggerel conveyed the charade's authentic character—empty flourish.

In the decade after Green's "true and exact account" other persons in other places also decided that the best way to rebuke Masonic pretension was by mockery. In London two societies of mimics formed: the Glamorgan Mock Masons and the Scald Society of Miserable Masons. Both took to the streets in caricature processions, displaying their own incomprehensible symbols and shamming profound dignity. The Boston gazettes featured their antics in the foreign news columns. *The Boston Evening-Post* of 14 June 1741, for instance, reproduced "A MANIFESTO" from the Scald Miserable Masons, declaring the society's precedence over the Freemasons in antiquity, and proposing an order of march for an annual parade. To wit:

> Two *Sackbutts*, vulgarly call'd *Cow's Horns*, in Liveries.
>
> An Ass, in proper Habiliments, led by two Pages, in the *Liveries* and *Ribbons* of the *Stewards* Colours; carrying a Pair of *butter Firkins*, on which a Youth in a neat Attire beat, with a Pair of *Marrow-bones*.
>
> A dextrous one legged Man riding on an *Ass*, and playing on a *Tinkling Cymbal*, viz. a *Salt box*.
>
> The TYLER, in a long Robe or Vestment, completely arm'd; on his Head a Cap of Maintenance, on which was Hieroglyphically depicted the mystical

Emblems of the CRAFT; in his Hand a wooden Sword, riding on a *Lean, Lame,* cropt Sorrel Nagg.

Three Stewards in *Proper Cloathing,* with *Jewels* and *Wands,* in a GOAT CART, drawn by Three Asses *beautifully* adorned, with Ribbons and Cockades. A *Postilion* on the first, which was led by two *Pages.*

Three more *Stewards* in a SAND CART, drawn as before.

GRAND GARDER, or *Tyler* to the Grand Lodge, in a *Huge Cap* of Skins, in his Hand a Truncheon; his Shoulders from both Sides *ornamented* with LAY-BANDS, like a *HambiCollonel,* riding on a *Fine* prancing Steed, well managed *in a Grain Cart.*

RAGGED BRETHREN in proper Cloathing, walking according to the Ancient Constitutions, THREE, THREE and THREE.

The Right Worshipful GRAND MASTER with his GRAND OFFICERS in a *superb magnificent, sable State Coach,* drawn by *Spavin, Splint, Swiftail, Bobtail, Oneeye,* and *None-eye,* all of various Colours and bedecked with *Azure Ribbons.*

This *Grand* and *Illustrious* Procession, was finish'd by vast numbers of different Instruments, which all together composed a *delectable* Symphony of ROUGH MUSICK. (Grand Master Pony [pseud.] June 14, 1741)

The following year the Scald Miserable Masons marched again and rebuked the Freemasons for imposing "their false Mysteries (for a Premium) on the Credulous and Unwary, under Pretence of being part of our Brotherhood, and still are determin'd with Drums, Trumpets, gild Chariots and other unconstitutional Finery to cast a Reflection on the primitive Simplicity and decent Oeconomy of our Ancient and Annual Peregrination" (Scald 1744). Boston's readers may have savored this mock complaint particularly. The spirit of the dissenters was still strong in Boston, and many Bostonians were peculiarly attuned to the rhetoric of dissent, even in its mock employments. The empty ceremony of Freemasonry did violate the primitive simplicity of life in the realm of the saints—or so the saints imagined.

Joseph Green's second satire on Freemasonry, composed and published in January 1750, exploited the popular sympathy of Boston toward dissenting religion. The title, *Entertainment for a Winter's Evening: Being a Full and True Account of a very Strange and Wonderful SIGHT, Seen in Boston on the Twenty-seventh of December, 1749. At Noon-Day. The Truth of which can be attested by a Great Number of People, who actually saw the same with their own Eyes,* playfully called to mind two traditional reformed Christian genres: Green's short title recalled seasonal works of piety such as Cotton Mather's *Winter-Meditations;* his subtitle brought to mind the literature of remarkable providences. In the body of the satire Green identifies Masonic doctrine with the "cheap-grace" theology of the latitudinarian wing of the Church of England; the immediate butt of the satire was the Reverend Charles Brockwell, "His Majesty's Chaplain in Boston" at Christ-Church. Yet the animus of Green's ridicule was the complacent optimism that constituted the Masonic creed. For this complacent optimism to be disrupted required a more violent corrosive than the good-humored mockery of a parade. Green borrowed the rude caricature of the Scald Miserable Masons and bound it to an astute parody of Brockwell's Masonic sermon. The result was an entertainment that both Old Light and New Light in Boston could savor.

Some literary historians have presented Green as a champion of the antitheological tendency in colonial letters; the opposite is the case.[5] Green was an Old Light Congregationalist who distrusted the optimism of deism, the enthusiasm of New Light evangelism, and the superstition of popery.[6] The poet's prejudices are readily seen in his *Entertainment*. The entire first section is controlled by a conceit conflating Freemasonry, the Church of England, and the Church of Rome.

Clio, the muse of history, presents the *Entertainment* as a Christmas tale—the premise itself would have been provocative for a readership that considered celebration of Christmas a "superstitious" rite. The tale relates how the brotherhood came

> To house of God from house of ale,
> And how the parson told his tale:
> How they return'd, in manner odd,
> To house of ale from house of God.

This confusion of sacred and profane is merely the first of several distinctions to be jumbled. The parade itself results from a confusion whether the Boston lodge should celebrate Saint John the Baptist or Saint John the Evangelist as its patron; the brotherhood's solution to the dilemma was to march indiscriminately for both Saints' days. The fact that the Freemasons feel compelled to celebrate a saint's day at all leads Green into a poetic suggestion that the Masons have taken on the trappings of popery, for "the day of Saint John's feast" was "Fix'd by the holy *Roman* priest" (6). We see how the morning of the feast dawns in "scarlet apron drest." We see the assembled brotherhood addressed by "Their *brother of the roll and rose*," Charles Brockwell.

> strange auditory!
> And yet we have as strange in story.
> For saints, as history attests,
> Have preach'd to fishes, birds and beasts;
> Yea stones so hard, tho' strange, 'tis true,
> Have sometimes been their hearers too.
> So good SAINT FRANCIS, man of grace,
> Himself preach'd to the *braying race*.

(7)

Notice how neatly Green recalls the Scald caricatures while investing the Masons with the (for New Englanders) bankrupt mystique of Catholic legend.

Literate Bostonians knew that Green did not seriously identify Freemasonry with the Church of Rome, for the Pope's proscription of the brotherhood was known to every reader of newspapers in British America; rather, New Englanders would have understood that Green saw the Freemasons embracing the ceremony and show of Roman Catholicism to dress their own woolly-minded doctrine. This doctrine is parodied in a mock sermon entitled "The Duties of *FREE MASONRY*," which comprises the central section of the satire. Here we are made to understand that the confusion of all distinctions results from the Masonic duty to love:

> While other sects fall out and fight
> About a trifling mode or rite,
> We firm by *Love* cemented stand,
> 'Tis *Love* unites us heart and hand.
> *Love* to a party not confin'd,
> A *Love* embracing all mankind,
> Both catholick and protestant,
> The *Scots* and eke *New-England* saint.
>
> (8–9)

The passage elaborates a section of *Brotherly Love Recommended*, the Reverend Charles Brockwell's Masonic sermon that was "Published at the Request of the Society" in January 1750.

> In some points or rather modes of worship we may differ or dissent from each other: yet still the LODGE reconciles even these—There we all meet amicably, and converse sociably together—There we harmonize in principals, though we vary in punctilioes—There we join in conversation and intermingle interests—There we discover no estrangement of behavior, nor alienation of affection—We serve one another most readily in all the kind Office of cordial Friendship. (13–14)

Green in his verse dramatizes the consequence of Brockwell's utopian politics of sympathy: all the significant controversies of faith troubling New England would be soothed in a Masonic embrace:

> RHODE-ISLAND's differing, motly tribes,
> Far more than ALEC. Ross describes.[7]
> And light that's *new,* and light that's *old,*
> We in our friendly arms enfold,
> Free, generous and unconfin'd
> To outward shape or inward mind.

Nor does the power of Masonic feeling cease here, for enlightened amiability can eradicate differences between individuals as well. Green has Brockwell make personal applications of his doctrines to members of the assembled brotherhood. Though the poet only supplies initials and dashes, the contemporary readers knew who was intended, for the names are written in most of the surviving copies of the satire.[8]

> The high and low and great and small,
> James Perkins short and Austin tall,
> Johnson as bulky as a house,
> And Wethred smaller than a louse,
> The grave and merry, dull and witty,
> The fair and brown, deform'd and pretty,
> We all agree, both wet and dry,
> From drunken Luke to sober I.
>
> (10)

When Brockwell's abstractions confront the particularities of the assembly, they reveal their transparency. A malicious auditor whispers, "Do they all meet and part in love?"

> "Quarrels oft times don't they delight in,
> "And now and then a little fighting?
> "Did there not (for the SECRET's out)
> "In the last LODGE arise a rout?
> "McKenzie with a fist of brass
> "Laid Trails nose level with his face,
> "And scarcely had he let his hand go,
> "When he receiv'd from Trail a dam'd blow.
> "Now, parson, when a nose is broken,
> "Pray, is it friendly *sign* or *token*.
>
> (11)

Green's arraignment of Brockwell's doctrine for its inapplicability to the personal conditions of the brother members reveals the satirist's reformed Christian sensibility. Reformed Christians, Old Light and New Light, believed that love existed only as the expression of grace, and that grace manifested itself preeminently in the lives of individuals. If the individuals lacked signs or tokens of regeneration, their ethics would be subject to question and their talk of love deemed merely protestation. Brockwell's recommendation to embrace the Masonic duty to love is specious because the duty has failed to alter the behavior of the persons it purported to direct. By showing the unregenerate pugnaciousness of certain members, Green reaffirms the power of depravity that New England's religion always recognized. He also implicitly confirms the old distinctions that governed New

England's judgment of person: those whose actions betoken regeneration v. those whose deeds do not; the sanctified sheep v. the depraved goats. With these distinctions come the other divisions that distinguish New England society—regrettable divisions, no doubt, but so weighted with significance that they cannot be dismissed lightly with acts of fellow-feeling. Rhode Island's motley tribes contend because even religious men cannot escape the effects of their sinfulness. Just as the profusion of languages after the fall of the Tower of Babel conveys a sad truth about human nature, so the divisions that beset New England religion figure a truth of social conduct too significant to be canceled by a Masonic embrace. Green rejects out of hand the enlightenment's faith in the will to love as a social corrective; human will of itself has no effectual power to do good. The politics of sympathy that the Masonic brotherhood espouse are a mask disguising the true grounds of their fellowship—a common appetite for the pleasures of the flesh—"Love—of the BOTTLE and the BOWL" (11).

Given the reformed Christian recourse to one's personal standing vis-à-vis grace in matters of judgment, we can understand why Green indulges in the sort of ad hominem satire that neoclassic critics denigrated throughout the century. Green's critical presumption is diametrically opposed to the demand to generalize satire; indeed the problem with Brockwell's sermon and Masonic ideals is that they speak so generally that they have no real bearing on the conduct or character of the members. When confronted with the actual behavior of the lodge, Brockwell defends his sermon by repeating the ancient dodge, "All general rules have an exception," then contradicts his argument on social perfectability by adding, *"Humanum enim est errare."* Having demolished Brockwell's homily, Green shows the brotherhood acting on their love of bottle and bowl, trekking to Stone's tavern to seek truth by drinking wine.

The several pages of personal reflections that comprise Green's survey of the procession no doubt had their pungency in the poet's day. But of the protraits only two retain vital interest: that of Luke Vardy, who as the custodian of the bottle and bowl is the true advocate of Masonic love—

> without Luke the LODGE is undone.
> 'Twas he who oft dispell'd their Sadness,
> And fill'd the *brethren's* hearts with gladness.
> For them his ample bowls o'erflow'd,
> His table groan'd beneath it's load.
>
> (14)

—and that of Apothecary Austin, known to the assembled multitude because he applies the trunnel pipe to the bottoms of all who suffer from a binding of the bowels. His scatological fame is measured in his exaltation among the brotherhood, "high rising o'er the rest" (13). The portrait prefigures what subsequent representations of the Masons would entail. It also prepares for Green's scathing portrayal of the crowd, whose gawking and cheering confirms the brotherhood in its convictions of self-esteem:

> WHENE'ER for aiding nature frail,
> Poor bawd must follow the cart's-tail,
> As through fair LONDON's streets she goes,
> The mob, like fame, by moving grows,
> They should 'ring close, press, stink and shove,
> Scarcely can the *procession* move.
> Just such the noise, just such the roar
> Heard from behind and from before,
> 'Till *lodg'd* at STONE's, nor more pursu'd,
> The mob with three huzzas conclude.
>
> (14–15)

Green treats the mob with Hogarthian rigor, refusing to sink to its level and find favor with the show.

His harsh representation of the multitude did not prevent the satire from becoming popular. *Entertainment for a Winter's Evening* quickly sold out, and demand warranted a second edition. This occurred despite the fact that Green's muse left off before revealing the mysteries the lodge enacted in their meeting at the tavern. Instead, Green concluded by hinting that Clio might "once more" elucidate Masonic doings: five years later Clio took up the tale where she left off, in the *Grand Arcanum Detected*.

Many Bostonians, Freemasons among them, believed that Green's muse did not wait so long to take flight. On 7 January 1751 a verse addressed "To Mr. CLIO, at North-Hampton, *In Defence of* masonry," appeared in the *Boston Evening-Post*. The verse was adorned with the first woodcut ever to be published in illustration of a poem in an American newspaper (Lemay 1972, 141–42): a Scald jackass looking over Apothecary Austin driving a trunnel up the exposed rump of a stooping mason. The obscenity of the illustration suited the scatology of the "defense": "I'm sure our TRUNNELS look'd as clean / As if they ne're up A——se had been," and "We don't TRUNNELs with a Sister, / When we make them, we give a Cl[yst]er." The debt this piece of scurrility owed to Green's portrait of Austin immediately led to the general conclusion that the satirist was the author, despite the fact that the piece was addressed to Clio/Green. On 9 January the lodge voted to boycott the offending newspaper and send a committee of its most powerful members to the lieutenant governor and council "to complain against a scandalous piece of ribaldry . . . and to pray their order for prosecuting the printer thereof" (Shepard 1917, 39). The rumor-mongering concerning authorship grew so great that Green was forced to publish a disclaimer in the *Boston Post-Boy* of 14 January (Lemay 1972, 142):

WHEREAS there is a Report spread by Benjamin Hallowell of Boston, Shipwright, That I the Subscriber wrote, or Was concerned in writing, a Piece intitled, In Defence of Masonry, printed in the Boston Evening-Post of the 7th Instant;

I hereby declare, That I was not any ways, directly or indirectly, concerned in writing or publishing the aforesaid piece . . . and that the aforesaid Report is a scandalous and malicious Lie, invented by evil-minded Persons, and industriously propagated by the said *Benjamin Hallowell*, in the most indecent and abusive manner.

Green's claims are true, for on the twenty first, in a brief poem Clio identifies the culprit author as Mr. Vini Doctor. To the cognescenti of Boston's literary tavern culture, the pseudonym would have been sufficient to reveal the author: John Hammock.

John Hammock, like other minor figures in Boston's literary tavern culture (Thomas Kilby and John Barrell, for instance) has been forgotten by literary history. Nothing is known of his birth, though he appears to have been a freeholder of Braintree during the 1730s. His vocation, that of a medicinal vintner, was sufficiently unusual in Boston to elicit wry comment; yet his wine was good enough to earn him a place at the club table of John Dowse and Thomas Hutchinson (Barrell). The assembled Scotsmen called him Bacchus and held him in the regard with which the Freemasons held Luke Vardy. In 1750 Hammock emerged from obscurity into a modest literary prominence with several satirical pieces signed V.D., the initials for "Vini Doctor."[9] Though he attempted serious poetry on occasion—"On some fine Peach-Trees being kill'd by the late cold Easterly Wind," *Boston Evening-Post*, 27 May 1754; "On the present EXPEDITION," *Boston Evening-Post*, 12 May 1755—his modest genius was best employed in satire. It is seen to best advantage in the series of poems rebuking Nathaniel Ames for supplying New Englanders with a recipe for wine made from raisins ("To Mr. Ames," *Boston News-Letter*, 25 December 1760; "Tale," *Boston Evening-Post*, 1 February 1762). About this time Hammock appropriated the honorific "Captain" and served in the most prominent of Boston's charitable societies (Rowe 256).[10]

Hammock's "In Defence of Masonry" appeared in print lacking his usual identifier; it may have been intended to implicate Green in trouble, for during the previous year Green became Hammock's literary nemesis. Their rivalry appears to have arisen from Green's pique at a poem published by V.D. in the *Evening-Post* of 23 April 1750. Entitled "Dream," Hammock's verse surveyed the principal literary controversies disturbing the public prints during the winter of 1750. He granted his own paltry satirical advertisements of vintner Jonathan Williams equal standing with Green's *Entertainment* and the controversy surrounding Jonathan Mayhew's famous *A Discourse Concerning Unlimited Submission*. Acting on his pique, Green composed a satire upon V.D.'s medicinal enterprises. Some sample remarks:

> It is very well known
> You have kill'd half the town
> With your *succum ex pomis vinosum;*
> And, to make good the slaughter,
> Your *gratis* tar-water
> Advertise in the papers to dose 'um.

The satire passed in manuscript among Green's circle until the author began to entertain second thoughts concerning it. When his sister Ruth requested a copy, "Clio" replied,

> The Naughty thing for which you sent,
> Being by some thought to be nocent,
> I in the flames the Same did throw,
> Where all the Naughty folks must go.
>
> ("The Answer," Barrell MS)

The original may have been destroyed, but some friend made a copy and forwarded it to the editor of the *Boston Post-Boy,* where it was published on 30 July 1750. Green contritely penned an apology to Hammock: "The writer grieves to hear you're purty, / And swears he'd no design to hurt ye." As part of his apology, Green offered to make amends:

> Say, shall I never write again?
> If so, I'll throw away my pen.
> Or shall I write a recantation?
> E'en this I'll do, to calm your passion.
>
> ("Apologia," Smith-Carter MSS)

Apparently Hammock's stipulation was that Green publish a poem disavowing authorship of the satirical address "To V.D." and criticizing its style. Green must satirize himself. This he did, submitting "To the POET in the Post Boy, in his own Style" to the *Boston Gazette* under the signature "J G——ne"—the only occasion during his life when a poem appeared in Boston bearing his name. Yet this penance did not prove sufficient, for Hammock published "A Defence of Masonry," embroiling his adversary in a public controversy about blasphemy. Green defended himself with the only means he had available, the sharpened quill:

> WHEN Masons write in MASONS Praise,
> The Theme dictates the noblest Lays;
> Their grand, their secret Myst'ries rowl
> In Numbers that must charm the Soul;
> That like an *Amphion's Orphaean* Lyre,
> Might Cities build or Groves inspire:
> But when weak Bards presume, in spite
> Of Nature and their Stars, to write;

> What Character soe'er they chuse,
> Whither of the MASON or the MUSE,
> They only show, and all must know it,
> They're neither MASON, WITT, nor POET.
>
> ("Mr. Vini Doctor," *Boston News-Letter,* 24 January 1751)

Clio's reply to V.D. presaged Green's next poetic effort, "An ADDRESS To the MASONS at HALLIFAX," wherein the satirist assumes Amphion's task and builds a city in poetry. Like Hammock in the "Defense," Green adopted the persona of a Mason for the poem in order to burlesque the grandiose mythology of Freemasonry. Green's "Address" is a panegyric to the Masons for their role in creating Halifax,

> which now appears
> To all who view, the Work of many Years,
> And from a Chaos may be justly said,
> A decent Form to rear its towering Head:
> May it in future Time, in Structures Vie,
> With antient *Greece,* or famous *Italy.*
>
> (*Boston News-Letter,* 22 August 1751)

Green's jest depended on the reader knowing that in 1751 Halifax was one of the least imposing outposts of the British Empire, a rude assemblage of minor dwellings and ill-constructed public buildings (Shipton 1933, 4:434–49). It possessed little claim to the promise of rising glory and a new classical age.

Panegyric poetry is not constrained by matters of fact, and Green invests Masonic Halifax with a glory few cities could match. He sees it as the sum of the great creation that began "When first from Nothing at th' Almighty's Call / Came this unbounded, this stupendous ALL." Green then surveys the biblical history as rewritten by Masonic expositors, telling how the Fall wrought the need for science and arts; how architecture flourished until buildings wrought the Tower of Babel; how confusion ensued. Then,

> At length, directed by Heaven's Architect,
> Great SOLOMON a Temple doth erect
> Surpassing ev'ry Structure far in Fame,
> As its wise Founder every other Name
> JEHOVA's Self inhabited the Shrine,
> And mark'd the consecrated Work Divine.
> To raise this Dome, rose from distant Parts
> The Emulous, and Excellent in Arts:
> But he whose Skill was most superlative
> From whom our sacred Secrets we derive,
> The most compleat MECHANICK known to Fame,
> Needless to tell you BRETHREN his NAME,
> Engrav'd Life's figuring Imag'ry most true.

Here Green follows closely the Masonic mythology concerning Solomon's request to King Hiram of Tyre for the workman to oversee construction of the temple. King Hiram sent "Hiram the Chief" who built the two cherubim and wings to the cover the ark, according to Masonic song. Green's account, however, highlights the pride in skill and vanity of secrecy that the Masons derive from their apochryphal past. The reader is left to wonder why they escaped the fate of the builders of Babel.

The artistry of Green's "Address" lies in its credibility as a Masonic oration. Rather than distort the Masonic mythology or caricature the brethren, Green has composed a piece faithful to the self-celebration of Masonic song. The irony lies in the fact that the creation of Halifax is a matter hardly worthy of celebration. The pseudoscriptural history that prepares us for the creation of Halifax is rendered empty in retrospect. And we recall that Freemasons are not literally masons at all and had little if any hand in the actual construction of that place which they congratulate themselves for creating.

One further point must be made about Green's choice of Halifax as the place of his satirical address: the international scope of Freemasonry was a source of anxiety to natives of New England. The principle of local autonomy that instructed congregational polity and the charter struggles of the eighteenth century bred suspicion of institutions that willingly acknowledged direction from overseas. Boston's lodge derived its authority from the Grand Mother Lodge of London; indeed it was the first chartered New World lodge. That it gloried in its London connection yet refused to reveal its mysteries, particularly its reason for being; that it counted among its membership the Belchers and other politically powerful persons yet repeatedly disavowed having any political program, despite the fact that the kings of France, Austria, Spain, and Belgium had taken action against lodges during the 1730s and 1740s, inspired among many a profound discomfort. The greatest causes of anxiety were "Those sacred, solemn Secrets we alone, / Enjoy from sure Traditions of our own" (ll. 38–39). These secrets Green would bring to light in his final anti-Masonic satire, *The Grand Arcanum Detected*.

Masonic secrecy invited curiosity. The mystique enticed numbers sufficient for Nathaniel Ames to issue a warning in his almanac for 1738:

When once our Friends do quit the living Shore
    We hear from them no more.
Do any curious Minds desire to know
    Where 'tis they go
    Or how they fare
Let them be pleas'd to die
    Only to trie,
Or else remain in Ignorance as they were.
    Thus whether they fare ill or well
    Since not allow'd to tell.

>   Who'd voluntary enter *Charon's* Boat.
>   So *Masonry* and *Death* are both the same
>   Tho' of a different Name.
>   If Good there is in their Society
>   'Tis free for those that try;
>   But like the Grave let not the Living know't.[11]

Ames's analogy invests Masonic secrecy with an ultimacy that only New England moralists could manage. Yet of all regions New England probably had the least to fear from the arcane knowledge protected by the cloak of secrecy.

Secrecy was a legacy of the guild protections afforded practical masons in earlier centuries. When speculative masonry developed during the late seventeenth century and the practical lodges became havens of Whig politics, the conversion of masonry to a clandestine social and political movement took place. Guild protections were invoked to hide the program of radical Whigs and proponents of the new science. In effect, the program of earlier political secret societies such as the Rota were grafted onto an already-existing secret organization.[12] As the Masonic movement spread throughout Europe in the early decades of the eighteen century, it became an agency for the most radical ideas of the Enlightenment: republicanism, anticlericism, materialism. An underground literature, including such works as the infamous *Treatise of the Three Imposters*, a tract debunking Moses, Jesus, and Muhammed, circulated in manuscript at Masonic meetings (Jacob 1981, 142-76). Hints of the subversive activities no doubt resulted in repeated attacks against the brotherhood by European authorities.

In New England many elements of the secret Masonic program may have seemed gratuitous. Tory politics and Jacobitism had only modest popular support; the public gazettes (for instance, the *Independent Advertiser* of Boston) printed republican tracts by the "Salem shoemaker" as volatile as any manuscript screed furtively passed among the brotherhood; and circles existed in the city (the Merchant's Club, for instance) that promoted Whig constitutionalism with a vigor the Masons could not rival. Local political circles, too, did not suffer from the onus of an international government, nor all the imperial baggage that attended Freemasonry's spread to outposts such as Halifax and Bombay.[13]

The issue of Freemasonry's role in the spread of freethinking was more problematic. Brockwell's large, loose principles of brotherly love lacked the philosophical rigor to be dangerous. Yet his insistence that "whoever is an *Upright Mason*, can neither be an Atheist, Deist, or Libertine" (14) suggests that suspicions floated about Boston that demanded refutation.

Green did not promote these suspicions, for aside from a passing allusion to Rosicrucianism, little is done in the satire with the notion that Masons were seriously engaged in a program of intellectual subversion—that they were undermining monarchial or theological authority. For Green, the Masonic mythology is so ludicrous in its pseudoscriptural fictionalizing that it does not merit refutation, but only mocking recitation instead. Brockwell, the one Masonic theorist encountered, is shown to be out of touch with the brotherhood in his vaporous idealizing. Ultimately the impression one receives from the satires is that the Masons are so given over to their appetites and passions that they are incapable of cultivating pernicious thought.

The Grand Arcanum Detected depicts how the Masonic brotherhood treats the issue of authority in the privacy of its own circle. The principle actions of the narrative are the obscene rites three candidates endure in order to win the right to sit as temporary Grand Master when the "Right Honourable" is away. Like Hammock before him, Green made use of a second tradition of rumor prompted by secret societies—that the circles occult themselves because they engage in obscenity. In the Grub-street fantasy literature about clubs, one finds many dark hints of illicit circles: assemblies of pederasts, covens of aristocratic Satanists, gaggles of sadomasochists. (Ned Ward's *History of clubs*, 1709, was the most comprehensive collection of rumors about clandestine circles.) The Masons enjoyed a peculiar reputation for sadistic initiation rites that included spankings and coprophilia. An episode in Philadelphia that touched Benjamin Franklin illuminates the sort of nonsense commonly believed. Daniel Ress, a "simple-minded apprentice," desired initiation into the Masonic mysteries. A group, including a renegade Mason and Rees's employer, Dr. Evan Jones, decided to stage a mock initiation. The ceremony included an "oath of allegiance to Satan" and a draught of purgative from a "sacramental cup," after which "one of the Company indecently discovered his Posteriors, to which the Lad . . . was led to kiss" (Labaree 1959–, 2:198). A second initiation resulted in the accidental death of the apprentice when a bowl of burning brandy (a prop to dramatize the appearance of a devil) spilled on Rees. Though the affair was enacted by mock Masons, Franklin and other Freemasons did not escape censure, for rumor held that Franklin had read the Satanic oath and had been much amused by it (Sachse 1906, 65–71). The popular tradition that Masonic initiations entailed bum-baring and scatology subserved Green's obscene revelation of Freemasonry's *Grand Arcanum*.

Green readies his reader for the descent into low matters by having Folly serve as guide to the Masonic proceedings, rather than Clio: "Rise Folly, Rise, for this prevails, / When every Muse in Heav'n fails" (4). Folly shows the brotherhood indulging in its love for bowl and board. After the revelry the clerk announces the circumstance that will generate the action of Green's satire:

"Brethren as by a sad Disaster,
"The L[odg]e deplores her absent Master.

> " 'Tis necessary, and no Wonder,
> "That one should keep the others under;
> "Therefore 'tis meet at present Sitting
> "To delegate a Person fitting.
>
> (7)

Four candidates rise for the honor. The clerk announces that the chair will be awarded to him

> "Who best can bear the Shock of Noses,
> "And tender Breech to Fist exposes;
> "And stems the Force of vile Grimace,
> "With most Serenity of Face.
>
> (8)

One would-be chairman demurs. Three resolve to face one another in combat. The candidates include brothers Box, Withred, and Atkins, "Whose hand" can give "the rudest Touch, / Whose callous Palm, can nobly boast, / The Nerves benumn'd, and Feeling lost." Green devotes 106 lines to the contest, describing Atkins's successful flogging of Box's rump, whose contents "struggling hard for vent" eventually burst on Atkins's face; we are also treated to a vicious nose-pulling match between Atkins and Withred. The poetic machinery of the sublime and a heavy slathering of classical allusion supply the combat with an appropriate bathetic portentiousness:

> So fierce the Blow, so dire the Fall,
> He wak'd up some, and startled all.
> Thus *Vulcan* from *Olympus* tumbel'd,
> While o'er his Head hoarse Thunder grumbel'd.
> So dar'd the Miscreants to rebell,
> And so the daring Miscreant fell.
> H[enry] up-scrambling eager fled,
> While A[tkin]s thundred at his Head.
>
> (13)

In triumph Atkins is installed as temporary chairman. His triumph through degradation is, of course, a hollow victory hard won. Thus the *Grand Arcanum* that Folly reveals is "Nothing" and the moral of the revelation is precisely that supplied by Green in the first stanza of the poem *Ex Nihilo, nam Nihil sit.*

The moral of Green's satires is that the Freemasonic show is much ado about nothing. The lodge's membership may include powerful men, but behind the closed doors they feed and brawl. Boston's Grand Master may heed authorities in London, but the orders amount to little more than march and revelry. Rumors may circulate about the pernicious doctrines protected by the Freemasonic vow of secrecy, but judging from the pastiche of scripture that serves as their warrant for antiquity and the idealist vaporizings of Brother Brockwell, they may be dismissed as puerile fantasy. The solemnities the lodge displays on the public streets are simply expressions of vanity—a pride that is shown to be groundless when the members are known in their true characters.

Throughout his career Green viewed the Freemasons as a travesty of society. Since the brotherhood itself was a travesty, Green could employ total irony and closely mimic the writings and descriptions generated by the order. When he desired to make his reflections more personal, he could employ burlesque, exaggerating Masonic traits into caricature. In terms of literary history his method of burlesque has the greater interest, for it prefigures the personal satire that so dominates revolutionary belles-lettres. Those historians who follow Bruce I. Granger and see Charles Churchill's satires of the 1760s inspiring the American literature of mock confessions and mad monarchial soliloquies ignore the native practitioners of the mode; practitioners whose writings predate Churchill's (Granger 1960, 9–10). Furthermore, they neglect to see the curious appropriateness of personal satire in eighteenth-century New England, where Augustan wit was tempered with Reformed Christian individualism.

NOTES

This essay is based on research undertaken as a Samuel Foster Haven Fellow of the American Antiquarian Society. The research into the career of John Hammock was underwritten by a Citadel Development Foundation grant. Thanks are due Professor J. A. Leo Lemay for graciously calling the Thomas Pemberton Notebook and the Smith-Carter Papers to my attention.

Excerpts of the Benjamin Walker diaries and the Joseph Green poems in the Smith-Carter papers are printed by permission of the Massachusetts Historical Society; the Green poem from the manuscript John Barrell Letterbook is quoted by permission of the New York Historical Society.

1. Saint Johns Lodge of Boston is the first chartered Masonic lodge in the Western Hemisphere, receiving its warrant from the Grant Mother Lodge of London in 1733. The Masonic activities in Philadelphia prior to this date were without official sanction.

2. Jonathan Belcher had been hired by Massachusetts as an agent to testify in hearings before the crown against Governor William Burnet, who had insisted that the General Court (legislature) of Massachusetts set a fixed gubernatorial salary in accord with royal instructions. Burnet died during the course of the hearings. The crown appointed Belcher governor. Belcher returned to Massachusetts and reiterated the royal demand for the fixed salary.

The surviving copies of these satires were addressed to Captain Samuel Pollard of Portsmouth, New Hampshire, and are included among the Smith Townsend manuscripts of the Massachusetts Historical Society. The idea for the pastiche may have come to Green after reading Rev. Samuel Mather's laudatory broadside poem, *A Country Treat Upon the Second Paragraph in His Excellency's SPEECH, Decemb. 17. 1730* [1731].

3. "The Poet's [Rev. Mather Byles] Lamentation for the Loss of his Cat, which he used to call his Muse" 1733, 579. *A Mournful Lamentation for the Sad and Deplorable*

Death of Mr. Old Tenor (1750b) is an instance of a mock instructive elegy. "Lines occasioned by a *Dr. Hudson* thy fellow rogue Howe, pilloried in Kingstreet for counterfeiting," manuscript copy of 1762 broadside print, Thomas Pemberton Notebook, Massachusetts Historical Society.

4. "Mr. Waghorn, Grand Sword Bearer." (Green's note.)

5. I endorse Clifford Shipton's interpretation of Green's career in *Biographical Sketches* against Samuel Briggs's evaluation in *The Essays, Humor, and Poems of Nathaniel Ames* (1891).

6. He satirized the Church of England in his popular "Inscription under Revd. John Checkly's Picture." New Light enthusiasm was rebuked in "The Disappointed Cooper"; see Lemay 1974. His sympathy for a champion of the Old Light cause is evident in *An Eclogue Sacred to the memory of . . . Jonathan Mayhew* ([1766]).

7. Green alludes to Alexander Ross 1696.

8. I depend on the annotated copy found in the collection of the American Antiquarian Society.

9. A satirical advertisement by "John Hamock, V.D." appeared in the *Boston Weekly News-Letter,* 18 January 1750. The ad appeared in all the Boston gazettes of that week. The subsequent issue of *BWNL* on 15 January carries a further satire.

10. John Rowe, whose diary for the 1760s provides the most comprehensive view of Boston society in the era before the revolution, identifies Captain Hammock as an officer of the Charitable Society (Rowe 1898, 142).

11. Ames may be commenting on the death of Daniel Rees in Philadelphia in 1737 during a mock Masonic initiation rite.

12. Founded in 1659 as a republican debating society, the Rota included among its membership Sir William Pery, Cyriac Skinner, John Milton, Andrew Marvell, and James Harrington. After the Restoration the authorities repressed the organization (Timbs 1872, 13–14).

13. The "Salem Shoemaker" appears throughout the entire run of the *Independent Advertiser,* but see especially no. 52 (26 December 1748) and no. 64 (9 January 1748/9). Isaiah Thomas believed the Shoemaker to have been the mouthpiece for a committee whose membership included Sam Adams (Thomas 1810, 256). The issue of the Masonic role in Boston's revolutionary agitations remains clouded. The lodge included notable Whigs among its members, lawyer Oxenbridge Thacher being the most conspicuous patriot. Yet the membership appears to have been of mixed persuasion on the eve of independence. The nationalist bias of American Masonic histories invalidates their judgments concerning the extent of Masonic participation in the patriot cause in New England.

The Secret Fall of Freemasonry in Dr. Alexander Hamilton's *The History of the Tuesday Club*

ROBERT MICKLUS

In the prevideo world of eighteenth-century England and colonial America the most popular form of entertainment was clubbing. The wave of fraternal feeling that characterized the Age of Reason during the 1720s and 1730s made conditions ripe for the establishment of various social organizations on both sides of the Atlantic, and not coincidentally it was during this time that Freemasonry became firmly entrenched in Great Britain with the unification of the four major lodges in England in 1717, the publishing of James Anderson's Masonic *Constitutions* in 1723, and the establishment of the Grand Lodge in Scotland in 1736. A Scotsman such as Dr. Alexander Hamilton, who came to Maryland in late 1738, therefore brought with him a natural penchant for clubbing. And he was not alone. In *The History of the Tuesday Club*, his huge mock-epic of the rise and fall of colonial Maryland's foremost gentleman's club, Hamilton wrote in 1755 that at the turn of the century "the Annapolitans were very much addicted to Clubbing, so that I shall speak within Compass, If I say, that there were then at least 40 clubs in that City." Hamilton nostalgically added, however, that since that time "the Clubbing humor is much abated among [the Annapolitans], there being now at this day, not above four or five Clubs, and, to make up this number, we must reckon the Free masons and Routs, which by many connoiseurs, are not in a strict sense reckoned Clubs, the first, dealing in mysteries, which they keep Intirely to themselves . . . [while] the latter are governed and managed Intirely by the Ladies, being mixed assemblies of male and female."[1] Hamilton's account of the tremendous proliferation of conviviality in early Annapolis is as exaggerated as most of the events he narrates in *The History of the Tuesday Club*, but the point still remains: in the early eighteenth century clubbing was the thing to do.

This, of course, is hardly news to anyone who has studied the social life of the eighteenth century. The point I wish to stress, however, is the simple but, I think, important one that Freemasonry, too, was first and foremost a form of clubbing in an age of clubbing. We read so often about the anxieties that Freemasonry caused the church or the state,[2] or about the ways in which Freemasonry was ridiculed by other social groups, or about all the nefarious rituals that Freemasons reputedly conducted behind closed doors, that we tend to regard it as some sort of outcast, subversive organization, when in fact, in an age when clubbing really was *the* thing to do, being a Freemason—to Freemasons, at least—was as much a part of the normal social fabric of eighteenth-century life as being a member of a club such as Hamilton's Tuesday Club. To be sure, Freemasons encouraged and no doubt were amused by the misconceptions that the uninitiated entertained about their being a clandestine, "secret" organization. That, after all, was part of the fun of belonging to that particular club, and Freemasons such as Hamilton did their best to exploit those misconceptions if only to better relish the joke. In the passage quoted above, for instance, Hamilton whimsically encouraged the notion that Freemasonry was a secret, subversive organization by suggesting that there were real clubs and then there were those Freemasons, about whom, since no one knew for certain what the devil they did behind closed doors, no one could determine whether they could rightfully be called clubs or not. Yet Hamilton, like most of the other Tuesday Club members, was deeply involved in Freemasonry and understood full well that it was just as much a club as the Tuesday Club itself. Hamilton was Master Mason of his Annapolis lodge, while other prominent Tuesday Club members such as Edward Dorsey and the Reverend Alexander Malcolm were wardens and Jonas Green was secretary. Indeed, even while Hamilton was keeping the minutes that he would eventually use as an outline for his *History*, which contains numerous remarks humorously suggesting his ignorance about the secrets of Freemasonry, he was also presiding over his lodge and listening to another Tuesday Club member, the Reverend John Gordon, deliver his Masonic sermon *Brotherly Love Explain'd and Enforc'd* (1750).

What intrigues me most, then, about Hamilton's allusions to Freemasonry in *The History of the Tuesday Club* is that, despite all the fuss that the Royal Art sometimes occasioned among uninitiated or paranoid outsiders, a staunch Freemason such as Hamilton apparently felt no great cause of alarm to defend the brotherhood against its opponents' charges. Rather, he felt comfortable and secure enough about the place of Freemasonry in eighteenth-century society not only to play upon many of the popular misconceptions about Freemasonry in *The History of the Tuesday Club* but also, as I hope to show, to construct in that book a narrative that, sometimes overtly and more often covertly, humorously subverts the very principle of that covert organization.

At first it is a bit difficult to recognize what the principles of Freemasonry have to do with Hamilton's comic portrayal of the fall of the Tuesday Club.

Nowhere in *The History of the Tuesday Club* does Hamilton explicitly develop the relationship between the two clubs. Rather, like a good Freemason he develops the relationship covertly and subversively. Like a good Freemason he refuses to indulge the secrets of the brotherhood in the pages of his *History;* he refuses, in fact, even once to mention that he and the other principal actors in *The History of the Tuesday Club* were also Freemasons. Instead, he plays the man of the street viewing Freemasonry from outside its private world. Yet he mentions Freemasonry so frequently in volume 1 of his *History* that only the most obtuse reader will fail to see the connection between the conventions of Freemasonry and what transpires in Hamilton's narration of the fall of the Tuesday Club. "As for that ancient and honorable Club, the Free and Accepted Masons," Hamilton notes early in *The History of the Tuesday Club* while discussing the wise maxims upon which all clubs are founded, "many are of opinion, (who perhaps know nothing of the matter) that, the main Excellence of their Constitution, and principal Cause of their Antiquity rests on their admirable Talent at keeping a Secret" (1:11). This, the first mention of Freemasonry in *The History of the Tuesday Club*, does two things at once: it establishes Hamilton as a narrator who will promote the popular perception of Freemasonry, while at the same time—as the parenthetical remark suggests—hinting at the popular ignorance; and it establishes the link between Freemasonry and other forms of clubbing, a link that becomes significant in understanding the themes and motifs that Hamilton develops in his *History*.

Hamilton develops the link between Freemasonry and other forms of clubbing sometimes implicitly and sometimes explicitly throughout volume 1 of *The History of the Tuesday Club*. Shortly after first mentioning Freemasonry he ludicrously examines the antiquity of clubbing, a topic that has always been of singular interest to Masonic historians. In his *Illustrations of Masonry* (1775), for instance, William Preston typically and laboriously traced the roots of Freemasonry back to the beginning of the world, demonstrating that Lamech, Tubal Cain, and Jubal were among the most noteworthy of the earliest Freemasons (see bk. 1, sec. 3); not satisfied with that, George Oliver took Masonic antiquity even one step further, arguing that "our science existed *before* the creation of this globe" (1854, 24). Hamilton, however, humorously parodies the Masonic obsession with antiquity, merely stating that

> We have no certain accounts of any particular Clubs before the general Deluge, tho' doubtless there were such Societies among the Antidiluvians, we meet with a dark hint of the sons of God cohabiting with the daughters of men, from whence sprung a Club or Association of Gyants . . . but this account being very obscure, I leave it just where I found it. Some Ingenious Historians have alledged, with some Show of probability, that there was an Antidiluvian Tradesman's Club, of which Tubal Cain was

president, who is said to have first formed a regular Lodge of Free masons. (1:37)

But, that account being equally obscure, Hamilton leaves that, too, just where he found it. A few pages later, though, he returns to the same idea, arguing that if the spirit moved him he could probably trace the ancient and honorable Tuesday Club back to the deluge and to "some Club or other, that met on Tuesday, and this I might do with the same propriety, as the ancient & honorable fraternity of Free and accepted Masons . . . trace their Society from Noe, Tubal Cain, king Solomon . . . down to those famous modern Architects, Inigo Jones, and Sir Christopher Wren" (1:41). Which, of course, is exactly what Masonic historians did. But rather than follow in such uncertain footsteps, Hamilton decides to leave such things "to the Reverend Doctor Warburton, and others more versed in antiquities and Critical learning, and also," he judiciously adds, "for another weighty reason I ommit it, that is, least I should make this work too voluminous and bulky" (1:41). Anyone who has dipped into the literature of Masonic antiquity knows that Hamilton's insinuation is, to say the least, mildly understated.

These sorts of whimsical jibes at Freemasonry from a man who was himself a Master Mason appear throughout volume 1 of *The History of the Tuesday Club* and illustrate not only the sophisticated sense of humor that allowed Hamilton to laugh at himself and his own circle of friends but also his security about the place of Masonry in the social life of colonial America. Rather than defend Freemasonry or seek to dispel the confusion about its secret practices, Hamilton casually jokes about many of the popular misconceptions concerning the brotherhood. In discussing the derivation of *longstanding member*, a term that the Tuesday Club members use in addressing each other, Hamilton insists that *longstanding member* is an honorable phrase and that no one should "misinterpret [his] words in the manner that some evil minded females, have done the mysteries of the Free Masons" (1:51). Similarly, while defending the Tuesday Club's fondness for anniversary feasts and processions, Hamilton again refers to the proceedings of "the ancient and honorable Club of free and accepted Masons, who used to strut in grand procession, with all their ornaments, Jewels, badges and ensigns on [their anniversary] day, Till the Burlesque fraternity of Scald Miserables, Instituted a comic procession, in Imitation of them; ornamented with riders on asses Arsy-versy, dungcarts, mops, broomsticks, dishclouts, and Soot-bags . . . which Gelastic pomp and pegeantry, put a stop to the other, and ever since, that Right worshipful fraternity have left the street clear" (1:255–56). As here, Hamilton humorously defends the absurd practices of the Tuesday Club throughout his *History*. But, again, nowhere in all of his manuscript's nearly nineteen hundred pages did he feel obliged to defend Freemasonry, humorously or not. Instead, he clearly felt confident enough about the place of Freemasonry in colonial life to use it, as in the above instances, as a foil to make the Tuesday Club's absurd practices seem less ridiculous than they might otherwise appear.

Aside from mocking the Masonic preoccupation with antiquity and ceremonies, Hamilton has a field day in his *History* mocking the Masonic fascination with such things as Rosicrucian lore, ancient charms, and the mystical powers of numbers. In his discussion of the men who have made the greatest contribution to the world's wit and wisdom, for instance, he at one point reels off a list of alchemists that runs nearly an entire printed page. He leaves out no one and even invents a name or two. Rather than assume the importance they do in Masonic history, in Hamilton's *History* these names become a jumbled mass of equal importance—none. Hamilton likewise toys with the Masonic penchant to dabble in cabalistic charms such as the wondrous *abracadabra*, which he explains works best when written thus:

    abracadabra
    abracadabr
    abracadab
    abracada
    abracad
    abraca
    abrac
    abra
    abr
    ab
    a.

The charm acquires a certain cumulative power that way, although "in these our degenerate days," Hamilton writes, it does not make much difference how it is written, since the charm has somehow "lost it's efficacy, probably from some necessary Circumstance being ommitted in the use of the Charm, such, perhaps, as repeating it in a certain hour of the day or night . . . or in a particular posture of body . . . or with two Stockings on one leg, or with a Jacket wrong Side outwards, or with one's face towards the east, west, South or North, the ommission of any the least part of which ceremonies, would render the Charm of no effect" (2:22–23).

To Hamilton, charms were charming and numbers were numbers. But, as he well knew, to more serious-minded Freemasons the mystical powers of charms and numbers were not to be taken lightly. Accordingly, in the character of Loquacious Scribble (Hamilton's persona in *The History of the Tuesday Club*) he fell into a veritable Masonic rapture over those "two Surprizing & Mystical numbers, three and Seven" (2:361). "My Lord," Scribble says, addressing his mystical speech to the club's president, you know, to begin with the heavens, there are the Seven great Globes of this planetary System, the Seven Stars of the Heiades [Sir John: What! what! the Hay days!] the Seven of the Pleiades, the Seven of Arcturus, there are the Seven liberal arts and Sciences, the Seven wonders of the world, the Seven Pyramids of AEgypt, the Seven Churches of Asia, There are the Seven wise men of Greece, the Seven Sages of Gotham, the Seven Champions of Christendom, the Seven kings of Rome, the Seven hills upon which that City was built, there are the Seven Sleepers & their dog, who slept in a Cave for 500 years [Sir John: The devil! they did!] the Seven days of the week, the Seven. . . . (2:363)

Scribble's Masonic swoon goes on for another two pages. Sir John (patterned after John Bullen, captain of a regiment of Annapolis foot soldiers), champion of the club's liberty and common sense, finds it impossible to sit and listen to Scribble's rhapsody without ungraciously interrupting him. Otherwise, all the club's members would surely have fallen asleep during Scribble's harangue, as would any sensible person reading the portion quoted here or the pages and pages of detailed analysis concerning the significance of numbers in popular Masonic literature.[3]

It would be tedious to discuss all the Masonic customs that Hamilton parodies in *The History of the Tuesday Club*. It is enough to say that he pokes fun at almost everything from the Masonic grip, which he calls the clubical "manuquassation," to the custom that was almost as sacred to Freemasons as their secrecy, the forbidding of women into their private assemblies. For one momentous evening it actually came to pass that the Tuesday Club not only admitted women into their sacred halls but even allowed them to preside over their meeting (see 2:432–48). According to Hamilton's burlesque account in *The History of the Tuesday Club*, several of the club's members, who were absent on that conspicuous occasion, were appalled to discover that during their absence the club was governed by women, and, suspecting "such Innovations to be dangerous to the constitution of this here Club," they voted to issue a warrant "*de ventre Inspiciendo*, for searching and Inspecting these females, in order to discover, whether or not they were Effectual, and true Longstanding members" (2:448). Those interested in discovering the upshot of their inspection will have to read the book.

So even Hamilton's bawdry is just a step away from poking fun at Masonic traditions. Yet the antics of the Tuesday Club members described in Hamilton's *History* do more than mock Masonic learning and customs; they mock the very core of Masonic values. As any well-schooled Freemason knows, the primary virtues to which all Freemasons should aspire are those three pillars of Wisdom, Strength, and Beauty. More than any other member of the brotherhood, the Grand Master should be the walking emblem of those virtues. The Tuesday Club's equivalent of the Grand Master, President Nasifer Jole (patterned after Charles Cole, an Annapolis merchant), is a walking travesty of all three virtues. Judging from Hamilton's description of Jole's physical appearance, it is possible that the club's illustrious president could venture out on Halloween without the aid of a mask. "Our heroes person," Hamilton writes, "sett off his dress, rather more than his dress his person, he is of a fair complexion, long and Sharp visage; somewhat Inclinable to a Square countenance, his nose aqueline, his chin of a Considerable length and prominent, in short, he is what many call in their vulgar Stile somewhat hatchet faced; his body is thick and well built . . . and every way proportional except a little . . . *prominentia chinium,* resembling somewhat the description of Rob Morris in the old Scots Song . . .: Auld Rob Morris, I ken him fou well, / His arse it sticks out like ony peet creel" (1:160). With compliments like that a man never needs to be insulted. Hamilton similarly compliments Jole in describing his walk as being "stately and upright, tho' alittle on the hobble, which is not natural but from a gouty weakness in his feet" (1:160). In short, Jole possesses all the physical beauty of a stereotypical "confidence man," and if he possesses any inner beauty it is difficult to detect beneath his vanity, affectation, and niggardliness. Whatever inner strength he possesses, moreover, is merely the dubious strength of being able to endure the insults and attacks of his fellow club members. Outwardly Jole possesses no physical strength whatsoever; rather, his most dominant physical trait is his effeminacy. While aboard a man of war, Hamilton says, Jole acquired "many useful arts, particularly that of Cookery, and he was such a proficient in that noble Science, that he understood as well as any notable husiff, how to stew a frecassee . . . or raise a pasty" (1:155). Now, many men are good cooks without being effeminate, but this Nasifer also "had a curious and elegant taste in cutting out patterns of work for Sempstresses," and he "understood perfectly well . . . how in the most charming and elegant taste to dress up a nosegay" (1:157, 156). Indeed, whenever he went to church he wore a nosegay "in his buttonhole . . . while he kept twirling a charming pink Iris, Jonquille, or Aenemonie betwixt his finger and thumb" (1:156–57). Many members of the congregation suspected that he "intended thus to lay traps" to ensnare the ladies, for which he also used "perfumes, such as musk, ambergrise, Civet, Bergamot, and the like" (1:157). But Jole preferred instead "a Society of Cats for his friends, fellows and playmates, both at bed and board, and so far did his extraordinary charity and benevolence extend to those Cats, that . . . he would stroke down their soft Skins [and] apply their mouths to his" (1:164–65). Still, it would be possible to excuse Jole of all this if he possessed a shred of wisdom, but we learn that "the chief of Mr Joles Learning, besides that of cookery pastry, and other parts of housewifery, consists in divinity and music, his knowledge in the first he picked up, from a Curious collection of old books of Sermons . . . which Sermons were chiefly preached . . . in the Halcyon days of King James I. when punning and quaint Sayings were very much in vogue. . . . For this reason Chiefly Mr Jole admires these Quaint Sermons, affirming that there were no such sermons to be met with now a days, which," Hamilton concurs with his learned leader, "every one will frankly own to be true" (1:161–62). As for his knowledge in music, the mellifluous Jole has acquired that "merely by the force of Genius, having never been taught," and has developed a remarkable talent for singing love songs, reciting them "with so lamentable a voice, as to draw tears from the eyes of the most flinty hearted, tho many affirmed that these tears flowed not from Commiseration, but from a certain gelastic conquassation" (1:162–63).

Jole seems to have been created by Hamilton purposefully to burlesque all the values that Freemasons considered essential for an individual to advance to positions of authority in their society, just as the Tuesday Club itself—as Hamilton fictitiously depicts it in his *History*—seems to have been created to burlesque the values that were essential to Freemasonry as an organization. If Wisdom, Strength, and Beauty are the foundation of individual worth to Freemasons, charity, benevolence, and brotherhood are the foundation of their society as a whole. But not in the Tuesday Club. From its president on down, the club's sense of charity extends only as far as its members' own pockets. Although its members, like Freemasons, collect regular dues for charitable purposes, and although much ado is made in *The History of the Tuesday Club* about the noble designs for which the money in the "charity box" is intended, that box is never used for any charitable purpose. Instead, the club's members propose to President Jole that the money should be used to purchase punch ladles. Jole reminds them that "it would be contradictory to the original design of the box, which was allotted for charity, to lay out that fund upon punch Ladles, or any such triffles" (1:337), but shortly thereafter, Hamilton snidely observes, Jole himself "gravely proposed . . . to buy with the box money a Club table Cloth and Club Napkins, of some very fine diaper, which he had in his own Store for Sale; I would only ask," Hamilton reflects, "what Sort of Charity this was" (1:338). Much to Jole's chagrin, the club eventually uses the pittance in the charity box to purchase lottery tickets. And so it goes when the club ignores the entreaties of one of its members, Signior Lardini (Thomas Bacon, who actually founded a charity school in Maryland), to contribute to the establishment of a charity school then under way. In reality, the Tuesday Club surely answered these and other appeals for charity generously. In fiction, however, Hamilton created one of the most stingy clubs known to man, in part, I am sure, to burlesque the charitable, benevolent purposes of an organization such as Freemasonry.

The ultimate affront to the principles of Freemasonry in *The History of the Tuesday Club* is the comic destruction of brotherhood that occurs in volume 2. The constant bickerings in club and the increasing antagonism between the club's members and President Jole lead to the ignominious decathedration of his lordship, a movement spearheaded by Philo Dogmaticus (the Reverend

Alexander Malcolm) and agitated by Loquacious Scribble, the club's secretary. In his exhaustive discussion of the various degrees of Freemasonry a century later, Albert Pike began his chapter on the degree of "Intimate Secretary" by instructing his fellow Masons that "You are especially taught in this Degree to be zealous and faithful; to be disinterested and benevolent; and to act the peacemaker, in case of dissensions, disputes, and quarrels among the brethren" (1871, 119). Loquacious Scribble, the Tuesday Club's version of the "intimate secretary," is just the opposite: "he was of a positive fractious and fiery temper, and often excited Commotions and disputes in Club, by making absurd and Phantastical motions, under pretence of checking the grouth of Luxury, and arbitrary power in the Club . . . [he was] a Sly, cunning, Insinuating, deceitful, mischief making member, the continual Author and promoter of Brawls, wrangles, Jealousies, Grumblings, heartburnings, hubbubs and hurly burlys in this here ancient and honorable Club" (1:193, 243). When Philo Dogmaticus, the club's chancellor, seeks to unseat Nasifer Jole from his presidential throne, Loquacious Scribble is the first to goad him on. Accusing Jole of tyrannical behavior, the chancellor, "with a Ghastly and Enraged countenance" (1:486), provokes the club to fight for their liberty:

> Gentlemen, must we submit to this . . . unparallelled tyranny and oppression—must we be such dupes, such Simpletons, such asses . . . will you Gentlemen—will you see me abused—trod upon, Insulted, contrould and brow beaten by that old Coxcomb in the Chair, will you suffer your faithful Chancellor . . . to be made a Cypher, a person of no Influence or Significancy in this here Club, by an arrogant Prig . . . for Shame! rouse up your heroic Spirits, dont suffer your selves to be piss'd upon—pull him down I say!—pull him down! if he knows not how to command, let him be taught to obey, evacuate the chair of such a load of absurdity. (2:487)

"During this furious extacy of the Chancellor," Hamilton notes, "his honor the president was fixed like a monument of marble in his Chair; he moved neither to one Side, nor to the other, but like one in a Catalepsy, seemed to have nothing left about him but the faculty of breathing . . . being fixed and Immoveable, as one thunderstruck or under some Strange diabolical fascination or Incantation" (2:490). Immoveable or not, his lordship does not remain in his seat long. Under the influence of the chancellor's inflammatory speeches, the club's members manhandle their president most piteously in their efforts to unseat him, tearing his ruffles and altering "the posture of his wig . . . much for the worse, having tail turned foremost" (2:493). But his lordship, holding fast to his chair, refuses to budge until one of the chancellor's allies, Quirpum Comic (Beale Bordley) surprises President Jole with an attack from the rear, delivering "such a Strong concussion and repercussion, to his Lordship's buttocks, that he rebounded at least half a foot from his

Seat at each blow, and was obliged to quit his Chair of State" (2:495). Thus ends the inglorious decathedration of the great Nasifer Jole. Properly acted, it is a scene that would make Freemasons everywhere weep.

Jole's decathedration brings the destruction of all brotherly feeling to the Tuesday Club. Following Jole's decathedration, the insurgent club members are constantly beset by suspicions and fears of each other. Their suspicions lead to numerous impeachments and trials against one another in volume 3 of *The History of the Tuesday Club* and create an air of constant unrest and dissatisfaction among the club's members. The state to which the Tuesday Club—and the principles of Freemasonry—succumbs by the end of volume 3 is deplorable indeed.

In this essay I have tried not to overemphasize the importance of Freemasonry in *The History of the Tuesday Club*. Rather, as I stated at the outset, the connection between Freemasonry and Hamilton's *History* is more of a covert, in-club joke than an explicitly developed theme. All of the Tuesday Club's members, most of whom were Freemasons, would have recognized the implications about Freemasonry privately nestled in the pages of Hamilton's *History*, as I suspect most of his readers would have if *The History of the Tuesday Club* had been published in Hamilton's lifetime. It is not necessary to understand those implications to appreciate a book that, with or without the presence of Freemasonry, humorously reveals a good deal about eighteenth-century culture. But those who are in on Hamilton's secret will be able not only to better appreciate his humor but also, I think, to better appreciate the right and worshipful place of Freemasonry in eighteenth-century life.

NOTES

1. Alexander Hamilton, *The History of the Tuesday Club*, ca. 1752–56, 1:85–86. All subsequent page references to this text are provided in parentheses. Also see my forthcoming (1987) edition of *The History of the Tuesday Club*, 3 vols. (Chapel Hill: University of North Carolina Press), which also appears in an abridged paperback version by the same publisher.

2. The popular literature of Freemasonry is full of these sorts of discussions, but the best scholarly analysis of the various controversies that Freemasonry provoked during the eighteenth century is Jacob 1981, esp. chap. 4, "The Origins of European Freemasonry."

3. No book better illustrates the Masonic preoccupation with numbers—especially the numbers three and seven—than Albert Pike's frequently reprinted *Morals and Dogma of the Ancient and Accepted Scottish Rite of Freemasonry* (1871). Pike's discussion of the number seven is remarkably similar to Hamilton's, minus the levity (see pp. 57–60).

Radicalism in Joel Barlow's
The Conspiracy of Kings (1792)

CARLA MULFORD

In his 6 March 1792 letter to William Hayley, Joel Barlow promised, "I shall send you the little mad poem when printed." He fulfilled the promise on 5 April, enclosing with his letter copies of *The Conspiracy of Kings* for both Hayley and James Stanier Clarke. Humorously he cautioned, "If you can find a secret corner in your house, to hide it from the view of your visitors, it may be no injury to your reputation. but it must not be known that you have any knowledge of such a reprobate as the Author must have been."[1] Barlow was finding himself increasingly unpopular with the British government, and for good reason, according to the conservatives. After the first part of Barlow's *Advice to the Privileged Orders* appeared in February 1792, Barlow's name was circulated with Thomas Paine's as a foremost reformer.[2] Horne Tooke, secretary of the Society for Constitutional Information, nominated Barlow on 9 March for membership in that reform group.[3] Printed mid-March to "a great noise," *The Conspiracy of Kings* no doubt aided Barlow's unanimous election to the Society for Constitutional Information. Barlow might have read with self-consciously jocular uneasiness Clarke's comments of 25 March: "I think I shall hear of you in the Tower before long. If so take care to procure good apartments for we will certainly come to see you often."[4] In mid-April Barlow traveled to Holland—as much to escape the increasingly conspicuous watchfulness of the British government over his activities as for business reasons.[5]

Yet despite Barlow's contemporary reknown (indeed his infamy, to conservatives like Edmund Burke and Timothy Dwight); despite his popularity and influence with the leading writers, political philosophers, reformers, and statesmen of his day (people like William Hayley, William Blake, William Godwin, Richard Price, Horne Tooke, Mary Wollstonecraft, Thomas Paine, Thomas Jefferson, Constantin Volney, Brissot de Warville, Marquis de Lafayette); and despite the recent appreciations of Barlow's poetry by scholars like J. A. Leo Lemay, Robert Arner, and Robert Richardson—Joel Barlow still continues to be mentioned among the conservative federalist contemporaries from his Yale days as a "Connecticut Wit" and continues to suffer the unhappy rubric as the "poet of cornmeal mush." This condescending attitude pervades the recent biographical and critical essay on Barlow in the *Dictionary of Literary Biography*.[6] Such condescension reveals more about critics' post-Romantic tendency to view as stultifying those poets who use neoclassic forms than it does about Barlow and his writings.

Perhaps more than any other of Barlow's poems, *The Conspiracy of Kings* reveals his belief that the poet should be not only the corrector of the old order but the seer and speaker of the new. The poem is not the stale "juvenalian" satire Cecelia Tichi calls "utterly lifeless" (1985, 37:26). Rather, like *The Hasty-Pudding* (1793), it shows Barlow's adept fashioning of radical ideology in a denunciation of Burke and the conservative tendencies that could lead to more war and to anarchy. Barlow developed in the poem the kinds of paradox the radicals, especially William Blake, were using at the time. He used the notion of the *Translatio Studii* changed to *Translatio Libertatis* (from America to France to England) popular with the radical initiate. He used images and conceptions from his readings of the *encyclopedistes*, Constantin Volney, and others. Finally, he informed the poem with a poetic voice (probably adopted as a result of reading Diderot) of a creator/seer, not a juvenalian complainer.

Perhaps Barlow wished the uninitiated audience—the audience not familiar with radical ideology—to be misled into thinking *The Conspiracy of Kings* was simply the invective of a juvenalian satirist. The poet-speaker says that he will not "croak with omen'd yell" (l. 25) about a future hell. And this poet-speaker says that "Indignant Man" (l. 57) now "Displays the unclad skeletons of kings" (l. 59). In the pamphlet edition of the *Conspiracy*, Barlow's annotation for this line reads: "Ossa vides regum vacuis exhausta medullis. Juvenal, Sat. 8." The mention of "croak[ing]" and of Juvenal's eighth satire might seem reason enough to conclude that Barlow wrote the poem as a juvenalian political satire. Indeed, Juvenal's eighth satire would have been a good satire for Barlow to have imitated in his antimonarchical satire on Burke and on the conservative politics that sought the continuation of an obsolete distinction by rank and title. Juvenal's eighth satire began with a similar message: that although we may derive rank and title from our ancestors, yet if we degenerate from the virtues by which they obtained them, we are not truly noble.[7] It is easy to understand why scholars have assumed that Barlow's poem is just another juvenalian satire after the manner of Pope or Swift.[8]

But Barlow's allusion to Juvenal's eighth satire is misleading. He did not have Juvenal—or the eighth satire—specifically in mind when he wrote the poem. In fact, Juvenal's line was supplied him by William Hayley late in (or after) the period of composition. In addition, Barlow (and perhaps Hayley) quoted inexactly. In his 6 March 1792 letter to Hayley, Barlow thanked Hayley for having given him the Latin line:

> I thank you, my dear friend, among all your kind attentions to me, that you was so good as to find to our good Santo padre the motto, *ossa vides regum vacuis exhausta medullis*. I shall make use of it in the little Poem, which is now with the printer, but it remains to know to what latin poet we are originally indebted for it, because I wish to make the account stand even with him as I go along, by placing it to his credit. Neither his Holiness nor myself were able to recollect the author.[9]

As Victor C. Miller has pointed out, Juvenal's original line (Satire 8.90) reads: *Ossa vides regum vacuis exsucta medullis,* You see the very bones of kings sucked dry, with the marrow extracted (appendix [107]). The inexactness of the quotation (i.e., "exhausta" for "exsucta") might perhaps have been intentional. But Barlow clearly did not intend his poem to be a slavish or even slightly derivative imitation of Juvenal. *The Conspiracy of Kings* is indeed a satire, but a satire of a different order.

The Conspiracy of Kings ostensibly addresses the French émigrés, largely of the nobility, who after the fall of the Bastille (14 July 1789), fled to Coblenz and there had been gathering forces under the assumed leadership of the Comte d'Artois, Louis XVI's brother. From Coblenz, the émigrés watched the uneasy agreements made between the Assembly and Louis XVI and quietly planned and worked for a restoration of the old regime in France, with or without Louis XVI as king. Barlow couples his attack against these émigrés with one against the potential royal coalition of Europe and the German states. He specifically targets Gustavus III; Catharine II of Russia; Frederick William II of Prussia; and Leopold of Austria, Marie Antoinette's brother, the persuasive force behind the coalition intended to restore power to the French monarchy. But though the speaker of the poem clearly attacks these devious, dying older orders, he more fervently abuses those English conservatives who followed Edmund Burke in supporting the sinking cause of royal servitude by attempting to get government backing for the émigrés and for a royal alliance against the French republic.

Burke's *Reflections on the Revolution in France* (1790) opened him to abuse from the radicals. His *Reflections* took as its starting point a denunciation of the dissenting minister Rev. Richard Price's "Discourse on the Love of Our Country" (preached before the Revolution Society at the Old Jewry 4 November 1789) and reached a rhetorical pitch in Burke's famous lament that "The age of chivalry is gone . . . the glory of Europe . . . extinguished forever." Radicals and moderate reformers were surprised at Burke's seeming shift away from the freedoms about which he had spoken as inalienable rights in support of the American cause against the British crown. When it became clear by July 1791 that Burke, interested in finding British government support for the French émigrés, was cooperating with Calonne, chief adviser to the Comte d'Artois, the radicals were outraged. They rallied to praise Price and the French Revolution, which they figured forth as the dawning of equal rights due men around the world.

The concept of *figuring forth* is an important one, for the referent—the historical event called the French Revolution and all the facts reported with regard to that event—is finally of less importance than the poetic language and images chosen by writers in order to persuade readers to accept or at least to entertain as acceptable those writers' political-ideological positions.[10] One example should suffice. Burke's correspondence, before, during, and after writing his *Reflections* reveals his distrust of Marie Antoinette and her propensities for, in his words, "Court Intrigue."[11] Yet, despite Philip Francis's urgings before publication that Burke remove the "pure foppery" about the queen, Burke held with his rhapsodic picture of the former dauphiness, the "persecuted woman" (1790, 164) who, with "All the decent drapery of life . . . rudely torn off" (171), "had but just enough time to fly almost naked, and through ways unknown to the murderers . . . to seek the refuge at the feet of the king and husband, not secure of his own life for a moment" (164).[12] Burke seems knowingly to have distorted the "facts," then, so he could create a rhapsodic and shocking lamentation that "the age of chivalry is gone"—in order to persuade his readers that an irreparable loss has been created by the revolutionaries, a loss that might take place in England if the English reformers like Richard Price are allowed to promote the revolution in France in behalf of their own interests in English constitutional reform.

The radicals were indeed seeking English constitutional reform. Conservatives held that these radicals shielded their intent for more extensive political revolution under the name of reform. Burke and other conservatives propagandized the popular conservative position that the English radicals were secret conspirators against the crown, their reform societies secret organizations preparing for the king's overthrow—as precedented, according to the conservative position, by the Gordon Riots of 1780.[13] The conservatives further implied that the necessary corollary of such conspiracy would be tyranny, the radicals supplanting one long-standing reign they wrongly called tyranny with a tyranny more threatening because new and untried and because it emanated from the masses, not the aristocracy (Paulson 1983, 20). Such a revolution, the conservatives held, would bring anarchy.

Barlow and other radical political philosophers flaunted such conservative propaganda by transvaluing its referents. That is, the radicals used the conservative propagandists' names to *re*name, to give different (often completely opposite) valuation to, the phenomenon discussed by the conservatives.[14] Their message to Burke and others was twofold: that if the inevitable revolution can be seen as a conspiracy, then conservative factions were in conspiracy against it; and that the so-called tyranny of mob rule (Burke's "swinish multitude," the fear of which was associated with Burke's terror of the sublime)[15] was no worse than the tyranny of a dead and dusty conservatism that led to suppression of the energies of free people. The anarchic forces, the radicals insisted, were those forces working against the necessary revolution for freedom.

So Barlow titled his poem *The Conspiracy of Kings* to indicate his own radical propagandist message that the conservators of the old orders were conspiring, not just against the politically radical groups, but against equality and liberty, the inalienable rights of every person. Barlow thus makes his own process of transvaluation apparent in the title. The speaker of the poem, too, makes known that the old orders have valorized events and beliefs by naming them in ways to suit their need for political and ideological power over the masses. Echoing Constantin Volney's *Ruins*, Barlow's speaker addresses the "Drones of the Church and harpies of the State" (10),

> Ye, who pretend to your dark host was given
> The lamp of life, the mystic keys of heaven;
> Whose impious arts with magic spells began
> When shades of ign'rance veil'd the race of man;
> Who change, from age to age the sly deceit
> As Science beams, and Virtue learns the cheat.
>
> (15–20)

The speaker makes aware his belief that officials of Church and State have been deluding the ignorant world, and as they found it necessary, have simply "change[d], from age to age the sly deceit," for their own political ends. The poet-speaker again alludes to such false valorization when he rhetorically asks:

> Where then, forsaken villains, will ye turn?
> Of France the outcast and of earth the scorn;
> What new-made charm can dissipate your fears?
> Can Burke's mad foam, or Calonne's House of Peers?
>
> (96–100)

The poet-speaker insists that the émigrés and the conservatives have run out of "new-made charm[s]," that they have run out of objects that they can name in order better to institutionalize their ecclesiastical and civil hierarchies. In this new age, the émigrés and conservatives are simply "forsaken villains," forsaken largely because of the false naming and the false valorizations they sought to impose on an ignorant populace. In other words, the age of the conservatives' naming is being replaced by an egalitarian age that will rename according to the instruction of "Eternal Truth" (1).

The Conspiracy of Kings is developed entirely as a transvaluation. The émigrés, "Drones of the Church and harpies of the State," have only been engaged in setting up "crested reptiles to a throne" (14). By the end of the second stanza, the speaker has suggested that a transvaluation—an appropriate renaming—is necessary because of the hypocrisy of Church and State officials who have made the people fear a god in whom the officials themselves do not believe:

> Think not I come to croak with omen'd yell
> The dire damnations of your future hell,
> To bend a bigot or reform a knave,
> By op'ning all the scenes beyond the grave.
> I know your crusted souls: while one defies
> In sceptic scorn the vengeance of the skies,
> The other boasts,—"I ken thee, Power divine,
> But fear thee not; th'avenging bolt is mine."
>
> (23–30)

The implied message is that such hypocrisy has by necessity to be devalorized, for

> The hour is come, the world's unclosing eyes
> Discern with rapture where its wisdom lies.
> . . . .
> No turn, no shift, no courtly arts avail,
> Each mask is broken, all illusions fail.
>
> (159–60; 169–70)

The implication of such a transvaluation openly announced is that the old myths—particularly with regard to politics and, especially, to religion—are now known to have been lies. It is an implication common to Enlightenment philosophers, available perhaps most notably in the *Encyclopédie*, entries from which Barlow carefully translated and entered into at least one notebook.[16]

Barlow's interest in comparative religion and mythology began as early as 1787, when he published *The Vision of Columbus*. Barlow there included a "Dissertation on the Genius and Institutions of Manco Capec" in which he asserted that "Those constitutions of government are best calculated for immediate energy and duration, which are interwoven with some religious system. The legislator, who appears in the character of an inspired person, renders his political institutions sacred, and interests the conscience as well as the judgement in support." As proof, Barlow examined the institutions of Moses, Lycurgus, Solon, Numa, Mahomet, and Peter of Russia, all of whom he unfavorably compared to the benevolent "Peruvian Lawgiver" Manco Capec. Early in his career, then, Barlow had acknowledged his belief that a religious system aided political power.[17] The "Dissertation" shows that

Barlow was conversant with Voltaire's *Philosophical Dictionary*, William Robertson's *History of America*, and Garcilaso de la Vega's *Royal Commentaries of Peru*.[18] A note in Book 11 of the *Vision* indicates that Barlow was reading Richard Price as well (1970, 2:241–44). Barlow's interest in theories of political philosophy common to Enlightenment political and religious philosophers thus seem to have begun as early as 1787. He was working with many theorists, in addition to those mentioned, as he revised *The Vision* for a 1793 Paris edition.

A more immediate source for some of Barlow's comments in *The Conspiracy of Kings* about religion and its political mystique might be Constantin Volney's *The Ruins, or, Meditation on the Revolutions of Empires*, published originally in Paris in 1791. J. A. Leo Lemay has suggested that Barlow knew the works of both Volney and Charles François Dupuis, author of *Mémoire sur l'origine des constellations et sur l'explication de la fable par le moyen de l'astronomie* (Paris 1791), well enough to use them while writing *The Hasty-Pudding* in 1793 (1982, 11). Both works argued that all cultures have based their religions on their incomplete knowledge of the natural world; Volney's *Ruins* premised upon this notion its criticism of political power based on the superstitious ignorance of the populace. Barlow published in 1802 a translation, which Jefferson had begun, of *The Ruins*. I suspect Barlow had done some careful reading of Volney—if not some translation (or reading of Jefferson's partial translation) of *The Ruins*—by February 1792, when he was writing *The Conspiracy of Kings*. Parts of his poem seem reminiscent of his translation of Volney's book: compare, for instance, lines 70–118 of *Conspiracy* with Volney's chapter 12, "Lessons of Times Past Repeated on the Present."[19] The working conception of both texts is that a "genius" of light and truth has arrived to tear "the strong bandage from the eyes of man" (Barlow, *Conspiracy* l. 272), has arrived to show truth to men who "walked with a bandage on our eyes" (Volney 1802, 72). Barlow, evidently fond of the metaphor of removing bandages from eyes, used it in Part 1 of his *Advice to the Privileged Orders*, published a month before the *Conspiracy* in February 1792. There Barlow had insisted, "The church in that country [France] was like royalty,—the prejudices in its favor were too strong to be vanquished at once. The most that could be done, was to tear the bandage from the eyes of mankind, break the charm of inequality, demolish ranks and infallibilities, and teach the people that mitres and crowns did not confer supernatural powers" (1970; 1:144–45). Both *The Conspiracy of Kings* and *Advice to the Privileged Orders*—in addition to *The Hasty-Pudding* written a year later—are based on conceptions about Church and State available in Volney's *Ruins*. What distinguishes the *Conspiracy* from the other two works is Barlow's relentless insistence that a re-visioning based on the knowledge of the history of religion and its political manipulability is unquestionably necessary.

In *The Conspiracy of Kings* Barlow bases this re-visioning on a transvaluation of the myth of creation and divinity. The poet-speaker makes of Burke at once a kind of Miltonic Antichrist and a creator of a false myth of creation. Like Milton's story (in *Paradise Lost,* Book 6) of Christ's battling Satan, the poet-speaker announces in explanation of Burke's demise (in l. 151, Burke is a "lost man"):

> . . . 'twas Heav'n's returning grace,
> In kind compassion to our injur'd race,
> Which stripp'd that soul, ere it should flee from hence,
> Of the last garb of decency or sense,
> Left thee its own foul horrors to display,
> In all the blackness of its native day,
> To sink at last, from earth's glad surface hurl'd,
> The sordid sov'reign of the letter'd world.
>
> (141–48)

Burke is Antichrist hurled from heaven as a kindness to the "injur'd race." But also, according to the "Muse indignant" (106), Burke has created his own world out of the fragments of crumbling chaos, like a would-be God. The poet-speaker's periodic construction adds emphasis to the indignation of the Muse:

> Oh Burke, degenerate slave! with grief and shame
> The Muse indignant must repeat thy name.
> Strange man, declare,—since, at creation's birth,
> From crumbling Chaos sprang this heav'n and earth
> Since wrecks and outcast relics still remain,
> Whirl'd ceaseless round Confusion's dreary reign,
> Declare, from all these fragments, whence you stole
> That genius wild, that monstrous mass of soul.
>
> (105–12)

Reminiscent of Milton's chaos-hell (*Paradise Lost,* Book 2), Burke's world, made of creation's leftovers, with "genius wild" and spread in the waste of extremes, is, the poet has assured the reader, a "weak delusion" (39). Burke is not the maker: "Burke leads you wrong, the world is not his own" (40). Nor is he the proper celebrator of such a "mad-man's thread-bare theme" (41). That is, like Milton's anarchic Satan, Burke has named events improperly: the world about which Burke speaks is one of his own creation, a creation made of chaotic fragments having no basis in any real creation that is "the gift of God" known to the Muse "Eternal Truth" (1), which guides the present speaker.

Thus by contrast, "the present world . . . prompt[ing] the song" is better described (better named) by the poet-speaker who has been "len[t]" the trumpet of "Eternal Truth":

"For heav'n and earth," the voice of God ordains,
"Shall pass and perish, but my word remains,"
Th'eternal WORD, which gave, in spite of thee [Burke],
Reason to man, that bids the man be free.

(137–40)

The poet-speaker who knows God's true word of reason has "come not to croak with omen'd yell / The dire damnations of a future hell" (23–24), for this is a speaker free of the "mad-man's thread-bare theme" that would "veil the race of man" in "shades of ign'rance" (18) so as to gain political power. That is, this speaker is not like Burke a "degenerate slave" to impotent and tyrannous custom, particularly religious custom, but one who has come to tell of "nations, rising in the light of truth, / Strong with new life and pure regenerate youth" (43–44). Burke's old myth has been transformed into a groundless lie; the poet-speaker's creation message about "MAN, exalted title! first and best" (175) is not only new but engendered by God, "On God's own image by his hand imprest" (176).

The poet-speaker of Barlow's poem conflates religious history and the history of political freedom in announcing and celebrating the rise of "MAN" in France. No longer will the politics of oppression be tied to a repressive religion, the poet-speaker implies. On one level, the poet-speaker celebrates the new political and religious history by renaming the events of the Christian myth. As Paulson has suggested, the revolutionaries found the assimilation of Christian symbolism a valuable means as propaganda because "Christian symbolism was the only available form known to large numbers of the poor and illiterate" (1982, 14). Barlow's poet-speaker announces that the change brought by the French Revolution "Make[s] patriot views and moral views the same" (260). That is, the views of State and Church will no longer be founded upon ignorance of seeming mysteries but upon reason, which will bring politics and religion in line with "Eternal Truth." According to the Bible, God's word was made flesh in Adam, thus freeing Adam from the earth. When Adam transgressed against God's word, he was punished but was redeemed by Christ. Like many of the radicals—most notably William Blake—Barlow plays on this generative/regenerative myth. This poet-speaker announces that God gave "*Reason* to man, that bids the man be free." In this transvaluation, Christ is no longer the redeemer, man's reason is: "'twas Heav'n's returning grace, / In kind compassion to our injur'd race" (141–42). The race, according to the poet-speaker's story, was not "injur'd" by the godhead because of a betrayal of God's word. Rather, the race was betrayed by its own ignorance into the hands of false gods like the conservative Burke. As indicated by the French Revolution, the poet-speaker's story goes, the race is regenerated: "nations [are] rising in the light of truth, / Strong with new life and pure regenerate youth" (43–44). Grace has come to man in the form of reason, as a "trust by Heav'n's own hand consign'd, / The great concentred stake, the interest of mankind" (47–48). The poet-speaker in the *Conspiracy* has thus renamed events in the Christ myth to fit the myth of the French Revolution. Man can redeem himself, in this myth, so that he becomes at once redeemer and redeemed in the new history of Adam.

Barlow conflates this transvalued Christian myth with another myth related to freedom and associated with the death of Osiris. The "great concentred stake" is the figure Barlow uses for this conflation. As Paulson has shown, the radicals (particularly Blake) attached import to the cause of freedom by imaging their position in terms of virile masculinity on the rise, bound upward to express its freedom or ascending or descending into bowels of darkness to bring into fruition light and energy (89–91). Light, energy, and sexuality are the images associated with the myth. Barlow uses such images throughout *The Conspiracy of Kings*.

He ties the figures to the rise of a new "religion" of man, basing on his study of comparative religion the transvaluation of the Christian myth into a masculine regenerative myth. Barlow's "Genealogy of the Tree of Liberty," as he recorded it in an undated notebook (the source I use below), provides an informative context for this aspect of the poem.[20] The "Genealogy" traces the basis of religious worship to the myth of Osiris (the sun), killed in a battle against Typhon (the power of darkness), who dismembered Osiris and threw him into the Nile. Isis (the moon), wife of Osiris, collected all Osiris's parts "except the precious fragment that was lost in the river," which "genitals . . . communicated a fecundating power to that river" and "became the source of life & vegetation to all Egypt." Barlow continues, "To commemorate at once the tragical death of Osiris and the great benefits that resulted to mankind from the posthumous power of his organs of generation a solemn feast was instituted in which the Phallus in a posture of strong erection was carried in procession. The same fable of Osiris was extended to other countries under different names with a little variation." When the fables reached Greece, the death and resurrection "were celebrated with a variety of ceremonies" in honor of "Bachus," and "the procession of the Phallus always made a conspicuous figure." The "freedom and licentiousness that reigned in these nocturnal assemblies" brought the god the name Eleutheros—"free" or "freedom," and, when carried to Rome, the god became "known by the epithet *Liber, (Free)*, so that the Phallus became the emblem of *Libertas*." Through the ages the original meaning was lost, and the English have attached to their maypole or liberty pole the simple notion of the "liberty of a frolick . . . without ever dreaming of the origin or *antetype* of this curious emblem." The pole passed to America in a more "venerable" fashion, where "it grew to an enormous mast" and came to be "a solid emblem of *political Liberty*. From thence it has recrossed the Atlantic to extend its blessings to its native continent [where] it is now placed in the public places all over France . . . inspiring with enthusiasm the hosts of heroes who swell the triumphs of that victorious Republic."

Barlow's readings in comparative religion and philosophy had indicated to him that all religious worship is based on worship of natural phenomena having natural causes. These phenomena, not understood by the mass of men, were mythologized to create mystical meaning, which enabled those who pretended interpretive powers to have political power. Manco Capec was for Barlow the best law-giver of former times because he used benevolent control over men, control gained because, knowing more than the savages he came to conquer, he assumed political power by implying he had mystical (religious) power. During the French Revolution, as political power was transferred from the king to the people, radicals hoped for what they figured forth as a freeing of the populace from this kind of religious superstition. Thus, revolutionaries sought to effect a shift from worship of Christian objects to a worship of liberty, figured forth for the populace as liberty poles, capped with red liberty caps. By attempting to have the people worship liberty poles, "patriot views and moral views [could become] the same," for the people would be worshipping their political freedom while engaging in a kind of religious practice in behalf of morality.

In the "great concentred stake, the interest of mankind," Barlow figured forth the phallus of the Osiris myth transformed as the stake of liberty for the masses. The "great concentred stake" was a trust "by Heav'n's own hand consigned" because (not Christ but) *"Reason,"* "Heav'n's returning grace," brought a regenerative redemption. By using a system of transvaluation, the poetic voice informing the poem insists by implication that if a religion is to exist, it should be a religion of man's worship of man's own ability, not of a substitute man (Christ) viewed as some mystical agent of redemption.

Arguing in behalf of the French Revolution and using metaphors that marked revolutionary philosophy, Barlow created a masculine and regenerative metaphor throughout the poem. The liberty pole in a state of erection is figured forth as the "great concentred stake." The men the poet speaks of have been "rous'd from sloth" (35) to use their "deep-descending steel" (37) to "teach dull nerves to feel" (37). Nations are "rising in the light of truth" (43), because "Indignant Man resumes the shaft" (57) to "Disarm the tyrant" (58). France has "rent the dark veil" (62) with the "great concentred stake" (48). In contrast with these images of virility and power are those of the conservative, dying orders. Leopold II of Austria, for instance, is "too wise to trust his sword" (84) against such powerful combatants. "Artois' sword" (101) "Burn'd with the fire of fame, but harmless burn'd / For sheath'd the sword remain'd, and in its sheath return'd" (103–4). The impotent Burke, who wields only an "infuriate quill" (129), is plunging like Phaeton a "wasting course, / The great Sublime of weakness and of force" (122–23). The forces that would oppose the French are not fiery and virile. In fact, "Dim, like the day-struck owl, [they] grope in light, / No arm for combat, no resource in flight" (163–64). They are weak against the "ascending bliss that waits [man's] call" (245), for they have "erect[ed] their thrones amid [a] sanguine flood, / And dip[ped] their purple in the nation's blood" (217–18). They are mere "unclad skeletons" (59), "Spectres of power, and serpents without stings" (60). They have only "infuriate quill[s]" to spend against "Heav'n's own bequest, the heritage of all" (249). For "Freedom at last, with Reason in her train" (249), has made "Gallia's sons" (251) "Start into men" (253).

The masculine, regenerative myth is reflected in the reference to Alcides of Greek mythology as well. In a series of rhetorical questions, the poet-speaker suggests the émigrés would be asking the impossible:

Bid young Alcides, in his grasp who takes,
And gripes with naked hand the twisting snakes,
Their force exhausted, bid him prostrate fall,
And dread their shadows trembling on the wall.

(65–69)

The mention of Alcides, a patronymic of Heracles (Hercules), recalls the many labors of this hero known for strength, courage, endurance, good nature, compassion, appetite, and lust. In his cradle, Heracles strangled two serpents, sent against him by Hera. The young Alcides, then, has fought the "crested reptiles" of the conservatives. Indeed, according to the *Century Dictionary*, Heracles has long been seen as the borrowed Phoenician sun-god. That is, Heracles is a type of Osiris and a type of Christ. All three of them are reflected in the liberty pole that represents for the first time in history, according to revolutionary mythology, the conflation of meanings religious and political in one emblem in behalf of reason and eternal truth.[21]

In *The Conspiracy of Kings* Barlow is using a revolutionary mythology that informs most of the writings of English supporters of the revolution, William Blake most prominently. David Erdman has indicated that Blake most likely attended some of the dinners that radical printer Joseph Johnson (Barlow's printer) offered his authors and that Blake surely knew of the Society for Constitutional Information (1969, 153–60). Erdman has shown that Blake was indebted to Barlow for aspects of the machinery and conception of *America: A Prophecy*, published in 1793 (1954, 94–98). I find Blake's *America, Song of Liberty*, and *The Visions of the Daughters of Albion*, all dating to 1793, reminiscent of Barlow's *Conspiracy*.[22] Blake's fiery Orc come to confront the hoary Urizen gives a particularlized picture of Barlow's more generalized "MAN" who confronts the old conservative orders represented by the émigrés and Burke. In addition, both poets stress the image shift from *Translatio*

Studii to *Translatio Libertatis*.[23] Barlow's poet-speaker announces that the voice

> . . . borne on western gales from that far shore
> Where Justice reigns, and tyrants tread no more,
> Th'unwonted voice, that no dissuasion awes,
> That fears no frown, and seeks no blind applause,
> Shall tell the gift that Freedom sheds abroad,
> The rights of nature and the gifts of God.
>
> (3–8)

Midpoem, the speaker reminds the listener:

> The hour is come, the world's unclosing eyes
> Discern with rapture where its wisdom lies;
> From western heav'ns th'inverted Orient springs,
> The morn of man, the dreadful night of kings.
>
> (159–62)

And in conclusion, the poet insists:

> And deign, for once, to turn a transient eye
> To that wide world that skirts the western sky;
> Hail the mild morning, where that dawn began,
> The full fruition of the hopes of man.
>
> (275–78)

The poet-speaker emphasizes throughout *The Conspiracy of Kings* that freedom has traveled from America to France, and it soon will arrive in England. The normal course of revolution from east to west has been inverted into a revolution west to east. Blake's *Visions of the Daughters of Albion* (1793) likewise derives from the attempt of the revolutionary principle to travel from America to Europe in a kind of *Translatio Libertatis* (see Paulson 1983, 89, 93). In Blake's poem, freedom's procreative impulses are frustrated; in Barlow's poem, that frustration surfaces as an acid attack against Burke and the conservatives and is coupled with an insistence that the morn of man has arrived. Barlow's poem suggests the fulfillment of the procreative urge:

> O Man, my brother, how the cordial flame
> Of all endearments kindles at thy name!
> In every clime, thy visage greets my eyes,
> In every tongue thy kindred accents rise;
> The thought expanding swells my heart with glee,
> It finds a friend, and loves itself in thee.
>
> (181–86)

The urge for procreative love is one Blake left frustrated in *The Visions of the Daughters of Albion*. In Blake's view, regenerative freedom was not available for the England of Edmund Burke (see Paulson 1983, 88–89).

Barlow's view was clearly propagandist. He adopted the metaphors used by leading radicals in order to convey a political message; he adopted the language of the revolutionaries to clarify that message. Thus, all men become for the poet-speaker "my brother" (181), all mankind the "fraternal family divine" (187). The "dark deception . . . the glare of state" (205) kept the "cordial flame / Of all endearments" (181–82) from burning in ages past. The message and language are radical and revolutionary; the implication is finally what most readers—if asked for a name—would call Romantic. Now that the poet has spoken the word of God (cf. 137–40) via the muse of "Eternal Truth," now that the poet has "name[d]" (182) "Man" in his "exalted title, first and best" (177)—a cordial flame "kindles at the name" and "kindred accents rise" (184). The poet concludes not by summarizing the message past but by forcing the listener-reader—along with the émigrés (and, by implication, all conservatives)—to engage in the poetic experience, the creative act both visual and imaginative. As Stanislaus of Poland "Points the progressive march, and shapes the way, / That leads a realm from darkness into day" (273–74), so the poet points the listener-reader to "turn a transient eye / To that wide world that skirts the western sky" (275–76). Whereas the poet had himself "hail[ed] Man" (177), the listener-reader now must participate and "Hail the mild morning, where the dawn began, / The full fruition of the hopes of man" (277–78). A participation on the listener-reader's part would replicate the poet's "thought expanding" (185) into the love of freedom and his fellow man. It would fulfill in the listening-reading act the poet's "sacred cause" emblematized in the seeming paradoxical "rare union, Liberty and Laws" and spoken "to the reas'ning race" in the message "to freedom rise, / Like them [Americans] be equal, and like them be wise" (281–82). In looking to freedom's model in America, the listener-reader would be himself engaging in the idol-worship the poet celebrates.

Barlow's *Conspiracy of Kings* is not a closed expression in a discursive mode but a progressive and revolutionary message encouraging active participation both political and philosophical. Barlow's "little mad poem" is based on the same politics as his *Advice to the Privileged Orders*, but it is based on a synthetic discourse that is emblematic and suggestive rather than analytical and discursive.[24] As early as 1752 Denis Diderot had said in his now famous passage in *Lettre sur les sourds et muets* that the primary characteristic of poetry is suggestiveness, the true poet a creator:

Il passe alors dans le discours du poëte un esprit qui en meut et vivifie toutes les syllabes. Qu'est-ce que cet esprit? j'en ai quelquefois senti la présence; mais tout ce que j'en sais, c'est que c'est lui qui fait que les choses sont dites et représentées tout à la fois; que dans le même temps que l'entendement les saisit, l'âme en est émue, l'imagination les voit et l'oreille les entend, et que le discours n'est plus seulement un enchaînement de termes énergiques qui exposent la pensée avec force et noblesse, mais que c'est encore un tissu d'hiéroglyphes entassés les uns sur les autres qui la peignent. Je pourrais dire, en ce sens, que toute poésie est emblématique.

Mais l'intelligence de l'emblème poétique n'est pas donnée à tout le monde; il faut être presque en état de le créer pour le sentir fortement.[25]

Diderot here spoke of the newer poetic aesthetic of the mid-eighteenth century. By the time of the French Revolution, poets like Blake were freely experimenting with language and poetic emblems as hieroglyphs of meaning, and poet-revolutionaries like Barlow were exploring the extent to which a renaming could propagandize a political message.

Part of that revolutionary message was that the people had the power to reinvent their world—as the French were reinventing time and street designations. Paine had announced in the *Age of Reason*, part 2, "The present age will hereafter merit to be called the Age of Reason, and the present generation will appear to the future as the Adam of a new world" (1894–96, 2:512). Barlow's poet-speaker insisted

> To thee, O Man, my heart rebounding springs.
> Behold th' ascending bliss that waits your call,
> Heav'n's own bequest, the heritage of all.

According to the poetic voice, each man had the power to call anew his world to freedom and to progress toward happiness. Revealed religion, in this view, could not offer the miracle that every man might find if he would only see ("Behold") and name ("call") that force to which his "heart springs"—freedom. The message of this poet and the poem *The Conspiracy of Kings* seems an unusually appropriate antecedent to Emerson's statement that "Society everywhere is in conspiracy against the manhood of every one of its members," to Thoreau's "The mass of men lead lives of quiet desperation," to Whitman's "Song of Myself." Barlow's *Conspiracy of Kings* is not an "utterly lifeless" poem. It utters life.

NOTES

The author wishes to thank Villanova University for generously supporting the research and initial writing of this essay. The author also wishes to thank the following institutions for permission to quote or cite manuscript holdings: the Beinecke Rare Book and Manuscript Library, Yale University; the Houghton Library, Harvard University; the Huntington; the Harold B. Lee Library, Brigham Young University.

1. Barlow reported in his 6 March letter to Hayley that *The Conspiracy of Kings* was

"now with the printers." The poem evidently had reached print by 18 March, when Barlow sent a copy of it to Thomas Jefferson. His accompanying letter to Jefferson read: "I know not what apology to offer for troubling you so often with my publications. I sent you last month a pamphlet, called 'Advice to the Privileged Orders' &c. I beg you now to accept a little poem entitled, The Conspiracy of Kings. Though one of my Kings died while the Poem was in the press, it was not my fault. If this had been the case with all of them, I should have been willing to have suppressed the publication for so good a cause" (Jefferson Papers, Manuscript Division, Library of Congress). I have retained the peculiarities of Barlow's spelling and punctuation in his manuscripts.

The *St. James Chronicle or British Evening Post* advertised the sale of *The Conspiracy of Kings* on 20 March. Barlow had become a correspondent with Hayley late in 1791; early in 1792, Barlow visited Hayley at his Eartham estate with Rev. John Warner. He there met Rev. James Stanier Clarke. Warner, Clarke, and Hayley continued to be Barlow's most trusted friends and critics of his poetry and politics. They offered advice as he reworked *The Vision of Columbus* (1787) for a Paris edition in 1793, and they introduced him to other radicals and poets.

The 6 March 1792 author's letter, signed (ALS), from Barlow to William Hayley is located at the Huntington Library, San Marino, California. The 5 April 1792 ALS from Barlow to Hayley and Clarke is at the Harold B. Lee Library, Brigham Young University, Provo, Utah. Barlow's 18 March 1792 ALS to Thomas Jefferson is in the Jefferson Papers, First Series, Library of Congress, Washington, D.C. Lewis Leary discussed some of the Barlow-Hayley correspondence, but evidently did not have the important Barlow letter of 5 April 1792.

Leon Howard wrote on Barlow in *The Connecticut Wits*, but the most detailed and accessible account of Barlow's life is *A Yankee's Odyssey* by James Woodress. Victor Clyde Miller's *Joel Barlow, Revolutionist, London, 1791–1792* and Milton Cantor's dissertation (chaps. 7 and 8) recount Barlow's 1791–92 London period. Cantor's dissertation provides an excellent background of Barlow's social and cultural milieu. Other studies that bear upon these years are: M. Ray Adams's "Political Romanticist," Kenneth R. Ball's "American Nationalism" and his dissertation, Percy Boynton's "Barlow Advises," and Robert F. Durden's "Barlow in the French Revolution."

2. Barlow announced that his *Advice to the Privileged Orders* would run to eight chapters. Joseph Johnson published the first four chapters in early February. Stationer's Hall registered the *Advice* on 4 February (Miller 1932, 6); the *Advice* was advertised in the London *Morning Chronicle* on 11 February. Barlow wrote only one more chapter, which was published in France in 1793 and in England in 1795.

Cantor has pointed out that the Howells's *State Trials* repeatedly couples Barlow's name with Paine's. The *Journal of the House of Commons* reported that "At a meeting of the Society for Constitutional Information for March 4, 1792, a letter was 'read from the Norwich Revolution Society, which said that Paine's Rights of Man and the Advice to the Privileged Orders have been read with attention and circulated with avidity'" (*Journal* 49:682; in Cantor 1957, 172). On 24 September 1792 Brissot de Warville wrote in his underground *Le Patriote François*, amidst reportage of minutes from the French National Convention, an entry on Barlow for the "List d'Anglois à qui la convention nationale pourroit accorder le titre de citoyen françois": "Joel Barlow, américain, auteur de l'*avis aux ordres privilièges*, presqu'égal en mérite a l'ouvrage des droits de l'homme par M. Paine" (348).

3. Barlow had begun *Advice to the Privileged Orders* at least as early as 17 October 1791, when he wrote to his brother-in-law Abraham Baldwin (a member of Congress): "I have endeavored to chin up to the level of the politics of Europe, & not to suffer these great events to pass by without leaving an impression & leading to reflection. Perhaps you may hear from me on this subject, as I intend folks shall on this side the

water. I am meditating an attack which will be announced in a manifesto something like this, *The renovation of Society, or an Essay on the necessity & propriety of a revolution in the governments of Europe*" (ALS Barlow to Baldwin, Houghton Library, Harvard University). Evidently having known that Barlow was working on a denunciation of Burke, Horne Tooke urged Barlow to join the Society for Constitutional Information (cf. Cantor 1957, 146–47). Barlow does not seem to have attended a meeting of this society until 9 March 1792, when he was nominated with James Mackintosh, the author of *Vindiciae Gallicae* (1791), considered by some scholars to have been "the most acute of Burke's early critics" (Burke 1790, 51; see also Fennessy 1963, 194ff).

4. ALS Clarke (with postscript by Hayley) to Barlow, 25 March 1792, Beinecke Rare Books and Manuscripts Library, Yale University.

5. Barlow's business reasons for leaving London are unclear. It seems likely that he was arranging the shipping, via Holland, to France of goods in English ports. (See biographies by Woodress 1958, 125–26 and Cantor 1957, 177–79.)

6. Lemay's "The Contexts and Themes of 'The Hasty-Pudding,'" Arner's "'The Smooth and Emblematic Song': Joel Barlow's *The Hasty Pudding*," and Richardson's "The Enlightenment View of Myth and Joel Barlow's *Vision of Columbus*"—all reassess Barlow's literary and ideological impulses, Lemay and Richardson by indicating his avant-garde religious, mythological, and political motifs. Cecelia Tichi's *New World, New Earth* provides a good but standard account of Barlow's millenialism (chap. 4). Tichi wrote the Barlow entry in the *DLB* (37:18–31).

7. A roughly contemporary (1802) translation of the eighth satire occurs in William Gifford's *The Satires of Decimus Junius Juvenalis* (267–304).

8. Miller finds similarities between Barlow's *Conspiracy* and Pope's *Rape of the Lock* and *Dunciad*, but his analysis consists of little more than line quotation and syllable calculation (81–86). Cantor's dissertation is as much a guide to Barlow's life as it is to Barlow's social and intellectual milieu. Cantor's analysis is most useful on Barlow's sources; his discussion of Barlow's use of Baron d'Holbach in the *Advice* is excellent. Less able a critic of poetry, Cantor finds the *Conspiracy* lacking simply because it does not replicate the kind of political analysis available in the *Advice:* "the work was no more than a thin rhymed summary of beliefs that Barlow had expressed in the *Advice;* it sacrificed accuracy for passion, simplicity for rhetoric" (175). For aesthetic reasons I discuss later, I believe that Barlow wished to keep his political treatise free of rhetorical fervor, his passionate poem free of analytical discourse.

9. Barlow's mention of "his Holiness" might be a reference to John Warner, with whom Barlow had visited Eartham and returned to London.

10. Ronald Paulson has described the phenomenon this way in *Representations of Revolution* (4). Paulson continues: "And so referentially what has to be taken into consideration is not (except for purposes of difference) what actually happened, as reported in available sources—what served as referent and as analogue for the writer or painter, and the concepts and abstractions to which he had access and for which he sought equivalents" (5). Paulson, pointing to Wittgenstein's famous statement about use over meaning, concludes that "writers and artists do not use images to name a thing so much as to persuade to some end" (5).

11. In a letter to his son Richard, 18 August 1791, Burke said, "That most unfortunate woman is not to be cured of the spirit of Court Intrigue even by a prison" (1958–70, 6:361). Alfred Cobban and Robert Smith, the editors of Burke's correspondence from this period, remark that "Burke's distrust of Marie Antoinette, despite the rhapsody in the *Reflections*, was profound" (1958–70, 6:xvii; see xvii–xix). William B. Todd's standard edition of Burke's *Reflections* has been conveniently reprinted, with an introduction by Conor Cruise O'Brien, by Penguin.

12. Philip Francis was among Burke's few friends who read the *Reflections* manuscript as it went to press. Burke was evidently troubled by Francis's comments, and

his letters to Francis, as Cobban and Smith note, changed in tone thereafter from familiar to formal. (See 1958–70, 6: xiii–xiv and Francis's 19 February 1790 letter to Burke [85–86] along with Burke's response [88–92].)

Paulson has pointed out that there was no evidence that Marie Antoinette fled "almost naked" from the chamber (60). See the account in the *Gazette Nationale ou Le Moniteur Universal,* 12 October 1789, 293–95.

13. See Paulson 1983, 40, 45. Margaret C. Jacob's *The Radical Englightenment* discusses the cultural and scientific context of "secret" societies. See also Robert Darnton (1982), John Redwood (1976, esp. 174–96), and J. M. Roberts (1972, esp. 146–202).

14. See Paulson 1983, 14–15, 97. About the process of transvaluing and renaming Paulson has asserted: "While the revolutionaries were trying to valorize their day-to-day actions, the émigrés were identifying them with the vices, licentiousness, anarchy, and despotism on the other side of the Greco-Roman coin" (12); "Day-to-day policies were therefore understood in terms of analogues or fictions which related to the shifting policies (foreign and domestic) of the government of the moment" (13); "In terms of language, revolution makes things mean something else" (15). See also Ellul *(Propoganda).*

15. This aesthetic point, to which I later return, is key. Of the propagandists who replied to Burke, Mary Wollstonecraft in her *Vindication of the Rights of Woman* seems to have had the deepest insight that Burke's categories of revolutionary activities were essentially his own aesthetics adapted from the *Enquiry.* Paulson has made a similar point (1983, 81; see 80–86 passim).

16. Barlow's extant notebooks are located at the Houghton Library, Harvard. One undated notebook (bMS Am 1448 [13]) contains entries evidently translated and copied from the *Encyclopédie* on *théiste, athées, athéisme,* among other terms; his "Genealogy of the Tree of Liberty"; and notes about the French Revolution. The notes regarding the French Revolution, a group of notes at the end of this notebook having to do with Algiers, and a note written in 1866 by Lemuel Olmstead and pasted into the notebook seem to date the notebook to around 1796.

A series of questions relating to religion, however, might indicate an earlier date, perhaps prior to the 1787 publication of the *Vision.* Here Barlow wrote: "*Darkness, Storms, whirlwinds, thundre, inundations,* were deified on the same principle [as the sun's deification]; being unexplained they were supposed to act from their own will or that of their masters, they were therefore feared & adored as beings whom we could not controul but might hope to soften by our prayers as we might a passionate master who had us in his power.——" (p. 10 recto). This passage resembles a section of the "Dissertation." There, after explaining the method of the sun-god ruler, Barlow asserts about ignorant savage nations: "they find a Deity only in the storm, the earthquake and the whirlwind; or ascribe to him the evils of pestilence and famine; they consider him as interposing in wrath to change the course of nature, and exercising the attributes of rage and revenge. They adore him with rites suited to these attributes . . . [and] imagine him pleased with the severity of their mortifications" (1970, 2:188). The similarity of the *Vision* passage to the notebook entry is striking. Barlow might have been reworking his 1787 "Dissertation" for the 1793 Paris publication of the *Vision.* It should be noted, however, that the 1807 *Columbiad* reprints unchanged this passage from the "Dissertation."

Kenneth R. Ball discusses Barlow's 1788 diary in "American Nationalism" and his dissertation. He presents a transcription of the diary and of Barlow's unfinished fragment, "Canal," in appendices to the dissertation.

17. The traditional assumption has been that Barlow's writings as a young man were free of "heterodoxy" until he traveled abroad. Merton Christensen was among the first to show that deism and other Enlightenment beliefs can be found in Barlow's

earliest writings (1956, 509–20). J. A. Leo Lemay has found "Barlow's early religious beliefs more anti-Christian than those of most deists" (1982, 21 n. 21 and passim).

See M. Ray Adams (1968) and Joseph Blau (1949) for standard discussions of Barlow's deism.

18. The *Vision of Columbus* (1787) is reprinted in facsimile by Bottorff and Ford, eds., 1970, 2:101–370). The quotation from the "Dissertation" appears in 2:180. Richardson has noted the influence of Voltaire (1978, 37). Leon Howard has discussed Barlow's use of Robertson and Garcilaso de la Vega (1943, 148–50).

19. Volney's *Ruins* used the motif of a man who viewed the world's cultures, past, present, and future, by way of a dream visitation by a benevolent Genius. (Barlow had used the vision motif in his 1787 *Vision of Columbus*.) In chapter 12 of the *Ruins*, the Genuis reveals to the man a war that has been "kindled between the empire of the Czars and that of the Sultans" (42; compare Barlow's *Conspiracy* l. 12). At sight of the wars and the alms-giving in celebration of battle victory, the Genius, enraged, shouts, "What accents of madness strike my ear? What blind and perverse delirium disorders the spirits of the nations? Sacrilegious prayers rise not from the earth! and you, oh Heavens, reject their homicidal vows and impious thanksgivings! Deluded mortals! is it thus you revere the Divinity? Say then; how should he, whom you style your common father, receive the homage of his children murdering one another? (44; cf. *Conspiracy* ll. 39, 42, 129–40, 191–94). Volney's Genius discusses religion with the man, who admits: "Imposters have arisen on the earth who have called themselves the confidants of God; and, erecting themselves into teachers of the people, have opened the ways of falsehood and iniquity; they have acribed merit to practices indifferent or ridiculous" (45). The Genius insists: "A handful of brigands devour the multitude, and the multitude submits to be devoured! Oh degenerate people! Know you not your rights? All authority is from you, all power is yours. Unlawfully do kings command you on the authority of God and of their lance—" (51; cf. *Conspiracy* ll. 35–39, 53–56, 105).

Kenneth R. Ball discusses the similarities between Barlow's unfinished poem "Canal" (1797) and Volney's *Ruins*.

20. This undated notebook is discussed in note 16 above. The "Genealogy of the Tree of Liberty" appears on notebook pages 10 verso to 14 recto. Paulson briefly discusses Barlow's "Genealogy" (1983, 149–50). The "Genealogy" is very briefly mentioned in James H. Billington (1980, 42, 52, 68, 525).

21. Barlow would likely have known Benjamin Franklin's *Libertas Americana* medal, struck in 1782, which pictures on its front a woman carrying on her shoulder a pole that has a cap at its end (a liberty pole and cap). On the reverse of the medal, the infant Hercules (America) is strangling two snakes (the British armies captured at Saratoga and at Yorktown) while being watched by a helmeted woman who fends off a lion. The legend, NON SINE DIIS ANIMOSUS INFANS, indicates that "Not without divine help is the child courageous."

Barlow's allusion to the Alcides/Hercules myth takes advantage of the myth as it had entered the popular imagination: that the strength and courage that brought freedom to a young nation was divinely inspired and protected, and so, in Barlow's version of that myth, freedom would never "prostrate fall." Barlow's use of the infant Hercules, then, makes of Hercules the referent of freedom and virility and of America.

For a recent discussion of the medal see Winfried Schleiner (1976–77). I wish to thank J. A. Leo Lemay for referring me to the Franklin medal.

22. A standard source for Blake's writings and the edition I cite below is Erdman's edition of *The Poetry and Prose of William Blake*. For interesting variations on similar conceptions, images, and words, compare:

Carla Mulford

The Conspiracy of Kings	America	Song of Liberty
14–16	15:15–20	
34–38	1:9; 2:1–6	
55–68	6:; 7:; 8:	
61–68	2:7–11, 15–17	
75–92	16:15–23	
110–18	2:18–21	
119–23, 143–48		15
136	canceled plate b	
141–48		8–17
191–95, 209–16	9:22–25	
229–42	canceled plates b and c	

Both Blake and Barlow echo the Bible and Milton's *Paradise Lost*. I disagree with John Howard's conclusion that "Blake's hero is the personified antithesis of all that Barlow believed in" (1984, 115). See Erdman 1954 and its recast version in 1969 (23–26).

23. Paulson has said that the conception that freedom has flown the world over was inspired in Blake by Paine's *Rights of Man* (1983, 89).

Paine uses the *Translatio Libertatis* motif, the movement of liberty from America to France to England, in *The Rights of Man*, part 2, which was published the month before Barlow's *Conspiracy*. Paine wrote:

> Government founded on a *moral theory, on a system of universal peace, on the indefeasible hereditary Rights of man*, is not revolving from west to east by a stronger impulse than the government of the sword revolved from east to west. It interests not particular individuals, but nations in its progress, and promises a new era to the human race (1894–96, 2:404).

> From a small spark, kindled in America, a flame has arisen not to be extinguished. Without consuming, like the *Ultima Ratio Regum*, it winds its progress from nation to nation, and conquers by a silent operation (ibid., 2:454).

> Never did so great an opportunity offer itself to England, and to all Europe, as is produced by the two Revolutions of America and France (ibid., 2:512).

Other aspects of Paine's *Rights of Man* reflect the revolutionary conceptions found in Barlow (and Blake). "Lay then the axe to the root, and teach governments humanity," wrote Paine. "It is their sanguinary punishments which corrupt mankind" (ibid., 2:295; cf. *Conspiracy*, ll. 218–42). Paine also spoke of an equivocal generation that was exalted into men by the French Revolution:

> The French Constitution says, *There shall be no titles;* and, of consequence, all that class of equivocal generation which in some countries is called *"aristocracy,"* and in others "nobility," is done away, and the *peer* is exalted into the MAN. . . . France has not levelled; it has exalted. It has put down the dwarf, to set up the man. (1894–96, 2:319–20)

The best background, of course, for Paine's life and politics is Alfred Owen Aldridge, *Man of Reason* (1959) and *Thomas Paine's American Ideology* (1984). Margaret Jacob has suggested that Paine might have been a Freemason (1981, 154).

For a discussion of the *Translatio Studii* and *Translatio Imperii* motifs as transformed in the eighteenth century see Aldridge's "The Concept of Ancients and Moderns" (1976) also in *Early American Literature* (1982).

24. Part of Barlow's (and Paine's and Wollstonecraft's) attack against Burke is an aesthetic attack. Burke, in this aesthetic view, broke aesthetic decorum by combining cant, rhapsody, and sentiment—aspects intended sensibly to move the reader—in a work of political philosophy. Barlow seems clearly to have sought the cool discourse of

political philosophy in the *Advice;* his prose is largely free of the emotion-charged and emotion-charging language that would distract from the reasoning in his argument. Barlow claims a self-conscious intention in keeping his language suited to his discourse. Early in the *Advice* he suggests that he is trying to control his contempt in the discussion of primogeniture: "It is difficult to express a suitable contempt for this idea, without descending to language below the dignity of philosophy" (1970, 1:125). When Barlow does insult the conservatives, he takes the high road, as when he denounced those who support the British legal system: "It is so fashionable . . . to speak in praise of English jurisprudence . . . that it may seem necessary for a person to begin with an apology for offering his ideas on that subject, if he means to deviate from the opinion so generally established. But instead of doing this, I will begin by apologizing for those who at this day support the established opinion: Your fairest apology, Gentlemen, is, that you understand nothing of the matter. To assign any other, would be less favourable to your characters as honest men" (1970, 1:193). In the *Conspiracy* Barlow used the entirely different mode of discourse, one suitable to incite an emotional response, particularly in the lower class of readers, thus (presumably) to engender the desire for freedom. The notion of separate discourses for separate purposes is in Diderot's *Lettre sur les sourds et muets* (1751).

It seems likely that, given the writers with whom Barlow associated, Barlow read or discussed Diderot's and other writers' aesthetics. Stuart Curran suggests that Barlow developed an aesthetic of epic poetry from Hayley's *Essay on Epic Poetry* and that Barlow's epics *The Vision of Columbus* and *The Columbiad* themselves influenced Shelley in the writing of *Queen Mab* (1986, 170–73, 247, 248).

25. Denis Diderot 1875–77, 1:374. For a discussion of Diderot's aesthetics see Crocker 1974, 52–74. Engell (1981) discusses the philosophical and aesthetic changes that occurred as the Enlightenment became a Romantic movement.

The Age of Reason versus *The Age of Revelation*
Two Critics of Tom Paine: David Levi and Elias Boudinot

RICHARD H. POPKIN

Tom Paine's *Age of Reason* was written during the horrendous days of the Reign of Terror in 1793–94. The author explained to Samuel Adams, on 1 January 1803, that he wrote the first part while expecting to be arrested and guillotined, as his friends were. However, he finished the first part of the book just before being arrested by the French authorities and the second part while recovering from the effects of his imprisonment. Paine further told Adams that he saw his mission at the time as that of preventing the people of France from running headlong into atheism (Paine 1894–96, 4:205). He sought to help them by supporting deism, debunking the "fabulous theology" of Judaism and Christianity, and exposing the dangers and follies of the priestcraft. This might bring people back to "the just and humane principles of the Revolution which philosophy had first diffused [but] had departed from" (4:85). The work was published first in 1793 or 1794 in French translation, and then in English in London in 1795.

Alfred Owen Aldridge has observed that the work was taken as a continuing part of the attack on Christianity from Bayle to Voltaire and Diderot, and that more than thirty answers were written to it, and that the printer was charged with blasphemy (Aldridge 1959, 234). He states that "the most serious and distinguished [answer] was *An Apology for the Bible*, 1796, by Richard Watson, bishop of Llandaff. Most theologians and authorities on Christian apologetics accept Watson's answer as the standard work" (1959, 234). It was published many times, including a cheap edition by the American Tract Society.[1] Paine wrote a reply that only appeared posthumously. In his letter to Samuel Adams, Paine pointed out that the bishop saw that Paine was not an infidel, but a deist (1894–96, 4:203).

Bishop Watson's answer is not impressive. It combines standard elements of the Anglican latitudinarian view of the reasonableness of Christianity that has been set forth from Chillingworth and Stillingfleet and Tillotson to Butler, with their commonsense defense of believing in the Bible as a most probable account of humanity's and the world's history. But, as Moncure D. Conway pointed out, the bishop accepted many of Paine's "heretical views" about difficulties in the biblical text and about its authorship (Paine 1894–96, 4:259). As a result, "as for Watson's 'Apology' it is well known in the history of 'Freethought' that the Bishop's work was second only to Paine's in the propagation of scepticism, partly, no doubt, through the extracts from the 'Age of Reason' contained in it. Indeed as the Bishop's own orthodoxy was suspected, his legitimate promotion was prevented" (1894–96, 4:260).

Two other orthodox critics of Paine rarely have been given consideration. They are the leading Anglo-Jewish polemicist David Levi (1740–1801) and one of the leaders of the American Revolution and later first director of the United States Mint, Elias Boudinot, (1740–1821). Both represent a radically different theological spirit than that of Paine or Bishop Watson. They were far more erudite and had read a vast variety of Jewish and Christian apologetics than Paine or Watson. They had thought through the crucial points raised by Paine from Spinoza, Bayle, Voltaire, and others. And they faced Paine's attack with equanimity since they were each in their own way convinced that they were living in providential history, predicted by the biblical prophecies, and that contrary to Paine, there was good reason to believe that they were living in the Age of Revelation, the end of times as foreseen in Daniel and Revelation. The French Revolution for them was part of the divine scenario, soon to be followed by the recall and reestablishment of the Jews to Palestine, and then the triumphant arrival of the first or second appearance of the messiah.

Levi and Boudinot lived in entirely different intellectual and spiritual worlds from Paine but nevertheless interacted with each other. Paine discussed Levi and saw that his scholarly knowledge about Judaism was relevant. Paine must have known about Boudinot because of his important role in the American Revolution and in the American government thereafter. Just as Paine returned to America from the debacle of his European experience, Boudinot was dropping out of the deist government of Thomas Jefferson in order to prepare for the Second Advent. Levi in turn was trying to save the London and American Jewish communities from the inroads of freethinking while defending Judaism from the Christian millenarians who wanted to convert the Jews as part of the finale of world history. Boudinot and Levi were part of a large group of theologians who saw the outbreak of "Enlightenment" of the American and French revolutions as the prelude to the culmination of God's plan. As these events were soon interpreted in secular terms, the theologians who took prophecy seriously were brushed aside and ignored. Clarke Garrett's *Respectable Folly* (1975) tries to show that some of these people were respectable and important, but were also part of the lunatic fringe. By now, with enough distance and understanding of the role of millenarian thinking from the Reformation onwards, we can perhaps appreciate how Paine's views looked to an intelligent Jew and an intelligent Christian who were living in the Age of Revelation rather than the Age of Reason. Combining hindsight with imagination, we may be able to grasp some of the power of the rise of fundamentalism in the midst of the world's most scientific age, and understand how, almost two centuries after Paine's works, people are seeing signs that we are nearing the apocalyptic times foretold in the Bible.

Levi's work appeared first. Boudinot's dedication, however, indicates that he started after he saw that Bishop Watson's volume had not stopped the tide of Paine's attack and after he saw that copies were being sold for a penny and a half in Philadelphia and would corrupt the poor and the young.

David Levi was unique for his time. He was a self-taught Jew who took it upon himself to provide the basic Jewish materials in English for the quickly expanding Jewish communities in London. He translated into English both the Aschenazi and Sephardic prayer books, as well as compilations of other Jewish religious texts. He wrote a three-volume dissertation on prophecies to show which prophecies about the future history of the Jews in the Old Testament had been fulfilled and which ones remained to be realized. He explained in great detail that the crucial prophecies about the coming of the messiah had not yet been fulfilled. Christian theologians, he insisted, had misread the material (Paine was happy to cite him on this). Levi's three volumes, finished in 1801, remained an authoritative source for a good part of the nineteenth century for both Jews and Christians. Levi himself devoted some of his great erudition to answering Dr. Joseph Priestley's letter to the Jews (urging them to convert), to answering those who answered his letter, and then to answering Tom Paine. Levi represents, I think, almost the end of a Jewish polemical tradition that grew up first in seventeenth-century Amsterdam and that fought off Christian conversionists by insisting that Jewish history is going on according to God's providential schedule and that argued that Christianity is based on a mistaken reading of some nonmessianic events.[2]

In fighting Paine, Levi combined some of his Judaized reading of world history with his practiced answer to freethinkers like Spinoza, Voltaire, Hume, and others. Levi's answers were finished on 30 August 1796 and published first in New York, then in London (1797), and finally in Philadelphia (1798) (Levi 1798). The introductory letter addressed to Tom Paine said that Levi had read Paine's opus some months ago, and "do not scruple to pronounce it one of the most violent and systematic attacks on the word of God that was ever made" (3). Levi said that there was nothing new in Paine's objections, but his work was more acrimonious, abusive, and impertinent. It was the more dangerous in that it came "from the pen of a man that has acted so distinguished a part on the theatre of the philosophical world." Since he was so widely read in Europe, he might destroy the faith of many (3).

Nonetheless, Levi reported that he had to finish his translation of the prayer book and the second volume of his *Dissertation on Prophecies* before answering Paine. The already-published answers had not impressed Levi. All he could see that Paine had done was to blindly follow Morgan, Tindal, Bolingbroke, Hume, Voltairé, and Spinoza, and had picked up all sorts of nonsense from them such as the belief that Jews engaged in human sacrifices and cannibalism (46).

The main point that Levi dealt with, and which he considered the cornerstone of Judaism, was the belief that Moses was the author of the Pentateuch and that it is a divinely inspired work. Paine devoted a great deal of energy in the beginning of *The Age of Reason*, Part 2—when he had access again to a Bible, which he found worse than he previously remembered it (Paine 1894–96, 4:88)—to giving reasons why Moses was not the author of the first five books and to demonstrating that they were not written until several hundred years later (4:93). This evidence, Paine claimed, would destroy the basis for biblical religion: "Take away from Genesis the belief that Moses was the author, on which only the strange belief that it is the word of God has stood, and there remains nothing of Genesis but an anonymous book of stories, fables, and traditionary or invented absurdities, or of downright lies" (4:102). Levi had told Joseph Priestley in his second answer to him that "if a Jew once calls in question the authenticity of *any part* of the Pentateuch, by observing that one part is authentic, i.e., was delivered by God to Moses, and that another part is not authentic, he is no longer accounted a Jew, i.e., a true believer" (1789, 14–15).

So Levi tried to answer Tom Paine's challenge in detail, addressing various points emerging from seventeenth-century biblical criticism from La Peyrère, Spinoza, Hobbes, and Richard Simon down to the Encyclopédists and the English deists—points like how Moses could describe his own death in Deuteronomy, how he could describe the events in Genesis (since they occurred long before his birth), and so on. Levi's central defense (after using his erudition to straighten out Paine's version of Aben Ezra's remarks, Paine's grammatical analyses, and purported contradiction in the biblical text) was to insist on one main point, which was that the Pentateuch reports a series of prophecies by Moses that have been exactly fulfilled. This could only be the case if Moses received divine information about both the past and the future (Levi 1798, 14).

The major prophecies deal with the future course of Jewish history, the later dispersion of the Jews all over the face of the earth, with the Jews nonetheless remaining a separate people, capable of being gathered together in the latter days. All other nations had been assimilated or destroyed when they were dispersed. So Levi proclaimed, "And now, sir, give me leave to ask you, how was it possible for Moses, without being divinely inspired, to foresee that, the dreadful punishment which he had denounced against them should be so fully accomplished, as they are allowed on all hands to be; because a number of accidents might have arisen to prevent their completion, which no human foresight could have foreseen?" (16). How could Moses have known about a Roman conquest of Judea and the expulsion of the Jews from their homeland? How could he have known about the persecutions of the Jews by the Romans, the Christians, and by others? And how could he have known that the Jews would not abandon Judaism under such miserable treatment and then be assimilated? Based on historical experience the Jews should have disappeared long ago. "But Moses," he wrote, "contrary to all human foresight, informs us, that notwithstanding the severe and almost unparalleled chastisements, that they should experience, yet should they still be preserved a distinct nation" (18). Anyone now can see that this is what has happened in the course of history, *but* Moses prophecized this three thousand years ago. Is it really possible that Moses or any other human being could foresee such a wonderful course of events by human means (since it is counter to all other human experience)? Can this be accounted for by anything other than divine prescience? (19)?

The evidence of Jewish dispersal, suffering, and survival is everywhere. Levi cited the Protestant Jacques Basnage, who wrote the first history of the Jews since Josephus and who pointed out that there is nothing comparable to Jewish survival in the annals of humanity (21, 25).[3] Levi insisted that Jewish survival in the Diaspora is a standing miracle, "exhibited to the view and observation of the whole world" (35):

> These sir, are manifest proofs of prophecies: of prophecies delivered above three thousand years ago: and which we nevertheless plainly see fulfilling in the world at this very time: and what stronger proof can we have, or desire of the divine legation of Moses? (36)

Having built his cases for Moses, the divinely inspired author of the Pentateuch, on his prophetic picture of the future course of Jewish history, Levi then answered Paine's many points about the Mosaic authorship and the historical content of the Pentateuch. Although these answers may not be as convincing as Levi believed them to be then, the author proudly declaimed,

> And now, Mr. Paine, and ye Deists and Infidels of every description, who have written with such acrimony, and indecent levity, against the authority of the books of Moses, what have ye to say? Will ye, with all this mass of evidence against you, and staring you in the face, still have the assurance to take up your pens, and continue to impose on the weak, the ignorant and unwary, by asserting, that the work of the inspired penman is naught but fiction, when it is as evident as demonstration can make truth appear,

that all is the work of God. What shadow of pretence have ye now to produce, for continuing the immoral and blasphemous charge? What have ye still to offer against the pure, just, moral, humane and truly benevolent religion of Moses? (131)

Levi had centered his case here and throughout his other theological writings on the contentions that the course of Jewish history was predicted by Moses and the prophets, that the course of Jewish history is unique among the histories of peoples on this planet, and that history up to now is the fulfillment of the prophecies in the Old Testament. Further, Levi insisted, no mere human being could have foreseen the course of Jewish history and the unique survival of the Jews as a distinguishable and separate group in their dispersion. This amazing conformity of the prophecies to the future course of Jewish history is the guarantee of the accuracy and reliability of the Bible. He ended his answer to Paine by declaring, "It is the wonderful accomplishment of these predictions, that hath established the truth and verity of these books: and caused them to be handed down to us for so many centuries, with respect and veneration; and which they ever will retain, in defiance of the utmost malice of the deists and infidels, till time shall be no more" (240).

Levi's *Defence* was in accord with many Christian millenarian theologians, including Jacques Basnage, Sir Isaac Newton, William Whiston, David Hartley, Joseph Priestley, and Elias Boudinot, who believed that the best evidence to prove that we are living in a providential world in which a divine drama is unfolding is the amazing way in which Scripture prophecies have been fulfilled, especially about the Jews. Shortly before Levi became known, both Bishop Thomas Newton and Bishop Robert Clayton used the case of Jewish history to convince people that the millenium would soon occur.

Levi, of course, denied that Christianity was the fulfillment of the prophecies about the coming of the messiah. He was cautious in his *Dissertations on the Prophecies of the Old Testament* not to calculate when these prophecies would be fulfilled. He gave the usual Jewish claim that the Almighty, in his great widsom, has thought it proper to conceal the date (1800, 3:139). However, God has made it evident that we are not yet living in the days of the messiah since there is no peace on earth. All one has to do is look at the events in France and the rest of Europe and the Middle East to see that the prophecies in Isaiah have not yet been fulfilled (1800, 3:138 and 240–41). But, as Levi examined the modern history that so actively engaged Paine, he finally wrote in 1800,

However when we see so many nations engaged in a war, carried on with almost unparalleled violence, desolating so many countries, and producing such extraordinary Revolutions, as having scarcely ever been witnessed, but which seem so much to accord with the events, that the different prophets have predicted are to take place at, or near the time of that great and important event, I can not but consider all those occurrences, as indications of the near approach of the redemption of the nation. It therefore, in my humble opinion, behooves every rational mind, to pay a due regard to those awful warnings, and to endeavour to deprecate the wrath of the Almighty by a thorough reformation, and an amendment of their lives. (1800, 3:140)

So Levi finally joined those who saw that they were living in the Age of Revelation, the end of the days prophecized in Daniel and Revelation. He appealed to every rational mind to see the supernatural course of history unfolding. Paine could pretend to be rational, but he was irrational in his attacks on the Bible. He did not see its force as the prediction of the course of human history, and he did not realize that the ultimate fulfillment was now taking place. Levi was uninterested in Paine's avowed mission to save the French from atheism by offering them humanistic deism instead of Judeo-Christianity. Too much was at stake, the end of human history was at hand, and everybody's possibility of salvation was at risk. So this was no time for frivolous, acrimonious infidel attacks on Scripture and its message.

Paine read Levi's attack and gave a brief answer in his letter to Mr. Erskine of September 1797. (Erskine was prosecuting Paine's publisher in London.) In defending his reading of Jewish history, Paine denied the providential or supernatural element so central in Levi's account. Paine said, "Levi the Jew, who has written an answer to the *Age of Reason*, gives a strange account of the Law of Moses. . . . The sum of the history of the Jews is this—they continued to be a nation about a thousand years, they then established a law, which they called the *law of the Lord given by Moses* and were destroyed. This is not opinion, but historical evidence" (Paine 1894–96, 4:220). The course of postbiblical Jewish history was ignored by Paine and hence did not have to be accounted for. (This is strange, since Paine was a close friend of the millenarian l'abbé Henri Gregoire, who wrote a good deal about Jewish history up to contemporary times to show that it was both providentially guided and was approaching its climax [Conway 1900, 217, 391–92, and 421]).

As for the detailed points Levi brought up, Paine briefly answered a couple and then commented,

Levi, like the Bishop of Llandaff, and many other guess-work commentators, either forgets, or does not know, what there is in one part of the bible, when he is giving his opinion upon another part. . . . I did not, however, expect to find so much ignorance in a Jew, with respect to the history of his nation, though I might not be surprised at it in a bishop. (Paine 1894–96, 4:220)

If Tom Paine was not impressed by the learned answer of David Levi to the *Age of Reason*, he paid no attention to the long-winded scholarly answer by the millenarian American Revolutionary leader Elias Boudinot, one of the founders of America fundamentalism. Boudinot was an important figure in his day who has passed into oblivion, probably because his religious views seemed out of keeping with the prevailing deism and liberal Christianity of his time. Boudinot was born in Philadelphia in 1740 to a Huguenot family. He was baptized by the great evangelist George Whitefield. He had a classical education and became a lawyer in 1760. A trustee of Princeton from 1772 to 1821, he was the patron of Alexander Hamilton, who as a youth came up from the Caribbean to live with Boudinot, who then guided his career. Boudinot was active in revolutionary affairs, and in 1775 was a member of the New Jersey Provincial Congress. In charge of prisoners during the Revolution, he was elected president of the Continental Congress from 1782–84, and in that capacity signed the peace treaty with Great Britain making the United States a free nation. He was elected congressman from New Jersey for the first three Congresses, and then was appointed first director of the U.S. Mint in 1795. He resigned from that position in 1805 when the deist Jefferson became president, and devoted himself to writing, Bible study, and preparing for the Second Advent by founding two of the first fundamentalist institutions in the United States, the American Bible Society and the Society for Ameliorating the Condition of the Jews.

His first publication was an answer to Paine, *The Age of Revelation or the Age of Reason shown to be An Age of Infidelity*, in 1801. This was followed in 1815 by *The Second Advent* and a year later by *A Star in the West*, the latter two dealing with the millenarian events in America and Europe. The *Dictionary of American Biography* lists Boudinot's religious writings and comments that they "may be read by those curious to do so" (Whittlesley). Boudinot's biographer, George Adams Boyd, calls him "without a peer as the foremost Christian layman of the United States" (1952, 261). Regarding his answer to Tom Paine, Boyd remarked that Boudinot "set forth what might be called the fundamentalist as opposed to the modernist viewpoint. The spirit of the age was against it. Tom Paine is still read; Boudinot's volume has become a curiosity" (261).

One would expect that Paine and Boudinot knew each other from their revolutionary activities. Paine was secretary of the Continental Congress committee on foreign affairs. After the Revolution he lived in New Jersey, where Boudinot was a leading politician. And when Paine returned from Europe in 1802 he again lived in New Jersey, where Boudinot retired in 1805. They obviously had many common acquaintances from their activities during the Revolution and the post-Revolutionary situation. However, there is no indication they had any intellectual contact, except for Boudinot's answer to the *Age of Reason*.

In the *Age of Revelation*'s dedicatory introduction, dated December 1795, written to his daughter Susan (the widow of the first American attorney general), Boudinot said that Paine rehashed old objections that had been answered a thousand times. In the preface Boudinot explained his reason for responding. He did not feel that the bishop of Llandaff would convince either young people or the lower ranks of the community that Paine was wrong. He first wrote his answer for his daughter when he heard that thousands of copies of *The Age of Reason* had been sold at auction at Philadelphia for a cent and half (Boudinot 1801, xix–xxi). Be that as it may, Boudinot's answer is of more than antiquarian interest, and rests on much the same basis as David Levi's.

To appreciate his answer, I think one has to see Boudinot in his religious world. He interpreted the American Revolution as part of the premillennial events in divine history. The American Revolution was a second deliverance from bondage that would bring about human freedom, the end of slavery, the equality of the sexes and of people of all religions. Christ's message "Thou shalt love thy neighbor as thyself" was about to be realized in America, and America would lead the way into the millennium. Its Indians were the Lost Tribes of Israel who would now be recalled and (joined with the Jews who would convert to pure Christianity) would prepare the messianic state. As he stated in *A Star in the West*,

> What could possibly bring greater declarative glory to God, or tend more essentially to affect and rouse the nations of the earth, with a deeper sense of the certainty of the prophetic declarations of the holy scriptures, and thus call their attention to the truth of divine revelation than a full discovery, that these wandering nations of Indians are the long lost tribes of Israel, but kept under the special protection of Almighty God. (1816, 279–80).

This vision was further reinforced by Boudinot's careful study of what was happening in France from 1789 onward. In the preface to the *Second Advent*, he said that in 1790 he was struck by the concordance between what was occurring in France and what was forecast in the *Book of Revelation*. He took careful notes and then wrote an interpretation of French revolutionary developments as the fulfillment of the prophecies in *Revelation* (preface). From his reading of both the American and French revolutions, Boudinot clearly believed he was living in the age when God's revelation in Scripture was coming to fruition. From such an outlook, Paine's attack seemed to have no merit, to have missed the point entirely by using secular events and standards to measure divine events. A crucial example occurs when Paine moves from pointing out that some human beings are imposters to claiming that Moses, Jesus, and Mohammed also were imposters. Moses and Jesus showed their divine mission through their works, especially by foretelling events that had occurred over the last two hundred years. Since Mohammed could not produce such prophetic evidence, he resorted to ordinary human military power. Hence he is properly classed as an imposter (Boudinot 1801, 35–36).

Next Boudinot went into great detail to show that if one was living in the prophetic Jewish world in late antiquity, one would expect the events reported in the New Testament. These were not believed by the early Christians on the basis of hearsay, but because those were the events Jews expected at the time of Jesus' future history have been fulfilled. The divine authority of Moses' books becomes the basis for acceptance of the rest of Scripture, and the remaining books show how many prophecies of Moses had already been fulfilled (326).

Boudinot carefully outlined his case against Paine as a lawyer's brief, establishing the divinity of the Pentateuch. One of his major points was "By the manner in which the particular and minute historical events of the Jewish people, as the chosen nation of God, are recorded; the evidence in favour of the great truths of revelation, are daily increasing, and will so continue till the secomd coming of the Lord Jesus, as he has promised" (329).

So for Boudinot and Levi and a host of other apologetic writers of the late eighteenth and early nineteenth century, it was not just the probability that the facts recorded in Scripture occurred more or less as recorded and that the texts had been carefully preserved, but more that the predictions about later events in biblical history did in fact occur and that the prophecies about postbiblical history—especially those concerning the Jews—have happened. The fulfillment of prophecies was offered as the strongest answer to all of Paine's points. And, he wrote, the fulfillment of the final prophecies about the Jews and the Gentiles were apparently occurring before one's very eyes in France and America. France was in the last throes of unbelief before the coming of the messiah and the recall of the Jews. The glorious liberation of peoples in the United States was probably also part of the final providential drama. Boudinot asked at the end of *A Star in the West*, "Who knows but God has raised up these United States in these latter days, for the very purpose of accomplishing his will in bringing his beloved people [the Jews] to their own land" (1816, 297).

If one compares Paine's attack with Levi's and Boudinot's replies, the differences in their world views becomes apparent.

The early Bible criticism emerging from Hobbes, La Peyrère, Spinoza, and Richard Simon had raised a point that Paine declared destroyed the foundation of all claims that Scripture was the revealed Word of God. The questioning or denial of the Mosaic authorship raised the question of whether the Pentateuch was a human production. If Moses was not the author, then maybe ordinary people with human motives were. The problem of authorship grew out of the fact that Moses' death is described in Deuteronomy. Hobbes had used this account to restrict the Mosaic authorship to just the lines Moses is said *in the text* to have written. La Peyrère and Spinoza went further and declared that Moses might not have been the author of any of the text if he was not the author of some part of it. This familiar problem was raised much earlier by the medieval Spanish Jewish scholar Aben Ezra. He pointed out the forty lines that deal with events after Moses' death and regarded them as a special kind of revelation, not as nonrevelation. Other rabbis and Christian Bible scholars offered the possibility that if God was able to inform Moses of what happened before his birth, he could also inform him of what would happen after his death. One Jewish commentary portrays Moses as weeping while he wrote the post-Mosaic verse as God revealed them to him.[4]

Paine grabbed on to the most negative interpretation of Aben Ezra's point, the formulation in Spinoza that denied the Mosaic authorship.[5] Levi merely insisted that the Mosaic authorship was crucial for Judaism and Boudinot showed how it could still be maintainted in the light of Bible scholarship up to the end of the eighteenth century.

A more fundamental difference between Paine and the two opponents discussed here is whether one is living in secular or providential history. From the mid-seventeenth century onward claims were being advanced that all history is secular history. Spinoza, Bayle, Voltaire, Hume, and Gibbon all reinterpreted so-called providential history as a primitive, barbaric, immoral history that was used by corrupt priests and rulers to keep people in bondage. The Age of Reason applied reason to so-called providential history and saw it as just an unfortunate case study of the ancient Hebrews and a catastrophic case study of how the glory that was Greece and the grandeur that was Rome were destroyed by the Christians. The Age of Reason liberated one from providential history and finally led to either deism or the religion of reason.

Paine's view has been part of the prevailing way of reading history from the Enlightenment onward. Those who still talk of revealed history are regarded as uninformed or unenlightened. However, at the time Paine wrote *The Age of Reason*, there was an enormous outpouring of interpretations of the American and French revolutions as critical developments in providential history.[6] These were preceded by almost two centuries of reading Church history (the Reformation), the Thirty Years War, the Puritan revolution, the end of the Turkish threat to Europe, the Glorious Revolution, and so on, as the unfolding of providential history approaching its predicted climax. One of the items seen as crucial was the role of the Jews in providential history as the dispersed, despised, but miraculously preserved group whose conversion and return to their ancient homeland would be part of the grand finale, the commencement of the millennium, the thousand-year reign of Christ. It is interesting that it was not until the mid-seventeenth century that there was an attempt to write a history of the Jews from Josephus to the present. Rabbi

Menasseh ben Israel of Amsterdam was planning to do it to show how the divine plan was proceeding on course. We do not know if he ever wrote the work, but he inspired a Hugenot millenarian, Jacques Basnage, to write *Histoire des Juifs*, whose overriding theory is the awesome evidence of God's presence in history aiming at a quite imminent conclusion.[7]

Many intellectuals in the eighteenth century believed they were living in the Age of Revelation. Isaac Newton, David Hartley, Bishop Clayton, Bishop Thomas Newton, William Whiston, Joseph Priestley, Ezra Stiles, to name a few in the English-speaking world, interpreted events in terms of the approaching apocalyptic finale. The American and French revolutions added more fuel to this and led to an enormous and little-explored literature about the role of Napoleon as Christ, or Antichrist, and the role of the Jews in this finale of providential history. Napoleon's calling the Sanhedrin to meet in Paris in 1806 had monumental reverberations at the time. These interpreters formed the position that emerged as modern fundamentalism (Popkin 1975 and Sandeen 1970).

In the present, because we have been raised only on Paine and other Enlightenment and "enlightened" interpreters, we find ourselves mystified by the sudden resurgence of fundamentalism and by its influences on today's political world. If we study the basic world views that were in conflict when David Levi and Elias Boudinot fought back against Tom Paine, we may be able to understand how those who believed they were living in the Age of Revelation were able to construct the histories of America, the Redeemer Nation (Tuveson 1968), of Napoleonic and post-Napoleonic Europe, of Poland as the Crucified Nation, or Russia as the Star in the East and Moscow as Third Rome, and so on. These kinds of interpreters have been in the background of American and European history for the last two centuries but have been essentially relegated to their church-oriented colleges, their seminaries and yeshivas, and the early Sunday television programs that go on while the secular and enlightened intellectuals catch up on their sleep. Those living in the Age of Revelation have become noticed by their unstinting support of the State of Israel and by their role in recent United States political history. The history of Zionism in the nineteenth and twentieth centuries is full of Christian millenarian characters playing their part in divine history. The State of Israel is seen as the fulfillment of the penultimate prophecies about the Second Coming. Books read by millions of Americans including President Reagan show how the battle of Armageddon will be fought between the evil empire, Russia, and Israel, supported by the forces of good led by the United States (Lindsay and Carlson 1976).

Tom Paine might shake his head in dismay or laugh at the latest follies and foibles of men. But I believe he would have missed the point. The argument of *The Age of Reason* did not convince those who believed they were living in providential history. The Age of Revelation may be at least as valid a characterization of the period from Newton to Einstein as Paine's title. If we are to live and work together on one planet we may be forced to study and understand the dynamics of the unflinching believers who considered themselves part of divine history. Jewish history from Moses to Begin, as interpreted by its participants, may be a key to realizing some of the dynamics of the present world. What for Paine was fabulous theology has been for them the inner core of world history. Paine's great admirer, Moncure Daniel Conway, said, "It is impossible to understand the religious history of England, and of America, without studying the phases of their evolution in the writing of Thomas Paine (Paine 1894–96, 4:9). No doubt this is true, but, for better or worse, it is impossible to understand the religious histories of England and America without studying the phases of their evolution in the writings of the opponents of Thomas Paine. David Levi and Elias Boudinot are two of the most intellectual and serious critics whose basic outlook has contributed greatly to present-day Jewish and Christian fundamentalism. We are again living in the Age of Reason versus the Age of Revelation and need to understand both sides. Perhaps if we examine how Paine's attack failed to convince his opponents and how their defense failed to impress Paine, we can begin to understand the different interpretations of history that divide us so much today and the possible consequences in our age of believing that one is living in secular history or providential history.

NOTES

1. The edition of Watson's "Reply to Paine; or An Apology for the Bible," in *Letters to Thomas Paine*, by the American Tract Society, lists the author as being bishop of Landaff and professor of divinity in the University of Cambridge. Adjoined to Watson's text is Starkie's "Examination of Hume's Argument of Miracles."

2. On Levi, see Singer 1896–98; Picciotto 1956; and Popkin (forthcoming).

3. Basnage's work came out in French and English in the first decade of the eighteenth century. Levi referred to Basnage as "an author of great note."

4. On the background of biblical criticism see Popkin 1964, chap. 11.

5. It is interesting that Paine cited Spinoza from the 1678 French translation of the *Tractatus Theologico-Politicus*, (1894–96, 272). An English translation had appeared in 1737, but Paine may not have had access to it in Paris.

6. This literature is beginning to be examined seriously.

7. See the preface to Jacques Basnage's *Histoire des Juifs* (1706–7) in both the French and English edition. Basnage used Menasseh as one of his main authorities.

Alfred Owen Aldridge: A Bibliography to 1986

1. Books

Shaftesbury and the Deist Manifesto. Philadelphia: American Philosophical Society, 1951.
Benjamin Franklin and His French Contemporaries. 1957. Reprint. Westport, Conn.: Greenwood Press, 1976. Rev. and enl. ed.: *Benjamin Franklin et ses contemporains français.* Paris: Didier, 1963.
Man of Reason: The Life of Thomas Paine. New York: J. B. Lippincott, 1959, and London: Cresset Press, 1960. Reprint: New York: Ladder Edition, Popular Library, 1963. French trans.: *La Voix de la Liberté: Vie de Thomas Paine.* Paris: Nouveaux Horizons, 1964. Also translated into Arabic (1964); Bengali (1965); and Urdu (1967).
Essai sur les personnages des "Liaisons Dangereuses" en tant que types littéraires. Paris: Les Lettres Modernes, 1960.
Jonathan Edwards. New York: Great American Thinkers Series, Washington Square Press, 1964. Reprint. New York: New York University Press, 1966.
Benjamin Franklin: Philosopher and Man. New York: J. B. Lippincott, 1965.
Benjamin Franklin and Nature's God. Durham, N.C.: Duke University Press, 1967.
Voltaire and the Century of Light. Princeton: Princeton University Press, 1975.
Comparative Literature Japan and the West (in Japanese translation). Tokyo: Nan'un Do Co., 1979.
Early American Literature: A Comparatist Approach. Princeton: Princeton University Press, 1982.
Thomas Paine's American Ideology. Newark: University of Delaware Press, 1984.
Fiction in Japan and the West (in Japanese translation). Tokyo: Nan'un Do Co., 1985.
The Reemergence of World Literature. Newark: University of Delaware Press, 1986.

2. Edited Books

Comparative Literature: Matter and Method. Intro. Urbana: University of Illinois Press, 1969.
The Ibero-American Enlightenment. Urbana: University of Illinois Press, 1970.
Anthony Ashley Cooper Third Earl of Shaftesbury. Complete Works. Advising coeditor. Standard ed., vol. 2, part 2. Stuttgart: Frommann-Holzboog, 1984.

3. Essays and Notes

A. Comparative Literature, East-West

"Comparative Literature East and West: An Appraisal of the Tamkang Conference." *Yearbook of Comparative and General Literature* 21 (1972): 65–70.

With Shunsuki Kamei. "Problems and Vistas of Comparative Literature in Japan and the United States: A Dialogue." *Mosaic* 5 (1972): 149–63.

"The Second China Conference: A Recapitulation." *Tamkang Review* 7 (1976): 481–92. Also in *Yearbook of Comparative and General Literature* 25 (1976): 42–48.

"East-West Literary Relations Conference Revisited." *Yearbook of Comparative and General Literature* 28 (1979): 50–56.

"East-West Relations: Universal Literature, Yes: Common Poetics, No." *Tamkang Review* 10 (1979): 17–33.

Foreword to *Chinese-Western Comparative Literature: Theory and Strategy*, iii–xx. Hong Kong: Chinese University Press, 1980.

Introduction to *China and the West: Comparative Literature Studies*. Edited by William Tay, Ting-hsiung Chou, and Heh-hsiang Yuan, iii–xiii. Seattle: University of Washington Press, 1980.

"Recapitulation of the Third International Comparative Literature Conference." *Tamkang Review* 10 (1980): 641–58.

"East-West Resonances in New York." *Tamkang Review* 13 (1982): 1–11.

"Balancing Careers or Comparatism Triumphant." in *Arcadia. Zeitschrift für Vergleichende Literaturwissenschaft*, 1983. (This is a special issue apart from series volumes as a Festschrift for Horst Rüdiger. All articles are short autobiographies. Aldridge's explains his dedication to East-West studies.)

"The Universal in Literature." *Neohelicon* 10 (1983): 9–31.

B. Western Comparative Literature

"The Debut of American Letters in France." *French-American Review* 3 (1950): 1–23.

"Polygamy in Early Fiction." *PMLA* 65 (1950): 464–74.

"La Signification historique, diplomatique et littéraire de la *Lettre addressée à l'Abbé Raynal de Thomas Paine.*" *Etudes Anglaises* 8 (1955): 223–32.

"Condorcet et Paine, leurs rapports intellectuels." *Revue de littérature comparée* 32 (1958): 47–65.

"Lolita and *Les Liaisons dangereuses.*" *Wisconsin Studies in Contemporary Literature* 2 (1961): 20–26.

"Le problème de la traduction au XVIIIe siècle et aujord'hui." *Revue belge de philologie et d'histoire* 29 (1961): 747–58. English résumé in *Actes de VIIe Congres de la Fédération Internationale des Langues et Littératures Modernes*, 189–91. Paris: Bibliothèque de la Faculté de philosophie et lettres de l'Université de Liège, no. 161, 1961.

"Benjamin Franklin and the Philosophes." In *Transactions of the First International Congress on the Enlightenment*, edited by Theodore Besterman, 1:43–65. Geneva: Institut et Musée Voltaire, 1963.

"The Brazilian Maxim." *Comparative Literature* 15 (1963): 46–59. Résumé in *Proceedings of the IIIrd Congress of the International Comparative Literature Association*, edited by Roland Mortier, 307. The Hague: 'S-Gravenhage, 1962.

"The Concept of Influence in Comparative Literature." In *Comparative Literature*

Studies, Special Issue of the Proceedings of the First Meeting of the American Comparative Literature Association, edited by Aldridge ["Special Advance Issue"] 1(1963): 143–46.

"Explication in France." In "Symposium on Explication de texte." *Books Abroad* 37 (1963): 261–65.

"*The Rights of Man* de Thomas Paine, symbole du siècle des lumières et leur influence en France." In *Utopie et institutions au XVIIIe siècle: Le Pragmatisme des lumières*, edited by Pierre Fancastle, 277–87. Paris: Mouton, 1963.

"Biography in the Interpretation of Poetry." *College English* 25 (1964): 412–20.

"Biography, the Criticism of Biography, and Comparative Literature." *Modern Language Journal* 50 (1966): 286–89.

"The Character of a North American as Drawn in Chile, 1818." *Hispania* 49 (1966): 489–94.

"International Influences upon Biography as a Literary Genre." *Proceedings of the IVth Congress of the International Comparative Literature Association*, edited by François Jost, 2:972–81. The Hague: Mouton, 1966.

"A Breakthrough in Comparative Literature." *Modern Language Journal* 51 (1967): 174-78.

"Camilo Henríquez and the Fame of Thomas Paine and Benjamin Franklin in Chile." *Inter-American Review of Bibliography* 17 (1967): 51–67.

"Apostles of Reason: Camilo Henríquez and the French Enlightenment." In *Transactions of the Second International Congress on the Enlightenment*, edited by Theodore Besterman, 1:65–87. Geneva: Institut et Musée Voltaire, 1968.

"The Background of Kleist's 'Das Erdbeben in Chile.'" *Arcadia* 3 (1968): 173–80.

"The Cloudy Spanish Enlightenment." *Modern Language Journal* 52 (1968): 113–16.

"Las ideas en la América del Sur sobre la ilustración Española." *Revista Iberoamericana* 24 (1968): 282–97.

"International and New Periodicals in Comparative Literature." *Yearbook of Comparative and General Literature* 17 (1968): 122–28.

With Melvin Zimmerman. "Foreign Influences and Relations: English and American." In *A Critical Bibliography of French Literature: The Eighteenth Century*, edited by D. C. Cabeen, 4A:212–37. *Supplement*, edited by R. A. Brooks. Syracuse, N.Y.: Syracuse University Press, 1968.

"Biography and Realism." *Les Problèmes des genres littéraires* 11 (1969): 6–22.

"The Comparative Literature Syndrome." *Modern Language Journal* 53 (1969): 110–16.

"Shifting Trends in Narrative Criticism." *Comparative Literature Studies* 6 (1969): 225–29.

"Chateaubriand, the Idea of Liberty, and Latin America." In *Proceedings of the Commemoration of the Bicentenary of the Birth of Chateaubriand*, edited by Richard Switzer, 201–13. Geneva: Droz, 1970.

"An Early Cuban Exponent of Inter-American Cultural Relations: Domingo del Monte." *Hispania* 54 (1971): 348–53.

"From Sterne to Machado de Assis." In *The Winged Skull: Bicentenary Conference Papers on Laurence Sterne*, edited by A. H. Cash and J. M. Stedmon, 170–85. Kent, Ohio: Kent State University Press, 1971.

"Thomas Paine, Edmund Burke and Anglo-French Relations in 1787." *Studies in Burke and His Time* 12 (1971): 1851–61.

"Fenimore Cooper and the Picaresque Tradition." *Nineteenth Century Fiction* 27 (1972): 283–92.

"The Modern Spirit: Kazantzakis and Some of His Contemporaries." *Journal of Modern Literature* 2 (1972): 303–13.

"Polly Baker and Boccaccio." *Annali dell'Istituto Universitario Orientale, Sezione Romanza* 14 (1972): 5–18.

"The State of Nature: An Undiscovered Country in the History of Ideas." *Studies in Voltaire and the Eighteenth Century* 98 (1972): 7–26.

"Voltaire and the Cult of China." *Tamkang Review* 3 (1972): 25–49.

"Ancients and Moderns in the Eighteenth Century." In *Dictionary of the History of Ideas*, 1:76–87. New York: Scribners, 1973.

"The Concept of Classicism as Period or Movement." *Neohelicon* 1–2 (1973): 230–43.

"The Concept of Literary Zones." *Neohelicon* 1–2 (1973): 149–52.

"Feijoó and the Problem of Ethiopian Color." In *Studies in Eighteenth-Century Culture, Racism in the Eighteenth Century*, edited by Harold E. Pagliaro, 263–77. Cleveland, Ohio: Case-Western Reserve Press, 1973.

"Primitivism in the Eighteenth Century." In *Dictionary of the History of Ideas*, 3:598–605. New York: Scribners, 1973.

"The Vampire Theme: Dumas père and the English Stage." *Revue des langues vivantes* 39 (1973): 312–24.

"The Collapse of the British Empire as Seen by Franklin, Paine and Burke." *Lex et Scientia: The International Journal of Law and Science* 10 (1974): 10–33, 52–56.

"The First American Interpretation of Boccaccio." In *Il Baccacio nella cultura inglese e anglo-americana*, edited by Giuseppe Galigani, 219–30. Firenze: Leo S. Ilschki, 1974.

"Cokain, Ovid, and the Vampire Theme." In *Teilnahme und Spiegelung. Festschrift für Horst Rüdiger*, edited by Dieter Gutzen et al., 217–25. Berlin: Walter de Gruyter, 1975.

"Feijoó, Voltaire, and the Mathematics of Procreation." In *Studies in Eighteenth-Century Culture*, edited by Harold E. Pagliaro, 131–138. Madison: University of Wisconsin Press, 1975.

"Mandeville and Voltaire." In *Mandeville Studies, New Explorations in the Art and Thought of Dr. Bernard Mandeville*, edited by Irwin Primer, 142–56. The Hague: Martinus Nijhoff. International Archives of the History of Ideas, 1975.

"Shaftesbury and the Classics." In *Gesellschaft, Kultur, Literature. Festschrift für Luitpold Wallach*, edited by Karl Bosl et al., 241–58. Stuttgart: Karl Bosl, 1975.

"The Vampire Theme in Latin America." In *Otros Mundos Otros Fuegos: Fantasía y realismo magico en Iberoamérica*, edited by Donald A. Yates, 145–52. East Lansing: Michigan State University Press, 1975.

"The Vogue of Thomas Paine in Argentina." In *Actes du VIe Congrès de l'Association Internationale de Littérature Comparée*, edited by Michel Cadot et al., 281–85. Stuttgart: Kunst und Wissen. Erich Breber, 1975.

"The Concept of Ancients and Moderns in American Poetry of the Federal Period." In *Classical Traditions in Early America*, edited by John W. Eadie, 99–118. Ann Arbor: University of Michigan Press, 1976.

"Thomas Paine and the Ideologues." *Studies on Voltaire and the Eighteenth Century* 151 (1976): 109–17.

"Thomas Paine and the French Connection." *French-American Review* 1 (1977): 240–48.

"Literature (Field of Study)." In *International Encyclopaedia of Higher Education*, edited by Asa S. Knoles, 6:2648–52. San Francisco: Jossey-Bass, 1978.

"Problems in Writing the Life of Voltaire: Plural Methods and Conflicting Evidence." *Biography: An Interdisciplinary Quarterly* 1 (1978): 5–22.

"The Enlightenment in the Americas." In *Proceedings of the 7th Congress of the International Comparative Literature Association*, edited by Milan V. Dimic and Juan Ferrante, 1: 59–67. Stuttgart: E. Bieber, 1979.

"Voltaire Then and Now: Paradoxes and Contrasts in His Reputation." In *Enlightenment Studies in Honour of Lester G. Crocker*, edited by A. J. Bingham and V. W. Topazio, 1–17. Oxford: The Voltaire Foundation at the Taylor Institute, 1979.

"Biographie." In *Dictionnaire International des Termes Litteraires*. Fascicule 2, 169–73. Bern: Editions Francke, 1980.

"Swift and Voltaire." In *Actes du VIIIe Congrès de l'Association Internationale de Littérature Comparée*, edited by Bela Kopeczi et al., 283–89. Stuttgart: Bieber, 1980.

"The Interplay of History and Literature." *CLIO, A Journal of Literature, History, and the Philosophy of History* 9 (1982): 261–70.

"Balancing Careers or Comparatism Triumphant." *Arcadia. Sonderheft for Horst Rüdiger.* 18 (1983): 1–5.

"Condorcet, Paine and Historical Method." In *Condorcet Studies* I, edited by Leonara Cohen Rosenfield, 49–60. Atlantic Highlands, N.J.: Humanities Press, 1984.

"European Poetry 1760–1820." *Arcadia* 19 (1984): 183–92.

"Some Aspects of the Historical Novel after Lukacs." In *Literary Theory and Criticism. Festschrift in Honor of René Wellek*, edited by Joseph P. Strelka, 677–87. Bern: Peter Lang, 1984.

C. Eighteenth-Century English Literature

"The Eclecticism of Mark Akenside's 'The Pleasures of Imagination.' " *Journal of the History of Ideas* 5 (1944): 292–314.

"Akenside and Imagination." *Studies in Philology* 42 (1945): 769–92.

"Lord Shaftesbury's Literary Theories." *Philological Quarterly* 24 (1945): 46–64.

"Shaftesbury and the Test of Truth." *PMLA* 60 (1945): 129–56.

"A Preview of Hutcheson's Ethics." *Modern Language Notes* 61 (1946): 153–61.

"Shaftesbury's Earliest Critic." *Modern Philology* 44 (1946): 10–22.

"Akenside and the Hierarchy of Beauty." *Modern Language Quarterly* 7 (1947): 65–67.

"Madame de Stael and Hannah More on Society." *Romanic Review* 38 (1947): 330–39.

"Addison's 'The Visions of Mirzah.' " *Explicator* 6 (1948): no. 6.

Explicator 6 (1948): no. 6.

"Akenside, Anna Seward, and Colour." *Notes and Queries* 193 (1948): 562–63.

"A French Critic of Hutcheson's Aesthetics." *Modern Philology* 45 (1948): 169–84.

"Polygamy and Deism." *Journal of English and Germanic Philology* 48 (1948): 343–60.

"The Pleasures of Pity." *ELH, A Journal of English Literary History* 16 (1949): 76–87.

"Population and Polygamy in Eighteenth-Century Thought." *Journal of the History of Medicine and Allied Sciences*, no. 4 (1949): 129–48.

"Shaftesbury, Christianity and Friendship." *Anglican Theological Review* 32 (1950): 121–36.

"Two Versions of Shaftesbury's Inquiry concerning Virtue." *Huntington Library Quarterly* 13 (1950): 121–36.

"The Meaning of Incest from Hutcheson to Gibbon." *Ethics* 61 (1951): 309–13.

"Shaftesbury and Bolingbroke." *Philological Quarterly* 22 (1952): 1–16.
"Shaftesbury's Rosicrucian Ladies." *Anglia* Band 103, Heft ¾ (1985): 297–319.

D. Thomas Paine

"Why did Thomas Paine Write on the Bank?" *Proceedings of the American Philosophical Society* 93 (1949): 309–15.
"Some Writings of Thomas Paine in Pennsylvania Newspapers." *American Historical Review* 56 (1951): 832–38.
"Thomas Paine and the New York Public Advertiser." *New York Historical Society Quarterly* 37 (1953): 361–82.
"The Poetry of Thomas Paine." *Pennsylvania Magazine of History and Biography* 71 (1955): 81–99.
"Thomas Paine's Plan for a Descent on England." *William and Mary Quarterly*, 3d ser., 14 (1957): 74–84.
"The Influence of Thomas Paine in the United States, England, France, Germany and South America." In *Comparative Literature, Proceedings of the ICLA Congress*, edited by Werner P. Friederich, 2:369–83. Chapel Hill: University of North Carolina Press, 1959.
"Thomas Paine." In *The Unforgettable Americans*, edited by John Arthur Garraty, 61–65. New York: Channel Press, 1960.
"Thomas Paine and Camus." *Pennsylvania Magazine of History and Biography* 85 (1961): 70–75.
"Thomas Paine and the Classics." *Eighteenth-Century Studies* 1 (1968): 370–80.
"The Religion of Thomas Paine (Summary)." *Akten des XIV. Internationalen Kongresses für Philosophie Wien* 5 (1968): 393–94.
"Thomas Paine in Latin America." *Early American Literature* 3 (1969): 139–47.
"Thomas Paine: A Survey of Research and Criticism since 1945." *British Studies Monitor* 5 (1975): 3–29.
"The Influence of New York Newspapers on Paine's *Common Sense*." *The New York Historical Society Quarterly* 60 (1976): 53–60.
"Paine and Dickinson." *Early American Literature* 11 (1976): 125–38.
"Thomas Paine." In *Heritage of '76*, edited by Jay P. Dolan, 16–22. South Bend, Ind.: University of Notre Dame Press, 1976.
"El Granadino que traduto la obra de Tomás Paine." *Inter-American Review of Bibliography* 31 (1981): 538–42.

E. Benjamin Franklin

"Benjamin Franklin and the *Maryland Gazette*." *Maryland Historical Magazine* 44 (1949): 177–89.
"Franklin as Demographer." *Journal of Economic History* 9 (1949): 25–44.
"Franklin's 'Shaftesburian' Dialogues Not Franklin's: A Revision of the Franklin Canon." *American Literature* 21 (1949): 151–59.
"Edwards and Franklin on Lightning and Earthquakes." *Isis* 41 (1950): 162–64.
"Franklin and the Ghostly Drummer of Tedworth." *William and Mary Quarterly*, 3d ser., 7 (1950): 559–67.
"Franklin's Deistical Indians." *Proceedings of the American Philosophical Society* 94 (1950): 398–410.

"Benjamin Franklin and Philosophical Necessity." *Modern Language Quarterly* 12 (1951): 292–309.

"Jacques Barbeu-Dubourg, a French Disciple of Benjamin Franklin." *Proceedings of the American Philosophical Society* 95 (1951): 331–92.

"Benjamin Franklin as Georgia Agent." *Georgia Review* 6 (1952): 161–73.

"A Humorous Poem by Benjamin Franklin." *Proceedings of the American Philosophical Society* 98 (1954): 397–99.

"The Sources of Franklin's 'The Ephemera.'" *New England Quarterly* 27 (1954): 388–91.

"Anecdotes sur Benjamin Franklin." *France-Amérique Magazine*, nos. 10–12 (1955): 153–55.

"Les Mémoires de Franklin." *France-Amérique Magazine*, nos. 1–3 (1956): 30–32.

"Benjamin Franklin and the Pennsylvania Gazette." *Proceedings of the American Philosophical Society* 106 (1962): 77–81.

"A Religious Hoax by Benjamin Franklin." *American Literature* 26 (1964): 204–9.

"Charles Brockden Brown's Poem on Benjamin Franklin." *American Literature* 38 (1966): 230–35.

"The First Published Memoir of Franklin." *William and Mary Quarterly*, 3d ser., 24 (1967): 624–28.

"Form and Substance in Franklin's Autobiography." in *Essays on American Literature in Honor of Jay B. Hubbell*, edited by Clarence Gohdes, 47–62. Durham, N.C.: Duke University Press, 1967.

"Franklin's Experimental Religion." In *Meet Dr. Franklin*, edited by Roy N. Lokken, 101–23. Philadelphia: The Franklin Institute, 1981.

F. Other American Literature

"Mysticism in Modern Times, L. I." *Americana* (1942): 355–70.

"George Whitefield's Georgia Controversies." *Journal of Southern History* 9 (1943): 357–80.

"Jonathan Edwards and William Godwin on Virtue." *American Literature* 18 (1947): 308–18.

"Phenomenology in America." *South Atlantic Quarterly* 48 (1949): 421–31.

"The Poet's Corner in Early Georgia Newspapers." *Georgia Review* 16 (1949): 45–55.

"Timothy Dwight's Posthumous Gift to British Theology." *American Literature* 22 (1950): 479–81.

"Edwards and Hutcheson." *Harvard Theological Review* 44 (1951): 35–53.

"Dickinson College and the Broad Bottom of Early Education in Pennsylvania." In *Early Dickinsonia*, 93–114. Carlisle, Pa.: Dickinson College Library, 1961.

"American Burlesque at Home and Abroad: Together with the Etymology of Go-Go Girl." *Journal of Popular Culture* 5 (1971): 565–75.

"The American Revolution and a Spurious Letter from Voltaire." *Studies on Voltaire and the Eighteenth Century* 124 (1974): 163–66.

"Massillon and S. S. Smith: French-Inspired Sermons in Early American Literature." *French-American Review* 6, no. 2 (1982): 147–59.

4. Selected Reviews

Essays in the History of Ideas, by Arthur O. Lovejoy. *Modern Language Notes* 65 (1950): 545–49.

Benjamin Franklin and a Rising People, by Verner W. Crane; *Franklin's Wit and Folly: The Bagatelles*, edited by Richard D. Amacher; and *Benjamin Franklin and American Foreign Policy*, by Gerald Stourzh (joint review). *William and Mary Quarterly*, 3d ser., 12 (1955): 145–50.

Benjamin Franklin and Italy, by Antonio Pace. *American Literature* 31 (1959): 345–47.

The Papers of Benjamin Franklin, by Leonard W. Labaree et al., vol. 1. *American Literature* 33 (1961): 208–10.

Benjamin Franklin in Portraiture, by Charles Coleman Sellers. *American Literature* 35 (1963): 372.

Pages d'ecriture, by Jean Tardieu. *Books Abroad* 42 (1968): 240.

Explication de Texte, edited by Jean Sareil. *Modern Language Journal* 52 (1968): 239–40.

Tradition and Innovation in Contemporary Literature. A Round Table Conference of International P.E.N., edited by Laszlo Kéry. *Books Abroad* 42 (1968): 174.

Le paradis perdu 1667–1967, edited by Jacques Blondel. *Books Abroad* 43 (1969): 80.

Puritans and Pragmatists: Eight Eminent American Thinkers, by Paul K. Conkin. *American Historical Review* 74 (1969): 200–201.

Le thème de Faust dans la Littérature européenne. 4: Du romantisme à nos jours. Part 2: De 1880 à nos jours. Books Abroad 43 (1969): 71.

The Americas Look at Each Other, by José A Balseiro. *Criticism, a Quarterly for Literature and the Arts* 12 (1970): 254–55.

Essais de litterature comparée. 2: Europaeana, by François Jost. *Books Abroad* 44 (1970): 256–57.

The Myth of the Golden Age in the Renaissance, by Harry Levin. *Modern Language Journal* 545 (1970): 444–45.

Perspectives in Literary Symbolism (Yearbook of Comparative Criticism, Vol. 1), edited by Joseph Strelka. *Journal of Aesthetic Education* 4 (1970): 150–52.

Roger Williams, by Henry Chupack. *Journal of American History* 61 (1970): 409–10.

T. S. Eliot and Charles Baudelaire, by Kerry Weinberg. *Books Abroad* 44 (1970): 313–14.

The Mathers: Three Generations of Puritan Intellectuals: 1596–1728, by Robert Middlekauff. *Manuscripta* 15 (1971): 119–20.

The Intellectual Development of Voltaire, by Ira O. Wade. *Comparative Literature* 23 (1971): 186–90.

Burke and Paine on Revolution and the Rights of Man, edited by Robert B. Dishman. *Studies in Burke and His Time* 13 (1971): 2042–45.

Benito Jeronimo Feijoó, by I. L. McClelland. *Modern Language Review* 64 (1972): 676–78.

The Waning of the Renaissance 1640–1740, by John Holyles. *Journal of the History of Philosophy* 10 (1972): 361–63.

Beyond Genre: New Directions in Literary Classification, by Paul Hernadi. *Books Abroad* 47 (1973): 363.

Grounds for Comparison, by Harry Levin. *Books Abroad* 47 (1973): 424.

A Literary History of Spain: The Eighteenth Century, by Nigel Glendinning. *Modern Language Review* (1973): 677–78.

Men of Letters in Colonial Maryland, by J. A. Leo Lemay. *Seventeenth-Century News* 31 (1973): 99–100.

Modern French Criticism from Proust and Valery to Structuralism, edited by John K. Simon. *Books Abroad* 47 (1973): 325–26.

The Papers of Benjamin Franklin, vol. 15, edited by William B. Wilcox et al. *American Historical Review* 78 (1973): 155–56.

The Unknown Distance: From Consciousness to Conscience. Goethe to Camus, by Edward Engelberg. *Books Abroad* 47 81973): 612.

The Colonial Legacy. Vol. 1. Loyalist Historians; Vol. 2. Some Eighteenth-Century Commentators, edited by Lawrence H. Leder. *American Historical Review* 79 (1974): 572.

Comparative Literature and Literary Theory, by Ulrich Weisstein. *Books Abroad* 48 (1974): 821–22.

La Poésie corps et âme, by Gabriel Germain. *Books Abroad* 48 (1974): 819.

Questions à la littérature, by Jean-Louis Curtis. *Books Abroad* 48 (1974): 424.

Voltaire Historian, by J. H. Brumfitt. *Revue belge de philologie et d'histoire* 52 (1974): 213–14.

Benjamin Franklin and the Zealous Puritans, by Melvin H. Buxbaum. *American Literature* 46 (1975): 446–48.

Comparative Literature Studies: An Introduction, by S. S. Prawer. *Yearbook of Comparative and General Literature* 24 (1975): 132–33.

Essais de littérature (vraiment) générale, by René Etiemble. *Books Abroad* 49 (1975): 188.

Rebel, by Samuel Edwards; *Thomas Paine. His Life, Work, and Times*, by Audrey Williamson; and *Paine*, by David Freeman Hawke. (Joint review). *Eighteenth-Century Studies* 8 (1975): 490–99.

Revolution and Romanticism, by Howard Mumford Jones. *American Literature* 46 (1975): 582–83.

The Selected Letters of Voltaire, edited and translated by Richard Brooks. *Eighteenth-Century Studies* 8 (1975): 360–62.

Velocities of Change: Critical Essays from MLN, edited by Richard Macksey. *Books Abroad* 49 (1975): 189–90.

Voltaire. Candide. Etude quantitative, by Pierre R. and Marie-Paule Ducretet. *Eighteenth-Century Studies* 8 (1975): 355–60.

Literary Landmarks: Essays on the Theory and Practice of Literature, by Francis Fergusson. *Books Abroad* 50 (1976): 961–62.

Lost Illusions: Paul Léautaud and His World, by James Harding. *Books Abroad* 50 (1976): 115.

The Oaten Flute: Essays on Pastoral Poetry and the Pastoral Ideal, by Renato Poggiolo. *Books Abroad* 50 (1976): 485.

The Oldest Revolutionary: Essays on Benjamin Franklin, by J. A. Leo Lemay. *Early American Literature* 11 (1976): 216–19.

The Private Franklin. The Man and His Family, by Claude-Anne Lopez and Eugenia W. Herbert. *New England Quarterly* 49 (1976): 295–97.

The Shape of the Puritan Mind: The Thought of Samuel Willard, by Ernest Benson Lowrie. *American Historical Review* 81 (1976): 651–52.

Univers parallèles II: Le point aveugle. Poésie roman, by Jean Paris. *Books Abroad* 50 (1976): 726.

American and French Culture, by Henry Blumenthal. *American Literature* 48 (1977): 120–22.

Sacred Discontent: The Bible and Western Tradition, by Herbert N. Schneidau. *World Literature Today* 51 (1977): 508.

American Literature, 1764–1789, edited by Everett Emerson. *Eighteenth-Century Studies* 11 (1978): 386–89.

The Cosmopolitan Ideal in Enlightenment Thought: Its Form and Function in the Ideas of Franklin, Hume and Voltaire, by Thomas J. Schlereth. *William and Mary Quarterly* 35 (1978): 578–80.

The Thomas Paine Collection of Richard Gimbel in the Library of the American Philosophical Society, compiled by Hildegard Stephans. *Studies in Burke and His Time* 19 (1978): 261–64.

Jonathan Boucher: Loyalist in Exile, by Anne Y. Zimmer. *Early American Literature* 14 (1979): 132–33.

La littérature et ses technocraties, by Georges Mounin. *World Literature Today* 53 (1979): 563.

The Secular Scripture: A Study of the Structure of Romance, by Northrop Frye. *World Literature Today* 53 (1979): 167.

Eighteenth-Century Spanish Literature, by R. Merritt Cox. *The Eighteenth Century: A Current Bibliography*, n.s., 5 (1980): 308.

Voltaire und Deutschland, edited by Peter Brockmeier, Roland Desne, and Jürgen Voss. *Yearbook of Comparative and General Literature* 28 (1980): 63–67.

Kazantzakis: The Politics of Salvation, by James F. Lea. *Clio* 10 (1981): 338–40.

Third Earl of Shaftesbury: Standard Edition. Complete Works. Vol. 1, edited by Gerd Hemmerich and Wolfram Benda. *Arcadia* 18 (1981): 324–28.

Proceedings of the 9th Congress of the International Comparative Literature Association 1980. In *Yearbook of Comparative and General Literature* 31 (1982): 134–36.

Jonathan Edward's Moral Thought and Its British Context, by Norman Fiering. *Eighteenth-Century Studies* 17 (1983): 89–92.

Voltaire et les grands, by Jean Sareil. *Revue Belge de Philologie et d'Histoire* 60 (1983): 3.

The Religious Life of Thomas Jefferson, by Charles B. Sanford. *American Literature* 56 (1985): 329–30.

The Third Earl of Shaftesbury, 1671–1713, by Robert Voitle. *Eighteenth-Century Studies* 19 (1985): 257–59.

Works Cited

Adams, M. Ray. 1968. "Joel Barlow, Political Romanticist." In *Studies in the Literary Backgrounds of English Radicalism, with Special Reference to the French Revolution.* New York: Greenwood Press.

Adams, Percy. 1962. *Travelers and Travel Liars 1660–1800.* Berkeley and Los Angeles: University of California Press.

Aesop. 1668. *The Fables of Aesop. Paraphrased in Verse,* by John Ogilby. Edited by Earl Miner. Los Angeles: William Andrews Clark Memorial Library.

Aldridge, Alfred Owen. 1949. "Benjamin Franklin and the *Maryland Gazette.*" 44: 177–89.

———. 1950. "Franklin's Deistical Indians." *Proceedings of the American Philosophical Society* 94: 398–410.

———. 1951. *Shaftesbury and the Deist Manifesto.* Philadelphia: American Philosophical Society (*Transactions,* n.s., 41, pt. 2).

———. 1959. *Man of Reason: The Life of Thomas Paine.* Philadelphia: J. B. Lippincott.

———. 1972. "Polly Baker and Boccaccio." *Annali dell'instituto universitario orientale, Seizione Romanza* 14: 5–18.

———. 1976. "The Concept of Ancients and Moderns in American Poetry of the Federal Period." In *Classical Traditions in Early America,* edited by John W. Eadie, 99–118. Ann Arbor: Center for Ancient and Modern Studies.

———. 1982. *Early American Literature: A Comparatist Approach.* Princeton: Princeton University Press.

———. 1984. *Thomas Paine's American Ideology.* Newark: University of Delaware Press.

Allen, Don Cameron. 1964. *Doubt's Boundless Sea: Skepticism and Faith in the Renaissance.* Baltimore: Johns Hopkins University Press.

Allison, C. F. 1966. *The Rise of Moralism: The Proclamation of the Gospel from Hooker to Baxter.* London: Society for Promoting Christian Knowledge.

Ames, Nathaniel. 1737. *An Astronomical Diary, or, an Almanack for . . . 1738.* Boston: Draper.

Aquinas, St. Thomas. 1948. *Introduction to Saint Thomas Aquinas.* Edited by Anton C. Pegis. New York: Modern Library.

Armstrong, Brian G. 1969. *Calvinism and the Amyraut Heresy: Protestant and Scholasticism and Humanism in Seventeenth-Century France.* Madison: University of Wisconsin Press.

Arner, Robert D. 1972. "The Smooth and Emblematic Song: Joel Barlow's *The Hasty Pudding.*" *Early American Literature* 7: 76–91.

———. 1976. "The Quest for Freedom: Style and Meaning in Robert Beverley's *History of Virginia.*" *Southern Literature Journal* 8, 2: 79–98.

Arnold, Matthew. 1962. *Lectures and Essays in Criticism*. Edited by R. H. Super. Ann Arbor: University of Michigan Press.

Ascham, Roger. [1563–68]. *The Scholemaster*. Edited by Edward Arber. Edinburgh: Muir & Paterson, 1870.

Atterbury, Francis. 1711. *A Representation of the Present State of Religion, with Regard to the excessive Growth of Infidelity . . . as it passed the Lower House of Convocation of the province of Canterbury*. London: J. Morphew.

Baine, Rodney. 1968. *Defoe and the Supernatural*. Athens: University of Georgia Press.

Balguy, John. 1719a. *Silvius's Defense of a Dialogue between a Papist and a Protestant*. London.

———. 1719b. *Silvius's Letter to the Reverend Dr. Sherlock*. London.

Ball, Kenneth R. 1967. "A Great Society: The Social and Political Thought of Joel Barlow." Ph.D. diss., University of Wisconsin.

———. 1969. "Joel Barlow's 'Canal' and Natural Religion." *Eighteenth-Century Studies* 2:225–39.

———. 1970. "American Nationalism and Esthetics in Joel Barlow's Unpublished 'Diary—1788.'" *Tennessee Studies in Literature* 15:49–60.

Barlow, Joel. 1792, 1795. *Advice to the Privileged Orders in the Several States of Europe, Resulting from the Necessity and Propriety of a General Revolution in the Principle of Government*. Edited by David B. Davis. Ithaca, N.Y.: Cornell University Press, 1956.

———. 1970. *The Works of Joel Barlow*. Edited by William K. Bottorff and Arthur L. Ford. 2 vols. Gainesville, Fla.: Scholars' Facsimiles and Reprints.

Barnard, F. M. 1971. "The Practical Philosophy of Christian Thomasius." *Journal of the History of Ideas* 32:221–46.

Barrell, Ruth Green. "To Clio." John Barrell Letterbook. New York Historical Society, Manuscript Collection, New York, N.Y.

Basnage, Jacques. 1706–7. *Histore des Juifs*. 5 vols. Rotterdam; and 1708. *The History of the Jews*. Translated by Thomas Taylor. London: J. Beaver and B. Lintot.

Bassett, John S., ed. 1901. *The Writings of Colonel William Byrd of Westover*. New York: Doubleday.

Bedford, R. D. 1979. *The Defence of Truth*. Manchester: Manchester University Press.

Berkeley, George. 1948–57. *The Works of George Berkeley, Bishop of Cloyne*. Edited by A. A. Luce and T. E. Jessop. 9 volumes. London: Nelson.

Berkhofer, Robert F., Jr. 1978. *The White Man's Indian: Images of the American Indian from Columbus to the Present*. New York: Knopf.

Berman, David. 1975a. "Anthony Collins and the Question of Atheism in the Early Part of the Eighteenth Century." *Proceedings of the Royal Irish Academy* 75:85–102.

———. 1975b. "Anthony Collins: Aspects of His Thought and Writings." *Hermathena* 119:49–70.

———. 1975c. "Anthony Collins' Essays in the *Independent Whig*." *Journal of the History of Philosophy* 13:463–69.

———. 1978. "The Genesis of Avowed Atheism in Britain." *Question* 2:44–55.

———. 1983. "David Hume and the Suppression of Atheism." *Journal of the History of Philosophy* 21:375–87.

———. 1984. "J. M. Robertson: Freethinker and Historian of Freethought." *New Humanist* 99:12–16.

———. 1985. "Tindal" and "Toland." *The Encyclopedia of Unbelief*. New York: Prometheus Press.

Berriman, William, 1733. *The Gradual Revelation of the Gospel . . . preached . . . at the lecture founded by the Honourable Robert Boyle esq.; in the years 1730, 1731, and 1732*. 2 vols. London: Ward and Wicksteed.

Betts, C. J. 1984. *Early Deism in France*. The Hague: Martinus Nijhoff.

Beverley, Robert. 1704. *A Ballad addres'd to the Reverend Members of the Convocation, held at Man's Ordinary at Williamsburg in Virginia; to defend G[overno]r N[icholso]n, And Form an Accusation against C[ommissary] B[lair]*. London.

———. 1705. *The History and Present State of Virginia*. Edited by Louis B. Wright. Chapel Hill: University of North Carolina Press, 1947.

Biddle, John. 1976. "Locke's Critique of Innate Principles and Toland's Deism." *Journal of the History of Ideas* 37:411–22.

Bigelow, John, ed. 1887–88. *The Complete Works of Benjamin Franklin*. 10 vols. New York: Putnam's.

Billington, James H. 1980. *Fire in the Minds of Men: Origins of the Revolutionary Faith*. New York: Basic Books.

Bjorck, Tobias Eric. 1943. *The Planting of the Swedish Church in America*. Translated and edited by Ira Oliver Nothstein. Rock Island, Ill.: Augustana College Library.

Blake, William. 1970. *The Poetry and Prose of William Blake*. Edited by David V. Erdman. Rev. ed. New York: Doubleday.

Blau, Joseph L. 1949. "Joel Barlow, Enlightened Religionist." *Journal of the History of Ideas* 10:430–44.

Blount, Charles. 1679. *Anima Mundi or an Historical Narration of the Opinions of the Ancients concerning Man's Soul*. London: William Cademan.

———. 1680a. *Great is DIANA of the Ephesians: or the Original of IDOLATRY*. London.

———. 1680b. *The Two First Books of Philostratus, Concerning the Life of Apollonius Tyaneus*. London: N. Thompson.

———. 1683. *Religio Laici Written in a Letter to John Dryden, Esq*. London: R. Bentley and S. Magnes.

———. [1686.] *A Summary Account of the Deists Religion*. [London.]

———. 1693. *Oracles of Reason*. Edited by Charles Gildon. London.

———. 1695. *Miscellaneous Works*. Edited by Charles Gildon. London.

Blount, Sir Henry. 1636. *A Voyage into the Levant*. London: Andrew Crooke.

Bonner, Hypatia. 1943. *Penalties upon Opinion*. London: Watts.

Boswell, James. 1971. *Boswell in Extremes 1776–1778*. Edited by Charles McC. Weis and Frederick A. Pottle. London: Heinemann.

Boudinot, Elias. 1801. *The Age of Revelation, or the Age of Reason shewn to be an Age of Infidelity*. Philadelphia: Asbury Dickens.

———. 1815. *The Second Advent, or Coming of the Messiah in Glory, shown to be a Scripture doctrine, and taught by divine revelation, from the beginning of the world*. Trenton, N.J.

———. 1816. *A Star in the West, or A Humble Attempt to discover the Long Lost Tribes of Israel, preparatory to their return to their beloved city, Jerusalem*. Trenton: D. Fenton, S. Hutchinson, and J. Dunham.

Boyd, George Adams. 1952. *Elias Boudinot, Patriot and Statesman, 1740–1821*. Princeton: Princeton University Press.

Boyle Lectures. 1739. *A Defence of Natural and Revealed Religion Being a Collection of the Sermons . . . 1691 . . . 1732*. Edited by Sampson Letsome and John Nickoll. London: D. Midwinter.

Boynton, Percy H. 1939. "Joel Barlow Advises the Privileged Orders." *New England Quarterly* 12:477–99.

Bredvold, Louis I. 1956. *The Intellectual Milieu of John Dryden: Studies in Some Aspects of the Seventeenth-Century Thought.* Ann Arbor: University of Michigan Press.

Briggs, Samuel. 1891. *The Essays, Humor, and Poems of Nathaniel Ames.* Cleveland: Privately printed.

Brockwell, Charles. 1750. *Brotherly Love Recommended in a Sermon Preached before the Ancient and Honourable Society of Free and Accepted Masons.* Boston: J. Draper.

Brooks, Richard. 1976. "The Relationships between Natural Philosophy, Natural Theology and Revealed Religion in the Thought of Newton and Their Historiographic Relevance." Ph.D. diss., Northwestern University.

———. 1978. "Newton, Newtonianism and Deism: Some Distinctions." Paper read at the annual ASECS meeting, Chicago.

Bunyan, John. 1678. *Pilgrim's Progress.* Edited by J. B. Wharey, rev. ed. by Roger Sharrock. Oxford: Oxford University Press, 1960.

Burdy, Samuel. 1792. *The Life of Philip Skelton.* Oxford: Clarendon Press, 1914.

Burke, Edmund. 1790. *Reflections on the Revolution in France and on the Proceedings in Certain Societies in London Relative to that Event (1790).* Edited by Conor Cruise O'Brien. London: Penguin, 1969.

———. 1958–70. *The Correspondence of Edmund Burke.* General editor Thomas Copeland. 9 vols. Chicago: University of Chicago Press.

Burton, Robert. 1621. *The Anatomy of Melancholy.* Edited by Floyd Dell and Paul Jordan-Smith. New York: Tudor Publishing Co., 1938.

Busson, Henri. 1957. *Les Sources et le développement du rationalisme dans la littérature française de la renaissance, 1533–1601.* Paris: Letouzey.

Calvin, John. 1962. *Institutes of the Christian Religion.* Translated by Henry Beveridge. 2 vols. London: James Clarke & Co.

Cantor, Milton. 1957. "The Life of Joel Barlow." Ph.D. diss., Columbia University.

The Century Dictionary and Cyclopedia. 1906. 10 vols. New York: Century.

Carabelli, Giancarlo. 1975. *Tolandiana: materiali bibliografici per lo studio dell' opera e della fortuna di John Toland (1670–1711).* 3 vols. Florence: La nuova Italia.

———. 1978., "Tolandiana . . . Errata, addenda e indici." *Pubblicazoni della Facolta di Magistero dell' universitá de Ferrara,* vol. 4. Ferrara: Universitá de Ferrara.

Carlile, Richard. 1819. "Letter of 24 November 1819." *The Republican* 1, no. 15 (3 December).

Carroll, Robert Todd. 1975. *The Common-Sense Philosophy of Religion of Bishop Edward Stillingfleet, 1635–1699.* The Hague: Martinus Nijhoff.

Cassara, Ernest. 1975. *The Enlightenment in America.* Boston: Twayne.

Cassirer, Ernst. 1951. *The Philosophy of the Enlightenment.* Translated by Fritz C. A. Koelln and James P. Pettegrove. Boston: Beacon Press, 1966.

Charbonnel, J. R. 1919. *La Pensée Italienne au XVIe siècle.* Paris: E. Champion.

Chillingworth, William. 1840. *The Works of William Chillingworth.* Philadelphia: Herman Hooker.

Chinard, Gilbert. 1911. *L'exotisme Américain dans la littérature française au XVIe siècle.* Geneva: Slatkine Reprints, 1970.

———, ed. 1931. *Dialogues Curieux entre l'Auteur et un Sauvage de Bon Sens qui a voyagé et Mémoires de l'Amerique Septentrionale,* by Louis-Armand de Lom D'Arce, Baron de Lahontan. Baltimore, Md.: Johns Hopkins Press.

———. 1934. *L'Ámerique et le Rêve Exotique dans la Littérature Française au XVIIe et au XVIIIe siècle.* Paris: E. Droz.

Christensen, Merton A. 1956. "Deism in Joel Barlow's Early Work: Heterodox Passages in *The Vision of Columbus.*" *American Literature* 7: 509–20.

Clarke, Samuel. 1716. *A Discourse Concerning the Unchangable Obligations of Religion.* 4th ed. London: J. Knapton.

Clayton, Robert. 1749. *Dissertation on Prophecy wherein the coherence and connexion of the Prophecies in both the Old Testament are fully considered.* London: J. Watts.

Clayton-Torrence, William. 1908. *A Trial Biography of Colonial Virginia.* Richmond: Virginia State Library.

Cobban, Alfred, and Robert A. Smith. 1967. Introduction to *The Correspondence of Edmund Burke.* Vol. 6. Chicago: University of Chicago Press.

Colie, Rosalie, 1957. *Light and Enlightenment: A Study of the Cambridge Platonists and the Dutch Arminians.* Cambridge: Cambridge University Press.

———. 1959. "Spinoza and the Early English Deists." *Journal of the History of Ideas* 20: 23–46.

———. 1963. "Spinoza in England, 1665–1730." *Proceedings of the American Philosophical Society* 107, no. 3: 183–219.

Collins, Anthony. 1707a. *Letter to the learned Mr. Henry Dodwell, containing some remarks on a (pretended) Demonstration of the immateriality and natural immortality of the Soul.* London: A. Baldwin.

———. 1707b. *A Reply to Mr. Clark's Defence of his letter to Mr. Dodwell.* London.

———. 1713. *A Discourse of Free-Thinking.* London [Holland?].

———. 1724. *A Discourse of the Grounds and Reasons of the Christian Religion.* London.

———. 1726. *The Scheme of Literal Prophecy Considered: in a View of the Controversy Occasioned by a Late Book, Intitled, A Discourse of the Grounds and Reasons of the Christian Religion.* London: Printed . . . by T. J.

———. 1729. *A Discourse concerning Ridicule and Irony in Writing.* London: J. Brotherton.

Commager, Henry Steele. 1977. *The Empire of Reason: How Europe Imagined and America Realized the Enlightenment.* Garden City, N.Y.: Anchor Press.

Conway, Moncure Daniel. 1900. *Thomas Paine (1737–1809) et la Révolution dans les Deux Mondes.* Paris: Plon-Nourrit.

Cremin, Lawrence A. 1970. *American Education: The Colonial Experience 1607–1783.* New York: Harper & Row.

Crocker, Lester G. 1974. *Diderot's Chaotic Order: Approach to Synthesis.* Princeton: Princeton University Press.

Curran, Stuart. 1986. *Poetic Form and British Romanticism.* New York: Oxford University Press.

Dahm, John J. 1970. "Science and Apologetics in the Early Boyle Lecturers." *Church History* 39: 172–86.

Darnton, Robert. 1982. *The Literary Underground of the Old Regime.* Cambridge: Harvard University Press.

Davis, Richard Beale. 1978. *Intellectual Life in the Colonial South 1585–1763.* 3 vols. Knoxville: University of Tennessee Press.

Defoe, Daniel. 1700. *The True-Born Englishman.* [London, 1700/1.]

———. 1703–5. *An Enquiry into Occasional Conformity, Shewing that the Dissenters Are in No Way Concern'd in it.* In *A True Collection of the Writings of the Author of the True Born English-man.* 2 vols. London.

———. 1705. *The Consolidator: Or, Memoirs*. London: B. Bragg.
———. 1712. *The Present State of the Parties in Great Britain*. London: J. Baker.
———. 1718. *Some Remarks upon the Late Differences among the Dissenting Ministers and Preachers*. London.
———. 1719. *The Farther Adventures of Robinson Crusoe*. London: W. Taylor.
———. 1721. *The Fortunes and Misfortunes of the Famous Moll Flanders*. London: W. Chetwood, [1722].
———. 1723. *The History and Remarkable Life of . . . Col. Jacque, Commonly Call'd Col. Jack*. London: J. Brotherton et al., [1722].
———. [1724.] *The Fortunate Mistress: Or, . . . the Lady Roxana*. London: T. Warner et al.
———. 1724–28. *A General History Of . . . Pyrates*. "By Captain Charles Johnson." 2 vols. London: Rivington et al.
———. 1726a. *An Essay on the Original of Literature*. London.
———. 1726b. *Mere Nature Delineated*. London: T. Warner.
———. 1726c. *The Political History of the Devil*. See 1727b, *The History of the Devil*.
———. 1727a. *An Essay on the History and Reality of Apparitions*. London: J. Roberts.
———. 1727b. *The History of the Devil*. 2d ed. London: T. Warner.
———. 1727c. *A System of Magick*. London: J. Roberts.
———. 1729. *Madagascar: Or, Robert Drury's Journal*. London: W. Meadows et al.
———. 1724. *A New Voyage round the World*. In *Romances and Narratives*, edited by George Aitken. London: Dent, 1895.
———. 1938. *Review*, 1704–13. Edited by Arthur W. Secord. 22 vols. New York: Facsimile Text Society.
Diderot, Denis, et al., eds. 1751–65. *Encyclopédie*. Paris: Briasson.
———. 1875–77. *Oeuvres complètes*. Edited by J. Assezat and Maurice Tourneux. 20 vols. Paris: Garnier.
Diket, A. L. 1966. "The Noble Savage Convention as Epitomized in John Lawson's *A New Voyage to Carolina*." *North Carolina Historical Review* 43:413–29.
Dryden, John. 1956–. *The Works of John Dryden*. Edited by E. N. Hooker; H. T. Swedenberg; and Alan Roper. Berkeley and Los Angeles: University of California Press.
Dunn, John. 1969. "The Politics of Locke in England and America in the Eighteenth Century." In *John Locke: Problems and Perspectives*, edited by John W. Yolton, 45–80. Cambridge: Cambridge University Press.
Dupuis, Charles François. 1781. *Mémoire sur l'origine des constellations et sur l'explication de la fable par le moyen de'astronomie*. Paris: Desaint.
Durden, Robert F. 1951. "Joel Barlow in the French Revolution." *William and Mary Quarterly*, 3d ser., 8:327–54.
Ehrenpreis, Irvin. 1962–82. *Swift: The Man, His Works, and the Age*. 3 vols. Cambridge: Harvard University Press.
Ellis, Frank. 1985. "Defoe's 'Resignation' and the Limitation of 'Mathematical Plainness.'" *Review of English Studies* n.s., 36:338–54.
Ellul, Jacques. 1965. *Propaganda: The Formation of Men's Attitudes*. Translated by Konrad Kellen and Jean Lerner. New York: Knopf.
Emerson, Roger L. 1968. "Heresy, the Social Order and English Deism." *Church History* 37:1–15.
Engell, James. 1981. *The Creative Imagination: Enlightenment to Romanticism*. Cambridge: Harvard University Press.

Ensor, George. 1801. *The Principles of Morality*. London: J. S. Jordan.
Erdman, David V. 1954. "Blake's Debt to Joel Barlow." *American Literature* 26: 94–98.
———. 1969. *Blake: Prophet Against Empire*. Rev. ed. Princeton: Princeton University Press.
Estienne, Henri. 1566. *Apologie pour Hérodote*. Paris.
Ewan, Joseph, and Nesta Ewan. 1970. *John Banister and His Natural History of Virginia 1678–1692*. Urbana: University of Illinois Press.
Fairchild, Hoaxie Neale. 1928. *The Noble Savage: A Study in Romantic Naturalism*. New York: Russell & Russell, [1955?].
Febvre, Lucien. 1942. *Le problème de l'incroyance au XVIᵉ siècle*. Paris: A. Michel.
Feest, Christian F. 1978. "Virginia Algonquians." In *Handbook of North American Indians*, edited by William C. Sturtevant; vol. 15, *Northeast*, edited by Bruce G. Trigger. Washington, D.C.: Smithsonian Institution.
Fennessy, R. R. 1963. *Burke, Paine, and the Rights of Man: A Difference of Political Opinion*. The Hague: Martinus Nijhoff.
Fiering, Norman. 1981. "The First American Enlightenment: Tillotson, Leverett, and Philosophical Anglicanism." *New England Quarterly* 54: 307–44.
Flannery, Regina. 1939. *An Analysis of Coastal Algonquian Culture*. Washington, D.C.: Catholic University of America Press.
Florida, R. E. 1974. "Voltaire and the Socinians." *Studies on Voltaire and the Eighteenth Century* 122: 1–275.
Foigny, Gabriel de. 1693. *A New Discovery of Terra Incognita Australis, or the Southern World. By James Sadeur, a French-man*. London: J. Dunton.
Foster, James. 1731. *The Usefulness, Truth and Excellency of the Christian Revelation defended against . . . Christianity as old as Creation*. London: J. Noon.
Frantz, R[ay] W[illiam]. 1934. *The English Traveller and the Movement of Ideas, 1660–1723. University Studies, vols. 32–33*. Lincoln: University of Nebraska.
Freemasons. 1736. News report concerning prohibitions against Masonic meetings in Amsterdam. *Boston Evening-Post*, no. 37 (26 April).
———. 1737. News report concerning anxiety caused by formation of a lodge in Paris. *Boston Gazette*, no. 902 (25 April).
———. 1743. News report concerning attempt to suppress lodge in Vienna. *Boston Evening-Post*, no. 411 (20 June).
———. *See also* "Scald Miserable Masons."
Free Thoughts on Mr. Woolston . . . To Which is Prefixed, A Catalogue of all the Books that have been wrote, pro and con, in the Woolstonian Controversy. 1730. 2d ed. London.
Fréret, Nicholas. 1758. *Défense de la chronologie fondée sur les monuments de l'histoire ancienne, contre le système chronologique de M. Newton*. Paris: Durand.
Gale, Theophilus. 1672–76. *The Court of the Gentiles*. 2 vols. 2d ed. London: T. Gilbert.
Garrett, Clarke. 1975. *Respectable Folly: Millenarians and the French Revolution in France and England*. Baltimore: Johns Hopkins University Press.
Gawlick, Günter. 1967. "Abraham's sacrifice of Isaac viewed by the English Deists." *Studies on Voltaire and the Eighteenth Century* 56: 577–600.
———. 1976. "The English Deists' Contribution to the Theory of Toleration." *Studies on Voltaire and the Eighteenth Century* 152: 823–35.
———. 1977. "Hume and the Deists: A Reconsideration." In *David Hume: Bicentenary Papers*, edited by G. P. Morice. Austin: University of Texas Press.
Gay, Peter. 1968. *Deism: An Anthology*. Princeton, N.J.: D. Van Nostrand Co.

———. 1973. *The Enlightenment: An Interpretation.* Vol. 1: *The Rise of Modern Paganism.* London: Wildwood House.

Gibbs, G. C. 1984. "The Radical Enlightenment." *British Journal for the History of Science* 17:67–81.

Gifford, William, trans. 1802. *The Satires of Decimus Junius Juvenalis.* London: G. and W. Nicol.

Gildon, Charles. 1705. *The Deist's Manual: or, A Rational Enquiry into the Christian Religion.* London: A. Roper, F. Coggan, and G. Strahan.

———. 1720. *Miscellanea Aurea: or Golden Medley.* [Ascribed to Thomas Killigrew.] London: A. Bettesworth.

Gordon, John. 1750. *Brotherly Love Explain'd and Enforc'd.* Annapolis, Md.: Jonas Green.

Granger, Bruce I. 1960. *Political Satire in the American Revolution, 1763–1783.* Ithaca, N.Y.: Cornell University Press.

Green, Joseph. [B.B.; Clio, pseud.] 1733. "The Poet's Lamentation for the Loss of his Cat, which he used to call his Muse." *London Magazine* 1 (November):579. Lemay, 1972a, no. 280.

———. [1750a.] *Entertainment for a Winter's Evening.* Boston: G. Rogers. American Antiquarian Society copy.

———. [1750b.] *A Mournful Lamentation for the Sad and Deplorable Death of Mr. Old Tenor.* Broadside. Boston.

———. 1750c. "To the POET in the Post Boy, in his own Style." *Boston Gazette* no. 1585 (31 July). Lemay, 1972a, no. 976: Lemay attribution.

———. 1750d. "To V. D." *Boston Post Boy* no. 816 (30 July). Lemay, 1972a, no. 975; incorrect attribution to H———k; Shields attribution.

———. 1751a. "Mr. Vini Doctor." *Boston News-Letter* no. 5346 (24 January). Lemay, 1972a, no. 997; Lemay incorrectly identifies "Vini Doctor" as Joseph Green. Shields attribution.

———. 1751b. "An ADDRESS to The MASONS at HALIFAX." *Boston News-Letter,* 22 August. Lemay, 1972a, no. 1041; Shields attribution.

———. 1755. *The Grand ARCANUM Detected: Or, A Wonderful Phoenomenon Explained, Which has baffled the Scrutiny of many Ages.* [Boston].

———. [1766.] *An Eclogue Sacred to the Memory of . . . Jonathan Mayhew.* Boston: Fleets.

———. 1792. "A True and exact account of the celebration of the Festival of St. John the Baptist, by the Ancient and Honourable Society of Free and Accepted Masons, at Boston in New-England, on June the 16th, 1739." *American Apollo* 1, no. 24 (22 June): 281.

———. "The Answer To the Writer of the Late Verses; whether *Man Woman or Hermaphradite.*" John Barrell Letterbook. New York Historical Society, Manuscript Collection, New York, N.Y.

———. "The Disappointed Cooper." Thomas Pemberton Poetry Notebook. Massachusetts Historical Society Manuscript Collection, Boston.

———. "Inscription under Rev. Jn. Checkly's Picture." Ezra Stiles Miscellanies. Yale University Library Manuscript Collection, New Haven. Also in Thomas Collins Notebook, American Antiquarian Society, Worcester, Mass.

———. "To V. D. Apologia." Smith-Carter Manuscripts. Massachusetts Historical Society Manuscript Collections, Boston.

Greene, Robert A. 1981. "Whichcote, Wilkins, 'Ingenuity,' and the Reasonableness of Christianity." *Journal of the History of Ideas* 42:227–52.

WORKS CITED

Greenly, A. H. 1954. "Lahontan: An Essay and Bibliography." *Papers of the Bibliographical Society of America* 48: 334–89.

Grotius, Hugo. 1815. *The Truth of the Christian Religion*. Edited by Jean Le Clerc and translated by John Clarke. 14th ed. Oxford: Law and Whattaker.

Hahn, Thomas, ed. 1981. *Upright Lives: Documents Concerning the Natural Virtue and Wisdom of the Indians (1650–1740)*. Augustan Reprint Society, nos. 209–10. Los Angeles: William Andrews Clark Memorial Library.

Hall, Max. 1960. *Benjamin Franklin and Polly Baker*. Williamsburg, Va.: The Institute of Early American History and Culture.

Hamilton, Dr. Alexander. *The History of the Tuesday Club*. Manuscript, John Work Garrett Library of The Johns Hopkins University, Baltimore, Md.

Hammock, John [V. D.; Vini Doctor; Bacchus, pseud.]. 1750. "Dream." *The Boston Evening-Post* no. 767 (23 April). Lemay, 1972a, no. 969; Green incorrectly identified as author.

―――. 1751. "To Mr: Clio, at North-Hampton. In Defence of Masonry."*Boston Evening-Post*, 9 January. MS copy in American Antiquarian Society copy of Joseph Green, *Entertainment for a Winter's Evening*. Boston: G. Rogers, [1750]. Lemay, 1972a, no. 990; incorrect suggestion of Green authorship.

―――. 1754. "On some fine Peach-Trees being kill'd by the late cold Easterly winds." *Boston Evening-Post* no. 978 (27 May). Lemay, 1972a, no. 1187; Green incorrectly identified as author.

―――. 1755. "On the present EXPEDITION." *Boston Evening-Post* no. 1028 (12 May). Lemay, 1972a, no. 1255; Green incorrectly identified as author.

―――. "Tale." 1762. *Boston Evening-Post* no. 1379 (1 February). Lemay, 1972a, no. 1850; Shields attribution.

Hammon, William. *See* Turner.

Hampshire, Stuart. 1951. *Spinoza*. London: Faber and Faber, 1956.

Hariot, Thomas. 1590. *Brief and True Report of the New Found Land of Virginia*. Edited by Paul Hutton. New York: Dover, 1972.

Harth, Phillip. 1961. *Swift and Anglican Rationalism: The Religious Background of A Tale of a Tub*. Chicago: University of Chicago Press.

―――. 1968. *Contexts of Dryden's Thought*. Chicago: University of Chicago Press.

Hayne, David M. 1966–. "Lom D'Arce de Lahontan, Louis-Armand de." In *Dictionary of Canadian Biography*, edited by Hayne, 2:439–45. Toronto: University of Toronto Press.

Head, Richard. 1961. *The English Rogue*. Edited by Michael Shinagel. Boston: New Frontiers Press.

Hoadley, Benjamin, Bishop of Bangor. 1713. *Queries Recommended to the Authors of a late Discourse of Freethinking*. London: James Knapton.

―――. 1716. *A Preservative against the Principles and Practices of the Nonjurors*. London.

―――. 1773. *The Nature of the Kingdom, or Church of Christ*. In *Works*, vol. 2. London.

Holberg, Ludvig. 1955. *Select Essays*. Translated by P. M. Mitchell. Lawrence: University of Kansas Press.

―――. 1970. *Ludvig Holberg's Memoirs*. Edited by Stewart E. Fraser. Leiden: E. J. Brill.

Holmes, Geoffrey. 1978. "Science, Reason, and the Religion in the Age of Newton." *British Journal for the History of Science* 11: 164–71.

Hornberger, Theodore. 1950. "The Enlightenment and the American Dream." In *The American Writer and the European Tradition*, edited by Margaret Denny and William H. Gilman, 16–28. Minneapolis: University of Minnesota Press.

Howard, John. 1984. *Infernal Poetics: Poetic Structures in Blake's Lambeth Prophecies.* Rutherford, N.J.: Fairleigh Dickinson University Press.

Howard, Leon. 1943. *The Connecticut Wits.* Chicago: University of Chicago Press.

Howell, T[homas] B[ailey], and Thomas Jones. 1809–26. *[Cobbett's] A Complete Collection of State Trials and Proceedings for High Treason and Other Crimes.* 33 vols. London: T. C. Hansard for Longman, Hurst, Rees, Orme & Co.

Hulton, Paul Hope. 1979. "Images of the New World." In *The Westward Enterprise: English Activities in Ireland, the Atlantic, and America 1480–1650,* edited by K. R. Andrews et al., 195–214. Detroit, Mich.: Wayne State University Press.

Hulton, Paul Hope, and David Beers Quinn. 1964. *The American Drawings of John White.* 2 vols. London: British Museum.

Hume, David. 1875. *The Philosophical Works of David Hume.* Edited by T. H. Green and T. H. Grose. 2 vols. London: Longmans, Green.

———. 1932. *Letters of David Hume.* Edited by J. Y. T. Greig. 9 vols. Oxford: Oxford University Press.

Hutcheson, Francis. 1728. *Illustrations in the Moral Sense.* London: John Smith and William Bruce.

———. 1788. "Letter to William Mace, 6 Sept. 1717." *European Magazine,* September, 158–60; partly reprinted in David Berman. 1974. "Hutcheson on Berkeley and the Molyneux Problem." *Proceedings of the Royal Irish Academy.* 74:259–65.

Hyde, Edward, Earl of Clarendon. 1727. *Contemplations and Reflections upon the Psalms of David.* In *A Collection of Several Tracts of the Right Honourable Edward, Earl of Clarendon.* London: Woodward.

Jacob, Margaret. 1976. *The Newtonians and the English Revolution 1689–1720.* Ithaca, N.Y.: Cornell University Press.

———. 1981. *The Radical Enlightenment: Pantheists, Freemasons and Republicans.* London: George Allen & Unwin.

Joost, Nicholas. 1951. "'Plain-Dealer' and *Free-Thinker*: A Revaluation." *American Literature* 23:31–37.

———. 1952. "William Parks, Benjamin Franklin, and a Problem in Colonial Deism." *Mid-America* 34:3–13.

Kammen, Michael. 1979. "In Pursuit of an Enlightenment Past." *History of Education Quarterly* 17:351–60.

Keen, Benjamin. 1971. *Aztec Image in Western Thought.* New Brunswick, N.J.: Rutgers University Press.

Kocher, P. H. 1953. *Science and Religion in Elizabethan England.* San Marino, Calif: Huntington Library.

Kroiter, Harry P. 1960. "Cowper, Deism, and the Divinization of Nature." *Journal of the History of Ideas* 21:511–26.

Labaree, Leonard W., et al., eds. 1959–. *The Papers of Benjamin Franklin.* New Haven: Yale University Press.

Lachèvre, Frédéric. 1909–24. *Le Libertinage au XVIIIe siècle.* 11 vols. in 13. Paris: H. Champion. Reprint. Geneva: Slatkin Reprints, 1968.

Lahonton, Louis-Armand de Lom D'Arce, Baron de. 1703, *New Voyages to North America.* Edited by Reuben Gold Thwaites. 2 vols. Chicago: McClerg & Co., 1905.

Law, William. 1753. *Three Letters to the Bishop of Bangor.* 9th ed. London.

Lawson, John. 1967. *A New Voyage to Carolina.* Edited by Hugh Talmage Lefler. Chapel Hill: University of North Carolina Press.

Leary, Lewis. 1949. "Joel Barlow and William Hayley: A Correspondence." *American Literature* 21:325–34.

Lee, William. 1869. *Defoe: His Life and Recently Discovered Writings*. 3 vols. London.
Leland, John. 1754. *View of the Principal Deistical Writers that have appeared in England*. London: B. Dodd.
Lemay, J. A. Leo. 1972a. *A Calendar of American Poetry in the Colonial Newspapers and Magazine and in the Major English Magazines Through 1765*. Worcester, Mass.: American Antiquarian Society.
———. 1972b. *Men of Letters in Colonial Maryland*. Knoxville: University of Tennessee Press.
———. 1974. "Joseph Green's Satirical Poem on the Great Awakening." *Resources for American Literary Study* 4: 173–83,
———. 1976. "The Text, Rhetorical Strategies and Themes of 'The Speech of Miss Polly Baker.' " In *The Oldest Revolutionary: Essays on Benjamin Franklin*, edited by Lemay, 91–120. Philadelphia: University of Pennsylvania Press.
———. 1979. "The Frontiersman from Lout to Hero." *Proceedings of the American Antiquarian Society* 88: 187–224.
———. 1982. "The Contexts and Themes of 'The Hasty Pudding.' " *Early American Literature* 17: 3–23.
Leslie, Charles, 1694. *The Charge of Socinianism Against Dr. Tillotson* . . . Edinburgh.
———. 1704. *Cassandra*, no. 1. London: Booksellers of London and Westminster.
———. 1730. *Letters Writ by a Turkish Spy*. 8 vols., 9th ed. London: Strahan, Mears, Ballard, Clay, Hooke, Wotte, Williamson, Rhodes. (The authorship is disputed. See Williams, Gwyn A.)
———. 1745. *A Short and Easie Method with the Deists*. 9th ed. London: G. Strahan. Also in *Infidelity*. New York: American Tract Society [c. 1836?].
Levi, David. 1789. *Letters to Dr. Priestley in Answer to his Letters to the Jews, Part II, occasioned by Mr. David Levi's Reply to the Former Part*. London: D. Levi.
———. 1798. *A Defence of the Old Testament in a Series of Letters addressed to Thomas Paine, Author of a Book entitled The Age of Reason, Part of the Second, being an Investigation of True and of Fabulous Theology*. Philadelphia: Hogan & M'Elroy.
———. 1800. *Dissertations on the Prophecies of the Old Testament*. Vol. 3. London: D. Levi.
Levine, Joseph M. 1977. *Dr. Woodward's Shield: History, Science and Satire in Augustan England*. Berkeley and Los Angeles: University of California Press.
Lindsay, Hal, and C. C. Carlson. 1976. *The Late Great Planet Earth*. Grand Rapids, Mich.: Zondervan.
Locke, John. 1689. *An Essay Concerning Human Understanding*. Edited by Peter H. Nidditch. Oxford: Clarendon Press, 1975.
———. 1690. *Two Treatises of Government*. Edited by Peter Laslett. Cambridge: Cambridge University Press, 1970.
———. 1695. *Reasonableness of Christianity*. London: Awnsham and John Churchil.
———. 1722. *Works*. 3 vols. London: A. Churchill and A. Manship.
———. 1794. *Essay for the Understanding of St. Paul's Epistles*. In *Works*. Vol. 7 of 9. London: T. Longman et al.
Locke, Louis G. 1954. "Tillotson: A Study in Seventeenth-Century Literature." *Anglistica* 4: 1–187.
Lough, John. 1975. "Reflections on *Enlightenment* and *Lumières*." *British Journal for Eighteenth-Century Studies* 8: 1–15.
[Lucas, Jean Maximilien]. 1777. *Traité des trois imposteurs, manuscrit clandestin du début de XVIIe siècle*. Edited by Pierre Retat. Saint-Étienne: Universités de la Région Rhône-Alpes, 1973.

Lundberg, David, and Henry F. May. 1976. "The Enlightened Reader in America." *American Quarterly* 28:262–93.

McAdoo, H. R. 1949. *The Structure of Caroline Moral Theology.* London: Longmans Green and Co.

———. 1965. *The Spirit of Anglicanism: A Survey of Anglican Theological Method in the Seventeenth Century.* London: Adam & Charles Black.

MacFarlane, Alan. 1978. *The Origins of English Individualism: The Family, Property and Social Transition.* Oxford: Basil Blackwell.

McKee, D. R. 1941. "Simon Tyssot de Patot and the Seventeenth-Century Background of Critical Deism." *Johns Hopkins Studies in Romance Languages and Literature* 40:11–101.

Macpherson, C[rawford] B[rough]. 1962. *The Political Theory of Possessive Individualism.* Oxford: Clarendon Press.

McTaggart, John M. E. 1906. *Some Dogmas of Religion.* London: E. Arnold.

Manuel, Frank E., and Fritzie P. Manuel. 1979. *Utopian Thought in the Western World.* Cambridge: Harvard University Press.

Marana, Giovannia Paolo. *See* Williams, Gwyn A.

Marshall, P. J., and Glyndwr Williams. 1982. *The Great Map of Mankind: Perceptions of New Worlds in the Age of Enlightenment.* Cambridge: Harvard University Press.

Martineau, James. 1901. *Types of Ethical Theory.* 3d ed. Oxford: Clarendon Press.

Mather, Cotton. 1693. *Winter-Meditations.* Boston.

Mather, Samuel. [1731.] *A Country Treat Upon the Second Paragraph in His Excellency's SPEECH, Decemb. 17. 1730.* [Boston.]

May, Henry F. 1976. *The Enlightenment in America.* New York: Oxford University Press.

Mayhew, Jonathan. 1750. *A Discourse Concerning Unlimited Submission.* Boston: Fowle and Green.

Mencken, H. L. 1976. *A New Dictionary of Quotations.* New York: Knopf.

Meyer, Donald H. 1976. *The Democratic Enlightenment.* New York: Putnam's Sons.

Miller, Victor Clyde. 1932. *Joel Barlow: Revolutionist London, 1791–92.* Hamburg: Friederichsen, de Gruyter and Co.

Moore, John Robert. 1960. *A Checklist of the Writings of Daniel Defoe.* Bloomington: Indiana University Press.

Morais, Herbert M. 1934. *Deism in Eighteenth-Century America.* New York: Russell & Russell.

Mossner, Ernest. 1967. Articles entitled "Deism," "Collins," "Toland," "Tindal," and "Blount." In the *Encyclopedia of Philosophy,* edited by Paul Edwards. 8 vols. New York: Macmillan Co.

Newton, Sir Isaac. 1728. *Sir Isaac Newton's Chronology, Abridged by Himself. Plus Observations by a Frenchman.* London: J. Peele.

Newton, Thomas, 1760. *Dissertations on the Prophecies which have been fulfilled, and at this time are fulfilling in the World.* 2d ed. London.

Nicholls, William. 1696–97. *A Conference with a Theist.* 2 vols. London: F. Saunders.

Novak, Maximillian E. 1982a. "Defoe's Authorship of *A Collection of Dying Speeches.*" *Philological Quarterly* 61:92–97.

———. 1982b. "The Unmentionable and the Ineffable in Defoe's Fiction." *Studies in the Literary Imagination* 15:85–103.

———. 1983. *Realism, Myth, and History in Defoe's Fiction.* Lincoln: University of Nebraska Press.

Nuttall, Geoffrey. 1965. *Richard Baxter.* London: Nelson.
O'Brien, Conor Cruise. Introduction to *Reflections on the Revolution. See* Burke, 1790.
O'Higgins, James, S.J. 1970. *Anthony Collins: The Man and His Works.* The Hague: Martinus Nijhoff.
———. ed. 1976. *Determinism and Freewill: Anthony Collins' A Philosophical enquiry concerning Human Liberty.* The Hague: Martinus Nijhoff.
Oliver, George. 1854. *The Antiquities of Freemasonry: Comprising Illustrations of the Five Grand Periods of Masonry, from the Creation of the World to the Dedication of King Solomon's Temple.* Philadelphia: Leon Hyneman.
Oxford Companion to Classical Literature. 1955. Compiled by Sir Paul Harvey. Oxford: Clarendon.
Paine, Thomas. 1791–92. *The Rights of Man.* Edited by Henry Collins. London: Penguin, 1969.
———. 1894–96. *The Writings.* Edited by Moncure Daniel Conway. 4 vols. New York: G. P. Putnam's.
Palmer, Robert R. 1939. *Catholics & Unbelievers in Eighteenth-Century France.* New York: Cooper Square Publishers, 1961.
Patey, Douglas Lane. 1984. *Probability and Literary Form.* Cambridge: Cambridge University Press.
Patrick, Simon. 1963. *A Brief Account of the New Sect of Latitude men.* Edited by T. A. Birrell. *Augustan Reprint Society,* publication no. 100. Los Angeles: Clark Memorial Library.
Paulson, Ronald. 1983. *Representations of Revolution (1789–1820).* New Haven: Yale University Press.
Pearce, Roy Harvey. 1965. *The Savages of America: A Study of the Indian and the Idea of Civilization.* Rev. ed. Baltimore: Johns Hopkins University Press.
Pepys, Samuel. 1929. *The Pepys Ballads.* 8 vols. Edited by Hyder E. Rollins. Cambridge: Harvard University Press.
Picciotto, James. 1956. *Sketches of Anglo-Jewish History.* Revised by Israel Finestein. London: Soncino.
Pike, Albert. 1871. *Morals and dogma of the Ancient and Accepted Scottish Rite of Freemasonry.* Charleston, S. C.: A.M. 5632.
Pintard, René. 1943. *Le Libertinage érudit.* 2 vols. Paris: Boivin.
Pocock, J. G. A. 1985. *Virtue, Commerce, and History.* Cambridge: Cambridge University Press.
Pole, J. R. 1981. "Enlightenment and the Politics of American Nature." In *The Enlightenment in National Context,* edited by Roy Porter and Mikulas Teich, 192–217, 257–59. Cambridge: Cambridge University Press.
Popkin, Richard. 1964. *The History of Scepticism from Erasmus to Descartes.* Rev. ed. New York: Harper Torchbooks.
———. 1975. "La Peyrère, the Abbé Grégoire and the Jewish Question in the Eighteenth Century." *American Society for Eighteenth-Century Studies* 4: 209–22.
———. Forthcoming. "David Levi, Anglo-Jewish Theologian." *Harvard Studies in 18th Century Judaism.*
Preston, William. 1775. *Illustrations of Masonry.* 2d ed. London: J. Wilkie.
Raleigh, Walter. 1614. *History of the World.* 2 vols. London: For Walter Burre.
Raven, Charles E. 1953. *Natural Religion and Christian Theology.* Cambridge: Cambridge University Press.

Redwood, John A. 1974. "Charles Blount (1654–93), Deism, and English Free Thought." *The Journal of the History of Ideas* 35:490–98.

———. 1976. *Reason, Ridicule and Religion: The Age of Enlightenment in England, 1660–1750*. London: Thames and Hudson.

Reedy, Gerard, S. J. 1977. "Socinianism, John Toland, and the Anglican Rationalists." *Harvard Theological Review* 70:285–304.

———. 1978–79. Review of "Irène Simon's *Three Restoration Divines: Barrow, South, Tillotson: Selected Sermons.*" *Eighteenth-Century Studies* 12:234–41.

Rex, Walter, 1965. *Essays on Pierre Bayle and Religious Controversy*. The Hague: Martinus Nijhoff.

Richardson, Robert D., Jr. 1978. "The Enlightenment View of Myth and Joel Barlow's *Vision of Columbus*." *Early American Literature* 13:34–44.

Robbins, Caroline. 1961. *The Eighteenth-Century Commonwealthman: Studies in the Transmission, Development and Circumstances of English Liberal Thought from the Restoration of Charles II until the War with the Thirteen Colonies*. Cambridge: Harvard University Press.

Roberts, J[ohn] M[orris]. 1972. *Mythology of the Secret Societies*. New York: Scribner.

Robertson, J. M. 1926. *The Dynamics of Religion*. 2d ed. London: Watts.

———. 1936. *A History of Freethought*. 2 vols. 4th ed. London: Watts.

Rosenberg, Aubrey. 1972. *Tyssot de Patot and His Work, 1655–1738*. The Hague: Martinus Nijhoff.

Ross, Alexander. 1696. *View of all Religions, with a Discovery of all known Heresies, and Lives of Notorious Hereticks*. London.

Rouse, Parke, Jr. 1971. *James Blair of Virginia*. Chapel Hill: University of North Carolina Press.

Rowe, John. 1898. *The Diary of John Rowe*. Boston: Wilson.

Roxburghe Ballads. 1869–99. Edited by Joseph Woodfall Ebsworth and William Chappell. 8 vols. London: The Ballad Society.

Rurak, James. 1980. "Butler's *Analogy*: A Still Interesting Synthesis of Reason and Revelation." *Anglican Theological Review* 62:365–87.

Sachse, Julius F. 1906. *Benjamin Franklin as a Free Mason*. Philadelphia.

Sandeen, Ernest R. 1970. *The Roots of Fundamentalism*. Chicago: University of Chicago Press.

Scaglione, Aldo. 1976. "A Note on Montaigne's 'Des Cannibales' and the Humanist Tradition." In *First Images of America: The Impact of the New World on the Old*. Edited by Fredi Chiappelli, 1:63–70. 2 vols. Berkeley and Los Angeles: University of California Press.

"Scald Miserable Masons." 1741a. News report of 1741 procession. *Boston Post-Boy*, no. 372 (25 May).

———. 1741b. [Grand Master Pony.] "A MANIFESTO By the Right Worshipful the Grand Master, Grand Officers, Stewards and Brethren of the SCALD MISERABLE MASONS." *Boston Evening-Post*, no. 306 (15 June).

———. 1744. Letter criticizing Freemasons. *Boston News-Letter*, no. 2105 (2 August).

———. *See also* Freemasons.

Schleiner, Winfried. 1976–77. "The Infant Hercules: Franklin's Design for a Medal Commemorating American Liberty." *Eighteenth-Century Studies* 10:235–44.

Scouten, Arthur H. 1978. "The Paradox of Deism in Colonial America." *Lex et Scientia* 14:215–28.

Segal, Howard P. 1978. "The American Enlightenment." *Canadian Review of American Studies* 9:84–89.

Shaftesbury, Anthony Ashley Cooper, third earl of. 1723. *Characteristics of Men, Manners, Opinions and Times.* 3 vols. 3d ed. London: [J. Darby].

Shapiro, Barbara. 1983. *Probability and Certainty in Seventeenth-Century England.* Princeton: Princeton University Press.

Sheehan, Bernard W. 1980. *Savagism and Civility: Indians and Englishmen in Colonial Virginia.* Cambridge: Cambridge University Press.

Shelley, Percy Bysshe. 1845. *Essays, Letters from Abroad.* Edited by Mrs. Shelley. London: Edward Moxon.

Shepard, Harvey. 1917. *History of St. John's Lodge of Boston.* Boston: Privately printed.

Sherlock, William. 1704. *A Discourse . . . containing the proofs of the immortality of the soul.* London: W. Rogers.

Shipton, Clifford K., and John L. Sibley. *Biographical Sketches of those Who Attended Harvard College.* 17 vols. Boston: Massachusetts Historical Society, 1873–1975. See "Jonathan Belcher," 4 (1933): 434–49; and "Joseph Green," 8 (1951): 42–53.

Simon, Irène. 1967–76. *Three Restoration Divines: Barrow, South, Tillotson: Selected Sermons.* 2 parts in 3 vols. Paris: Société d'Edition "Les Belles Lettres."

Simon, Richard. 1682. *Critical History of the Old Testament.* London: W. Davis.

Singer, S. 1896–98. "Early Translations and Translators of Jewish Liturgy in England." *Jewish Historical Society of England, Transactions* 3:56–71.

Skelton, Philip. 1749. *Ophiomaches, or Deism Revealed.* 2 vols. London: A. Millar.

Small, Judy Jo. 1983. "Robert Beverley and the New World Garden." *American Literature* 55:525–40.

Soman, Alfred. 1967. "Arminianism in France: The D'Huisseau Incident." *The Journal of the History of Ideas* 27:597–600.

Sparks, Jared. 1836–40. *The Works of Benjamin Franklin.* 10 vols. Boston: Hilliard, Gray, & Co.

Spiller, Michael R. G. 1980. *"Concerning Natural Experimental Philosophie": Meric Causabon and The Royal Society.* The Hague: Martinus Nijhoff.

Spink, John Stephenson. 1960. *French Free-Thought from Gassendi to Voltaire.* London: University of London, Athlone Press.

Spinoza, Benedictus de. 1883. *A Theologico-Political Treatise.* Translated by R. H. M. Elwes. New York: Dover Publications, 1951.

Stebbing, Henry. 1720. *An Appeal to the Word of God for the Terms of Christian Salvation: or, A Discourse, Proving that Sincerity, Exclusive of the Method of Religion which a Man Follows, is not Sufficient to Entitle Him to the Kingdom of Heaven.* London: J. Bowyer.

Stephen, Leslie. 1876. *History of English Thought in the Eighteenth Century.* 2 vols. New York: Putnam's Sons.

Stillingfleet, Edward. 1662. *Origines Sacrae.* London: Henry Mortlock.

———. "A Sermon on Luke 16:31." Ms. 0.81, St. John's College (Cambridge), fols. 25–49.

Stoddard, Roger E. 1982. "Poet and Printer in Colonial and Federal America: Some Bibliographical Perspectives." *Proceedings of the American Antiquarian Society* 92:265–361.

Strauss, Leo. 1952. *Persecution and the Art of Writing.* Glencoe, Ill.: The Free Press.

Stromberg, Roland M. 1954. *Religious Liberalism in Eighteenth-Century England.* Oxford: Oxford University Press.

Sullivan, Robert E. 1982. *John Toland and the Deist Controversy: A Study in Adaptations*. Cambridge: Harvard University Press.

Sutherland, James. 1950. *Defoe*. 2d ed. London: Methuen.

———, ed. 1975. *Oxford Book of Literary Anecdotes*. Oxford: Oxford University Press.

Swanton, John Reed. 1946. *The Indians of the Southeastern United States*. Bureau of American Ethnology *Bulletin* no. 137, Washington, D.C.

Swift, Jonathan. 1709. *A Project for the Advancement of Religion and the Reformation of Manners*. London: B. Tooke.

———. 1713. *Mr. C———ns Discourse of Free-Thinking, Put into Plain English*. London: John Morphew.

Sykes, Norman. 1959. *From Sheldon to Secker: Aspects of English Church History 1660–1768*. Cambridge: Cambridge University Press.

Thomas, Isaiah, 1810. *History of Printing in America*. Edited by Marcus A. McCorison. New York: Weathervane Books, 1970.

Thomson, James. 1726. *Winter*. London: For J. Millan.

Tichi, Cecilia. 1979. *New World, New Earth: Environmental Reform in American Literature from the Puritans through Whitman*. New Haven: Yale University Press.

———. 1985. "Joel Barlow." *Dictionary of Literary Biography*. vol. 37: *American Writers of the Early Republic*. Edited by Emory Elliott. Detroit, Mich.: Gale.

Tillotson, John. 1676. *The Rule of Faith or an Answer to the Treatise of Mr. I. S. [John Sargeant] entitled sure-Footing*. 2d ed. London: D. Gellibrand.

———. 1722. [*Sermons.*] *The Works of . . . Tillotson containing Two Hundred Sermons . . . with Tables*. Edited by Ralph Barker. 2 vols. 3d ed. London: Tooke, Pemberton, Valentine and Tonson.

———. 1820. [*Works.*] *The Works of . . . Tillotson with the Life*. Edited by Thomas Birch. 10 vols. London: R. Priestly.

Timbs, John. 1872. *Clubs and Club Life in London*. London: Chatto and Windus.

Tindal, Matthew. 1712. *The Nation Vindicated from the Aspersions cast on it in a late pamphlet, entitled A Representation . . . Part 2*. London: A. Baldwin.

———. 1730. *Christianity as Old as Creation*. London.

Toland, John. 1695. *Two Essays sent in a Letter from Oxford*. London: R. Baldwin.

———. 1696. *Christianity Not Mysterious*. London: Sam. Buckley.

———. 1702. *Vindicius Liberius: or Mr. Toland's Defence of himself, against the late Lower House of Convocation . . .* London: Bernard Lintot.

———. 1704. *Letters to Serena: containing . . . II. The History of the Soul's immortality among the Heathen*. London: Bernard Lintot.

———. 1718. *Nazarenus*. London: J. Brown.

———. 1720. *Tetradymus. Containing . . . II. Clidophorus; or of the external and internal doctrine of the antients: the one open and public, accomodated to popular prejudices and established religions; the other private and secret, wherein to the few capable and discrete, was taught the real truth stript of all disguises*. London: J. Brotherton and W. Meadows.

———. 1726. *A Collection of Several Pieces*. 2 vols. London: J. Peele.

Les Trois Imposteurs. See Lucas.

Turner, Matthew. 1782. *Answer to Dr. Priestley's Letters to a Philosophical Unbeliever*. By William Hammon [pseud.]. London.

Tuveson, Ernest. 1968. *Redeemer Nation: The Idea of America's Millenial Role*. Berkeley and Los Angeles: University of California Press.

Urban, Linwood. 1971. "A Revolution in English Moral Theology." *Anglican Theological Review* 53:5–20.

Vairasse [or Veiras] d'Allais, Denis. 1702. *Histoire des Sevarambes*. Amsterdam: E. Roger.

Van Gelder, H. A. Enno. 1961. *The Two Reformations of the Sixteenth Century*. The Hague: Martinus Nijhoff.

Van Leeuwen, Henry G. 1970. *The Problem of Certainty in English Thought 1630–1690*. 2d ed. The Hague: Martinus Nijhoff.

Van Lennep, William. 1960–70. *Index to the London Stage 1660–1800*. Carbondale: Southern Illinois University Press.

Venturi, Franco. 1972. "Radicati's Exile in England and Holland." In *Italy and the Enlightenment*, edited by Stuart Woolf and translated by Susan Corsi. London: Longman Group.

Viret, Pierre. 1564. *Instruction chrestienne en la doctrine de la loy et de l'Évangile: & en la vraye philosophie & théologie tant naturelle que supernaturelle des Chrestiens*. 3 vols. Geneva: I. Rivery.

Volney, Constantin F. 1802. *The Ruins, or, Meditations on the Revolutions of Empires: And the Law of Nature*. [Translated by Joel Barlow.] New York: Peter Eckler, 1926.

Wade, Ira O. 1930. *The Clandestine Organization and Diffusion of Philosophic Ideas in France from 1700 to 1750*. New York: Octagon Books, 1967.

Walker, Benjamin. 1737. *Journal*. "June 24, 1737." 3 Vols. Manuscript Collection of the Massachusetts Historical Society, Boston.

Walker, D[aniel] P[ickering]. 1964. *The Decline of Hell*. Chicago: University of Chicago Press.

Walpole, Horace. 1954–83. *Correspondence*. Wilmarth S. Lewis, gen. ed. 48 vols. New Haven: Yale University Press.

Walters, Robert. 1985. "The Allegorical Engravings in the Ledet-Desbordes Edition of *The Elements de la philosophie de Newton*." In *Voltaire and His World*, edited by R. J. Howells et al., pp. 27–49. Oxford: Voltaire Foundation.

Warburton, William. 1742. *The Divine Legation of Moses Demonstrated*. 3 vols. 3d ed. London: Executor of late Mr. Fletcher Gyles.

Ward, Edward ["Ned"]. 1709. *The History of the London Clubs*. 2 vols. London. Reprinted in 1710 as *The Secret History of clubs*.

Webster, Charles. 1975. *The Great Instauration: Science, Medicine and Reform 1626–1660*. London: Duckworth.

Welsh, Clement. 1956. "A Note on the Meaning of 'Deism'." *Anglican Theological Review* 38:160–66.

Westfall, Richard. 1958. *Science and Religion in Seventeenth-Century England*. New Haven: Yale University Press.

———. 1980. *Never at Rest: A Biography of Isaac Newton*. Cambridge: Cambridge University Press.

Whiston, William. 1723. *A Supplement to Mr. Whiston's Late Essay towards Restoring the True Test of the Old Testament*. London.

White, Morton. 1978. *The Philosophy of the American Revolution*. New York: Oxford University Press.

Whittlesley, Walter Lincoln. "Elias Boudinot." *Dictionary of American Biography*, 2:477–78.

Williams, Gwyn A. 1982. "Prince Madoc and the Turkish Spy." *Times Literary Supplement*, 24 December, 1415–16.

Wills, Garry. 1978. *Inventing America: Jefferson's Declaration of Independence*. Garden City, N.Y.: Doubleday & Co.

Winsor, Justin. 1889. *Narrative and Critical History of America*. 8 vols. Boston: Houghton, Mifflin.

Wodrow, Robert. 1842–43a. *Analecta; or, Materials for a history of remarkable providences*. Edited by Matthew Leishman. 4 vols. Maitland Club Publication no. 60. Edinburgh.

———. 1842–43b. *Correspondence of the Rev. Robert Wodrow*. Edited by Thomas M'Crie. 3 vols. Edinburgh: Wodrow Society.

Wollaston, William. 1722. *The Religion of Nature Delineated*. London: Privately printed.

Woodress, James. 1948. "The 'Cold War' of 1790–1791." *Duke University Library Notes* no. 20 (July): 7–18.

———. 1958. *A Yankee's Odyssey: The Life of Joel Barlow*. New York: Greenwood.

Wright, Dudley, et al., eds. 1936. *Gould's History of Freemasonry*. New York: Scribner.

Wright, Thomas. 1936. *Caricature History of the Georges*. New York: Scribner.

Yolton, John. 1956. *John Locke and the Way of Ideas*. Oxford: Oxford University Press.

———. 1983. *Thinking Matter: Materialism in Eighteenth-Century Britain*. Minneapolis: University of Minnesota Press.

Notes on Contributors

DAVID BERMAN, fellow and senior lecturer in philosophy at Trinity College, Dublin, has published articles on seventeenth- and eighteenth-century philosophy, theology, and iconography.

ROGER L. EMERSON is a professor of history at the University of Western Ontario. He has published a number of articles on the Scottish Enlightenment, the most recent of which contain a history of the Philosophical Society of Edinburgh.

J. A. LEO LEMAY, H. F. du Pont Winterthur Professor of English, teaches American Literature at the University of Delaware. His most recent books are *"New England's Annoyances": America's First Folk Song* (1985) and *The Canon of Benjamin Franklin 1722–1776: New Additions and Reconsiderations* (1986).

ROBERT MICKLUS is assistant professor of English at SUNY-Binghamton. His edition of *The History of the Tuesday Club* is scheduled for publication in 1987 by the Institute of Early American History and Culture.

CARLA MULFORD is assistant professor of English at the Pennsylvania State University, University Park, Pa. While preparing a three-volume edition of Joel Barlow's letters, Professor Mulford has edited two forthcoming volumes: *John Leacock's* The First Book of the American Chronicles of the Times *1774–1775* (1987) and *The Poetry of Annis Boudinot Stockton* (1987).

MAXIMILLIAN E. NOVAK, professor of English at UCLA, is currently at work on a biography of Daniel Defoe. His most recent books are *English Literature in the Eighteenth Century* (1984) and volume 13 of *The California Edition of the Works of John Dryden* (1984) with Alan Roper and George Guffey.

RICHARD H. POPKIN, professor emeritus of philosophy and Judiac studies at Washington University, Saint Louis, and adjunct professor of philosophy and history at UCLA, is the author of *The History of Scepticism from Erasmus to Spinoza* (rev. ed., 1964). He has completed a book-length study entitled

"Isaac La Pevrére and the Development of Biblical Criticism" and is now writing a book on Jewish messianism and Christian millenarianism from the sixteenth to the nineteenth centuries.

GERARD REEDY, S.J., is professor of English at Fordham University and Dean of Fordham College. He has recently published *The Bible and Reason: Anglicans and Scripture in Late Seventeenth-Century England* (1985) and finished a book-length study of Robert South.

DAVID S. SHIELDS is assistant professor of English at The Citadel. He has published articles on a variety of early American literary subjects. His study of Joseph Green's antimasonic satires was undertaken while a Samuel Foster Haven fellow of the American Antiquarian Society.

Index

Adams, M. Ray, 152 n.1, 155 n.17
Adams, Samuel, 126 n.13, 158
Adario, 81. *See also* Lahontan, Baron De
Addison, Joseph, 101, 106. See also *Spectator*
Aesop, 88
Alcides, 148, 155 n.21
Aldridge, Alfred Owen, 7, 8, 9, 11, 15, 45, 79, 91, 91 n.1, 94, 96, 156 n.13; *Benjamin Franklin and His French Contemporaries*, 7; *Benjamin Franklin and Nature's God*, 8; *Benjamin Franklin: Philosopher and Man*, 8; "Benjamin Franklin's Deistic Indians," 79; *Comparative Literature: Japan and the West*, 8; *Comparative Literature: Matter and Method*, 8; *Comparative Literature Studies*, 7; "Concept of Ancients and Moderns," 156 n.23; *Early American Literature: A Comparatist Approach*, 8, 156 n.23; *Essai sur les personnages des "Liaisons Dangereuses,"* 8; *Fiction in Japan and the West*, 8; *Ibero-American Enlightenment*, 8; *Jonathan Edwards*, 8; *Man of Reason: The Life of Thomas Paine* 7, 156 n.23; *The Reemergence of World Literature*, 8; *Shaftesbury and the Deist Manifesto*, 7, 94; "Shaftesbury's Rosicrucian Ladies," 7; *Thomas Paine's American Ideology*, 8, 156 n.23; *Voltaire and the Century of Light*, 8
Allen, Don Cameron, 45 n.4
American Magazine, (1741), 90
Ames, Nathaniel, 121, 122, 126 n.11
Anderson, James, 127
Anne (queen of England), 44
Annet, Peter, 63
Applebee's Journal, 93, 96
Arians, 42, 94, 96, 103
Arminianism, 32, 41
Armstrong, Brian, 29
Arner, Robert D., 82, 137, 153 n.6

Arnold, Matthew, 51
Ascham, Roger, 23, 24, 28
Asgill, John, 44
Atheism, 21, 22, 23, 24, 26, 27, 29, 45 n.7, 46 n.8, 46 n.13, 46 n.14, 74, 76, 77, 122
Atterbury, Francis, 68, 74
Aubrey, John, 104
Augustine, Saint, 33, 41
Austin (apothecary of Boston), 116, 117

Bacon, Francis, 29
Bacon, Thomas, 134
Baine, Rodney, 93, 94
Baldwin, Abraham, 152 n.3
Balguy, John, 95
Ball, Kenneth R., 152 n.1, 154 n.16, 155 n.19
Banister, John, 82, 85, 86, 87
Barlow, Joel, 14, 15, 91, 110, 137–57; *Advice to the Priviledged Orders*, 137, 143, 150, 152 n.1, 152 n.2, 152 n.3, 156 n.4; "Canal," 154 n.16, 154 n.19; *Columbiad*, 14; *Conspiracy of Kings*, 14, 137–57; "Dissertation on the Genius and Institutions of Manco Capac," 142, 154 n.16, 155 n.18; "Genealogy of the Tree of Liberty," 146, 154 n.16, 155 n.20; "Hasty Pudding," 110, 138, 143; *Vision of Columbus*, 91, 142, 143, 152 n.1, 154 n.16, 155 n.18, 157 n.24
Barrell, John, 118, 125
Barrow, Issac, 47 n.22
Basnage, Jacques, 162, 163, 169, 170 nn. 3 and 7
Baxter, Richard, 35, 101
Bayle, Pierre, 19, 25, 28, 45 n.6, 159, 168
Bedford, R. D., 46 n.9
Belcher, Jonathan, 109, 121, 125 n.2
Belfrage, Bertil, 78 n.17
Bentley, Richard, 23, 27, 46 n.12, 74
Berkeley, George, 45 n.4, 69, 72, 74, 75

INDEX

Berkhofer, Robert F., 79
Berman, David, 12, 45 n.1, 47 n.24, 61–78, 90
Berriman, William, 27
Betts, C. J., 46 n.6
Beverley, Robert, 12, 13, 15, 79–92; *Ballad Addres'd to the Reverend Members of the Convocation*, 91 n.4; *History of Virginia*, 12, 79–92
Bible, 11, 37, 51–52, 62, 73, 80, 97, 100–102, 155 n.22, 160, 163, 167–68; Abraham, 47 n.17, 52; Adam, 34, 106, 145, 146, 151; Amos, 53; David, 58; Eve, 106; Hosea, 53; Issac, 47 n.17; John, 109, 110, 113; Joshua, 105; Lamech, 129; Lazarus, 52; Micah, 51; Moses, 14, 24, 25, 51, 55, 103, 105, 122, 161, 162–63, 166–68; New Testament, 26, 31, 32, 40, 61, 62–63, 96, 102, 167; Noah, 103, 130; Old Testament, 31, 32, 51, 53, 56, 58, 62–63, 96–97, 102–3, 160, 163; Paul, 39, 65, 68; Peter, 37, 47 n.17; Solomon, 73, 121, 130; Tubal-Cain, 129, 130. Books of: Acts, 42; Daniel, 42, 53, 159, 164; Deuteronomy, 55, 161, 167; Genesis, 59, 106, 161; Isaiah, 51, 53, 163; Luke, 52; Matthew, 39; Psalms, 24, 58; Revelation, 42, 159, 164, 166; Song of Songs, 100. *See also* Christ
Bigelow, John, 91 n.3
Billington, James H., 155 n.20
Bjorck, Tobias Eric, 90
Blake, William, 102, 137, 138, 145, 149, 151, 155 n.23; *America: A Prophecy*, 14, 148, 156 n.22; *Song of Liberty*, 14, 148, 156 n.22; *Visions of the Daughters of Albion*, 14, 148–49, 150
Bland, Richard, 15
Blasphemy Act (1697), 62
Blau, Joseph, 155 n.17
Blount, Charles, 12, 26, 27, 29, 45 nn. 2 and 4, 46 n.10, 61–62, 65–68, 69, 72, 74, 76–77, 86; *Anima Mundi*, 65, 66, 67, 68, 76, 78 n.8; *Miscellaneous Works*, 25, 46 n.11, 78 n.8; *Oracles of Reason*, 25, 46 n.11, 76, 86; *Summary Account of the Deists Religion*, 25, 46 n.11; *Two First Books of Philostratus*, 25. *See also* Deism
Blount, Sir Henry, 46 n.10
Blount, Sir Thomas, 46 n.10
Bolingbroke, Lord, 15, 161
Bolling, Robert, 15
Book of Common Prayer, 11, 41, 42

Bordley, John Beale, 135
Boston Evening Post, 111, 117, 118
Boston Gazette, 110, 119
Boston News-Letter, 118, 120
Boston Post-Boy, 119
Boston Weekly News-Letter, 126 n.9
Boswell, James, 71
Boudinot, Elias, 14, 159, 160, 163, 169, 170; *Age of Revelation*, 165, 166; *Star in the West*, 165, 166–67
Boyd, George Adams, 165
Boyle Lecturers, 26, 27, 30, 42, 44, 46 n.13, 105
Boyle Lectures: *Defence of Natural and Revealed Religion*, 46 n.12
Boynton, Percy, 152 n.1
Bradford, Andrew, 46 n.12, 90
Briggs, Samuel, 126 n.5
Brockwell, Rev. Charles, 113–16, 122, 123, 125
Bruno, Giordano, 24, 29
Bull, George, 42
Bullen, John, 132
Bunyan, John, 101
Burdy, Samuel, 78 n.11
Burke, Edmund, 14, 137, 139–41, 144–45, 147, 149, 150, 154 n.15, 156 n.24; *Enquiry*, 154 n.15; *Reflections on the Revolution in France*, 139–40, 153 nn. 11 and 12
Burnet, Thomas, 105
Burton, Robert, 24, 29, 30, 43
Busson, Henri, 45 n.6
Butler, Joseph, 47 n.20, 159
Byles, Mather, 125 n.3
Byrd, William, 80, 81

Calonne, Charles Alexandre de, 140, 141
Calvin, John, 32, 33, 34, 41, 47 n.16
Cantor, Milton, 152 nn. 1 and 2; 153 nn. 5 and 8
Capec, Manco, 142, 147
Carlile, Richard, 74, 78 n.12
Carroll, Robert Todd, 47 n.18
Cassirer, Ernest, 54, 78 nn. 3 and 17
Catherine II (empress of Russia), 139
Cervantes: *Don Quixote*, 78 n.15
Charbonnel, J. R., 45 n.6
Charitable Society (of Boston), 126 n.10
Chillingworth, William, 19, 25, 29, 33, 41, 159
Chinard, Gilbert, 91 n.2
Christ (Jesus), 24, 26, 28, 31, 33, 36, 37, 38, 39, 40, 42, 47 n.17, 51, 55, 56, 57, 58, 59, 61, 66, 69, 71, 90, 94, 95, 102,

202

INDEX

122, 144, 145, 146, 147, 148, 166, 167, 168, 169. *See also* Bible
Christensen, Merton A., 154 n.17
Chubb, Thomas, 78 n.9, 90
Churchill, Charles, 125
Clarendon, earl of, 58
Clarke, James Stanier, 137, 152 n.1
Clarke, Samuel, 23, 27, 46 n.12, 69, 70, 74
Clayton, Robert, 163, 169
Cobban, Alfred, 153 n.11, 153–54 n.12
Colden, Cadwallader, 90
Cole, Charles 132. *See also* Jole, Nasifer
Colie, Rosalie L., 51, 55
Collins, Anthony, 12, 13, 19, 20, 22, 27, 28, 29, 43, 45 n.1, 47 n.24, 61–63, 65, 66, 67, 69–71, 72, 73, 74, 76, 77, 78 nn. 1, 3, and 4; 97, 98, 100, 102, 103; *Discourse Concerning Ridicule and Irony in Writing*, 62; *Discourse of Free-Thinking*, 61, 62, 69, 78 nn. 2, 5, and 10; *Discourse of the Grounds and Reasons of the Christian Religion*, 106; *Free Thoughts*, 78 n.5; *Letter to the Learned Mr. Henry Dodwell*, 69; *Reply to Clark's Defence*, 70; *Scheme of Literal Prophecy Considered*, 70, 94. *See also* Deism
"Connecticut Wits," 138
Conway, Moncure D., 159, 170
Coward, William, 78 n.9
Crocker, Lester G., 157 n.25
Curran, Stuart, 157 n.24

Dahm, John J., 46 n.12
d'Artois, Charles Phillipe (later Charles X, king of France), 139–40
DeBry, Theodore, 12, 81, 82, 83, 84, 85, 87
Defoe, Daniel, 13, 20, 93–108; *Apparition of Mrs. Veal*, 93; *Colonel Jack*, 106; *Enquiry into Occasional Conformity*, 107 n.4; *Essay on the History and Reality of Apparitions*, 93, 104, 105; *An Essay on the Original of Literature*, 13, 97, 98, 103, 106; *Farther Adventures of Robinson Crusoe*, 106; *History of Pirates*, 106; *Journal of the Plague Year*, 94; *Mere Nature Delineated*, 13, 98, 99, 100; *Moll Flanders*, 106; *New Family Instructor*, 13, 99, 101, 105; *New Voyage Round the World*, 106; "Orthodox" (Defoe pseudonym), 96; *Political History of the Devil*, 13, 93, 100–102; *Present State of the Parties in Great Britain*, 94; *Robert Drury's Journal*, 106; *Robinson Crusoe*, 69; *Roxana*, 106; *Some Remarks upon the Late Differences*, 13, 96, 107 n.3; *System of Magick*, 13, 93, 102–4; *True Born Englishman*, 108 n.10

Deism, 11, 12, 13, 15; and Amerindians, 79–92; and atheism, 76–77, 90; backgrounds of, 19–25, 43–45; and Barlow, 154 n.17; and Beverley, 79–92; and Blount, 65–68; and Collins, 61–62, 68–70; definition of, 23–24, 80; and Defoe, 93–108; and Hume, 70–75; and insinuation, 61–78; and Latitudinarianism, 19–48; and Locke, 70–72; and Paine, 161, 162, 164, 165; and Shaftesbury, 62–64; and Tillotson, 31–43; and Tindal, 68–70
Derham, William, 46 n.12
Descartes, René, 33
Desmaizeaux, Pierre, 43
Diderot, Denis, 138, 150–51, 156–57 n.24, 157 n.25; *Encyclopedie*, 142
Dissenters, 95, 96, 102
Dorsey, Edward, 128
Dowse, John, 118
Dryden, John, 80, 90; "Absalom and Achitophel," 90; *The Indian Emperour*, 80; *Plays*, 81; "Religio Laici," 80; *Works*, 81
Dunn, John, 91 n.3
Dupuis, Charles François, 143
Durden, Robert F., 152 n.1
Dwight, Timothy, 137

Einstein, Albert, 170
Ellis, Frank, 107 n.1
Ellul, Jacques, 154 n.14
Emerson, Ralph Waldo, 151
Emerson, Roger L., 11, 14, 19–48
Emlyn, Thomas, 102
Enlightenment, 11, 12, 14, 15, 21, 45, 48 n.25; American, 79–91, 97, 122; and Barlow, 142, 143, 154 n.17, 157 n.25; defined, 49–60; and Paine 169
Ensor, George, 74, 78 n.12
Epicureanism, 24, 67
Epicurus, 28, 68
Erasmus, 25, 28
Erdman, David, 148, 155 n.22
Estienne, Henri, 45 n.6
Evelyn, John, 52
Ewan, Joseph, 82, 85
Ewan, Nesta, 82, 85
Ezra, Aben, 161, 168

Fairchild, Hoaxie Neale, 80

203

Febvre, Lucien, 45 n.6
Fielding, Henry, 108 n.8
Fiering, Norman, 47 n.16
Firmin, Thomas, 42
Florida, R. E., 46 n.8
Foster, James, 78 n.6
Francis, Philip, 140, 153 n.12
Franklin, Benjamin, 7, 8, 9, 11, 91 n.3, 92 n.7, 123, 155 n.21; "Captivity of William Henry," 91; "Remarks Concerning the Savages of North America," 91; "Speech of Miss Polly Baker," 90
Frantz, R. N., 80
Fredrick William II (king of Prussia), 139
Freemasonry, 11, 13, 15, 22, 43, 44, 47 n.24, 156 n.23; *Constitutions* (Anderson), 127; and Joseph Green, 109–26; and Dr. Alexander Hamilton, 127–36. *See also* Glamorgan Mock Masons; Grand Lodge; Scald Society
Freethinkers, 12, 19, 22, 25, 26, 46 n.11, 54, 62, 63, 65, 69, 72, 73, 74, 79, 80, 81, 87, 100, 159, 160. *See also* Deism
Freret, Nicholas, 97

Gale, Theophilus, 106
Garcilasco de la Vega, el Inca, 143, 155 n.18
Garrett, Clarke, 159–60
Gastrell, Francis (Boyle Lecturer, 1697), 46 n.12
Gawlick, Günther, 20
Gay, Peter, 28, 78 nn. 1, 3, and 17
Gazette Nationale, 154 n.12
General Magazine (Franklin's), 92 n.7
George I (king of England), 94
Gibbon, Edward, 168
Gibbs, G. C., 44, 48 n.25
Gifford, William, *Satires of Decimus Junius Juvenalis*, 153 n.7
Gildon, Charles, 26, 27, 45 n.4, 70, 72; *Deist's Manual*, 25, 65, 78 n.9; *Miscellanea Aurea*, 25
Glamorgan Mock Masons, 111. *See also* Freemasonry
Glorious Revolution, 22, 168
Godwin, William, 137
Goodwin, Timothy, 54
Gordon, John, 128
Gordon, Thomas, 44
Gordon Riots, 140
Grand Lodge of Freemasons, 23
Granger, Bruce I., 125

Green, Jonas, 128
Green, Joseph, 13–15, 109–26; "Clio" (pseudonym), 117, 119, 120, 123; "The Disappointed Cooper," 126 n.6; "The Duties of FREE MASONRY," 114; *An Eclogue Sacred to the memory of . . . John Mayhew*, 126 n.6; *Entertainment for a Winter's Evening*, 110, 112–13, 117, 118; *Grand Arcanum Detected*, 117, 121, 123; "Inscription under Revd. John Checkly's Picture," 126 n.6; "Lines Occasioned by a *Dr. Hudson*," 126 n.3; *A Mournful Lamentation*, 125 n.3; "To the Poet in the Post Boy," 119
Greene, Robert, 24
Gregoire, Henri, 164
Gribelin, Simon, 81, 82, 85
Grotius, Hugo, 46 n.13
Gueudeville, Nicholas, 81
Gustavus III (king of Sweden), 139

Hahn, Thomas, 92 n.5
Hales, John, 19
Halley, Esmond (astronomer), 103
Hallowell, Benjamin, 111, 118
Hamilton, Alexander (statesman), 165
Hamilton, Dr. Alexander, 13, 15, 91 n.1, 127–36; "Discourse Delivered from the Chair in the Lodge-Room," 13; *History of the Tuesday Club*, 13, 127–36; as "Loquacious Scribble," 131–32, 135
Hammock, John, 13, 118–19, 120, 123, 125, 126 n.9; "An Address to the Masons at Halifax," 120, 121; "A Defence of Masonry," 119–20; "Dream," 118; "On Some Fine Peach-Trees," 118; "On the Present Expedition," 118; "To Mr. Clio, at North-Hampton, *In Defence of Masonry*," 117, 118; as "VD," 13, 118–20, 126 n.9; as "Vini Doctor," 118, 120
Hampshire, Stuart, 55
Hariot, Thomas, 82, 83, 84, 87; *Brief and True Report*, 12, 81, 83, 85
Harley, Robert, 98
Harrington, James, 126 n.12
Harth, Phillip, 45 nn. 3 and 4; 46 nn. 10 and 11; 47 nn. 18 and 20
Hartley, David, 163, 169
Hayley, William, 137–39, 151–52 n.1, 153 n.4, 157 n.24
Head, Richard, 45 n.7
Henry, Patrick, 15
Hera (wife of Zeus), 148

Heracles (Hercules), 148, 155 n.21
Herbert, Edward, first Baron Herbert of Cherbury, 24, 29, 46 n.9
Hill, Christopher, 46 n.15
Hiram (king of Tyre), 121
Hoadley, Benjamin, 69, 78 n.10, 94; *Nature of the Kingdom*, 95; *Preservative against the Principles*, 95; *Queries Recommended*, 78 n.1
Hobbes, Thomas, 25, 95, 161, 167
Holbach, Paul Henri, Baron d', 22, 153 n.8
Holberg, Ludvig, 43
Homer, 104
Hooker, Richard, 20, 27, 33, 41
Horace, 24
Hornberger, Theodore, 91 n.3
Howard, Leon, 152 n.1, 155 n.18
Howells's *State Trials*, 152 n.2
Hume, David, 12, 62, 70–77, 78 nn. 4 and 11; 160, 161, 168; "Of the Immortality of the Soul," 70; *Treatise of Human Nature*, 75, 78 n.4
Hutcheson, Francis, 15, 63, 78 n.7
Hutchinson, Thomas, 118
Hyde, Edward. *See* Clarendon, earl of

Ibbot, Benjamin (Boyle Lecturer), 46 n.12
Independent Advertiser, 122, 126 n.13
Isis (mythology), 146

Jacob, Margaret, 22–23, 30–31, 41–44, 45 nn. 2 and 4; 46 n.13; 47 n.24, 48 n.25, 136 n.2, 156 n.23; *Newtonians and the English Revolution*, 45 n.25; *The Radical Enlightenment*, 43, 44
Jacobites, 95, 106, 122
James I (king of England), 133
Jefferson, Thomas, 15, 137, 143, 152 n.1, 159, 165
Jewel, John (bishop of Salisbury), 33, 41
Johnsen, Joseph, 148, 152 n.2
Johnsen, Thomas, 43
Jole, Nasifer, 132–33, 134, 136. *See also* Cole, Charles
Jones, Dr. Evan, 123
Jones, Inigo, 130
Joost, Nicholas, 91 n.1
Journal literaire, 43
Jupiter, 88
Juvenal, 138–39

Keen, Benjamin, 80
Kierkegaard, Sören, 33

Kilby, Thomas, 118
Kocher, P. H., 45 n.6
Kors, Alan, 45 n.8

Lafayette, Marquis de, 137
Lahontan, Baron De, 43, 47 n.23, 81, 82, 91 n.2; *Dialogues Curieux*, 43, *New Voyages to North America*, 81. *See also* Adario
Lalor, Stephen, 78 n.17
La Peyrère, Isaac de, 161, 167, 168
Latitudinarianism, 11, 19–48, 112, 159
Law, William, 95
Lawson, John, 80, 90
Leary, Lewis, 152 n.1
Leland, John, 78 nn. 3 and 9
Lemay, J. A. Leo, 79–92, 125, 126 n.6, 137, 148, 153 n.6, 154 n.17, 155 n.21
Leopold (king of Austria), 139, 147
Leslie, Charles, 45 n.4
Levellers, 22
Levi, David, 14, 159–70, 170 nn. 2 and 3; *Defence*, 14; *Dissertation on the Prophecies of the Old Testament*, 161, 163
Liberatas Americana, 155 n.21
Locke, John, 15, 19, 20, 29, 30, 49, 50, 59, 70, 71, 73, 80, 81, 82, 86, 89, 91 n.3, 99; *Essay Concerning Human Understanding*, 49, 50, 86; *Essay for the Understanding of St. Paul's Epistles*, 49; *Reasonableness of Christianity*, 49; *Second Reply to Stillingfleet*, 71; *Two Treatises of Government*, 59, 91 n.3
Locke, Louis, 46 n.16
London Magazine, 90
Lough, John, 49, 50, 60
Louis XIV (king of France), 32
Louis XVI (king of France), 139
Lucan, 105
Lucas, Jean M., *Treatise of the Three Imposters*, 122
Lucretius, 68
Lundberg, David, 92 n.6
Luther, Martin, 19
Lycurgus, 142

McAdoo, H. R., 47 nn. 19 and 22
M'cala, Robert, 107 n.1
McCamus, Elizabeth, 47 n.23
Macfarlane, Alan, 45 n.5
Machiavelli, Niccolò, 29
Mackintosh, James, 153 n.3
Macpherson, C. B., 45 n.5
McTaggart, John M. E., 77, 78 n.14

INDEX

Madison, James, 15
Mahomet, 25, 142
Malcolm, Alexander, 128, 135
Manco Capec. *See* Capec, Manco
Marie Antoinette (queen of France), 139, 145, 154 n.12
Marshall, P. J., 47 n.23
Martineau, James, 78 n.7
Marvell, Andrew, 126 n.12
Maryland Gazette, 91 n.1
Mason, George, 15
Massé, Jacques, 43
Mather, Cotton: *Winter-Meditations*, cited, 112
Mather, Samuel, 125 n.2
Maximilla (early Christian prophetess), 56
May, Henry F., 79, 92 n.6
Mayhew, Jonathan: *Discourse Concerning Unlimited Submission*, 118
Menasseh ben Israel, 170 n.7
Merchants' Club (Boston), 122
Mesange, Pierre de, 43
Micklus, Robert, 13, 127–36
Millar, Andrew, 78 n.11
Millennialism, Christian. *See* Boudinot, Elias
Millennialism, Hebrew. *See* Levi, David
Miller, Victor C., 139, 152 n.1, 153 n.8
Milton, John: attacked by Defoe, 13, 101–2, 106; as member of the Rota, 126 n.12; *Paradise Lost*, 101, 106, 144, 156 n.22
Mist's Journal, 93
Mohammed, 122, 166–67
Mohamedans, 88
Molesworth, Robert, 44
Montaigne, Michel de: *Essays*, 80
Montanus (early Christian prophet), 56
Moore, John Robert, 97
Morais, Herbert M.: *Deism in Eighteenth-Century America*, 80, 91 n.1, 92 n.6
Morgan, Thomas, 161
Morning Chronicle (London), 152 n.2
Morris, Rob (in old Scotch song), 133
Mortalism, 76–77. *See also* Atheism
Mossner, Ernest, 78 nn. 1, 3, and 17
Muhammed. *See* Mohammed
Mulford, Carla, 14, 137–57

Napoleon, 169
Nashe, Thomas: as alleged libertine, 24
Naturalism, Renaissance, 22
Nelson, Robert, 42
Nemmattanow (Virginia Indian), 89
New England Company, 40
New England Courant, 110
Newton, Isaac: and biblical chronology, 97 n.4; as Christian millenarian, 163 n.7, 169; 170 n.3; and deism, 21 n.5; 30 n.1; and science 99 n.6; 103 n.2
Newton, Thomas, 163, 169
Newtonians, 22, 23, 26
New York Gazette, 90
Noble savage, 79
Norwich Revolution Society, 152 n.2
Novak, Maximillian E., 13, 93–108
Numa, 142

O'Brien, Conor Cruise, 153 n.11
O'Higgins, James, S.J., 19, 20, 23, 42, 43, 44, 45 nn. 1 and 2; 47 n.24, 70, 78 nn. 3 and 5
Oliver, George, 129
Olmstead, Lemuel, 154 n.16
Osiris, 146–48
Ouellet, Real, 47 n.23
Oxford Movement, 21

Paine, Thomas, 8, 11, 15, 137, 156 n.24, 158–70; *Age of Reason*, 14, 151, 158, 161, 164, 165, 168, 169; "Letter to Mr. Erskine," 164; *Rights of Man*, 152 n.2, 156 n.23
Pantheism 22; of John Toland, 20
Parker, James, 90
Pascal, Blaise, 33
Patey, Douglas: *Probability and Literary Form*, cited, 108 n.8
Paulsen, Ronald, 153 n.12, 154 n.13, 155 n.20, 156 n.23; *Representations of Revolution*, 145, 146, 153 n.10
Pelagians, 26, 32, 35
Pennsylvania Gazette, 91 nn. 1 and 3
Pepys, Samuel, 52
Percy, Thomas, 69
Pery, Sir William, 126 n.12
Peter (czar of Russia), 142
Peter the Wild Boy, 98–99
Picart, Bernard, 48 n.24
Picciotto, James, 170 n.2
Pike, Albert: *Morals and Dogma*, cited, 135, 136 n.3
Pintard, René, 45 n.6
Plato, 71
Pliny, 68
Plutarch, 105

Pocock, J. G. A., 108 n.10
Pole, J. R., 91 n.3
Pollard, Samuel, 125 n.2
Pope, Alexander, 138; *Dunciad*, 153 n.8; *Rape of the Lock*, 153 n.8
Popkin, Richard H., 14, 29, 158–70
Preston, William: *Illustrations of Masonry*, 129
Price, Richard, 137, 140, 143; "Discourse on the Love of Our Country," 139
Priestly, Joseph, 161, 163, 169

Quakers, 107

Radicati di Passerano, Alberto (count), 43, 74
Raleigh, Sir Walter: *History of the World*, 103
Randolph, Sir John, 15; his will, 91 n.1
Reedy, Gerard, S.J., 11, 45 n.3, 49–60
Rees, Daniel, 123, 126 n.11
Reformation, 160; and the rise of deism, 19, 29
Restoration, the, 11, 45 n.7, 52, 53, 108 n.8, 126 n.12
Retz, Cardinal de, 75
Rex, Walter, 29
Richardson, Robert, 137, 153 n.6, 155 n.18
Richardson, Samuel, 108 n.8
Richelieu, Cardinal, 101
Robbins, Caroline, 44
Robertson, J. M., 78 nn. 3 and 16
Robertson, William: *History of America*, 143
Rochester, John Wilmot, second earl of, 76
Rosicrucianism, 122, 131
Ross, Alexander, 126 n.7
Ross, Ian, 78 n.17
Rota (republican debating society), 122, 126 n.12
Rouse, Parke, 91 n.4
Rowe, John, 126 n.10
Royal Society of London, 30
Rurak, James, 47 n.20

St. James Chronicle, 152 n.1
"Salem Shoemaker," 122, 126 n.13
Savonarola, 53, 56
Scaglione, 80
Scald Society of Miserable Masons, 111–14, 117. *See also* Freemasonry

Schleiner, Winfried, 155 n.21
Schopenhauer, Arthur, 77
Scots Magazine, 90
Scottish SPCK, 40
Scouten, Arthur H., 92 n.6
Second Advent, the, 165, 166
Seneca, 76
"Serena" (Sophia, queen of Prussia), 66
Sevarambians, 43
Shaftesbury, third earl of (Anthony Ashley Cooper), 23, 43, 44, 67, 72, 98; *Characteristics of Men, Manners, Opinions and Times*, 63, 78 n.4, 96; *Shaftesbury and the Deist Manifesto* (Aldridge), 11
Shapiro, Barbara, 29, 30
Shaw, George Bernard, 76
Shelley, Percy Bysshe, 77, 78 n.14
Sherlock, William, 74
Shields, David S., 13, 109–26
Shipton, Clifford K., 126 n.5
Simon, Richard, 43, 59, 161, 167; *Critical History of the Old Testament*, 52, 55
Singer, S., 170 n.2
Skelton, Philip, 72, 74; *Phiomaches, or Deism Revealed*, 63, 71, 73, 78 n.11
Skinner, Cyriac, 126 n.12
Small, Judy Jo, 82
Smith, (Captain) John, 81
Smith, Robert, 153 nn. 11 and 12
Society for Constitutional Information, 153 n.3
Society for the Propagation of Christian Knowledge, 40
Society for the Propagation of the Gospel in Foreign Parts, 40
Socinianism, 32, 43, 57, 95, 96; and deism, 19, 20, 21, 42, 46 n.10; in France, 46 n.8; idolatry of, condemned by Blount, 25; Toland goes beyond, 45 n.3
Solon, 142
Sophia (queen of Prussia), 66
Sparks, Jared, 91 n.3
Spectator, 101
Spink, John S., 45 n.6
Spinoza, Benedictus de, 11–12, 25, 28, 43, 49–60, 159–61, 167, 168, 170 n.5; *Ethics*, 51; *Theological-Political Treatise*, 11, 50–55; *Tractatus Theologico-Politicus*, 170 n.5
Spinozism, 22, 51, 55
Stanislaus (king of Poland), 150
Starkie, Thomas, 170 n.1

207

Stebbing, Henry, 27, 95
Stephen, Leslie, 12, 77, 78 nn. 3 and 17; on catagories of deism, 80
Stephens, William, 45 n.4
Stiles, Ezra, 169
Stillingfleet, Edward, 11–12, 42, 49–60, 159; *Fifty Sermons*, 54; *Origines Sacrae*, 54, 106
Strauss, Leo, 52
Stromberg, Roland: his definition of deism, 80
Sturtevant, William C., 81, 85, 87
Sullivan, Robert, 20, 21, 23, 31, 32, 42, 44, 45 n.2; 78 n.6
Sutherland, James, 93, 94
Swanton, John R., 81, 84, 87
Swift, Jonathan, 103, 138; *Mr. C——ns's Discourse of Free-Thinking*, 78 n.10; *Project for the Advancement of Religion*, 107 n.5

Tenisin, Bishop Thomas, 46 n.12
Tertullian, 33
Tichi, Cecelia, 138, 153 n.6
Tillotson, John, 19, 27, 31–35, 37–40, 42, 46 n.16, 47 nn. 18, 21, and 22; 49, 57, 159; "Discourse to his Servants concerning the Sacrament," 41; "Religious and Divine Faith," 47 n.17; *Rule of Faith*, 36
Tindal, Matthew, 12, 20, 27, 44, 61, 62, 69, 71, 72, 76, 77, 78 n.2, 161; *Christianity as Old as Creation*, 74; *Nation Vindicated*, 68
Tipton, Ian, 78 n.17
Tissot, Georges, 47 n.23
Thacher, Oxenbridge, 126 n.13
Thomas, Isaiah, 126 n.13
Thomas Aquinas, Saint, 33, 35, 41
Thomson, James: *Winter*, 101
Thoreau, Henry David, 151
Todd, William B., 153 n.11
Toland, John, 12–13, 20–22, 27–29, 43–44, 45 nn. 2 and 3; 49, 61, 63, 65, 67, 69, 70, 71, 72, 76, 78 nn. 1, 15, and 16; 90, 98, 100, 108 n.10; "Account of the Indians at Carolina," 80; *Christianity Not Mysterious*, 84; "Clidophorus: or of the Exoteric and Esoteric philosophy," 62, 64, 78 n.4; *Consolidator*, 94; "History of the Soul's Immortality among the Heathens," 66; *Letters to Serena*, 66, 77; *Nazarenus*, 94; *Tetradymus*, 62; *Vindicus Liberius*, 64

Tomlinson, Robert, 109
Tompkins, Martin, 102
Tooke, Horne, 137, 153 n.3
Tourneur, Cyril: *The Atheist's Tragedy*, 24
Trenchard, John, 44
Trumbull, Jonathan: *M'Fingal*, 110
Tuckney, Anthony, 46 n.10
Tuesday Club of Annapolis, 127–36
Tully, 105
Turkish Spy, 43
Turner, Matthew: *An Answer to Dr. Priestley's Letters*, 78 n.13
Tyssot de Patot, Simon, 19, 43

Unitarians, 21
Urban, Linwood, 47 n.19

Vairasse d'Allais, Denis, 19
Van Gelder, H. A. Enno, 45 n.6
Vanini, Lucilio, 24, 49
Van Leeuwen, H. G., 29
Van Lennep, William, 45 n.7
Vardy, Luke, 109, 111, 116, 118
Viret, Pierre, 23, 28, 29; "Epistle Dedicatory," 45 n.6; *Instruction chestienne*, 45 n.6
Virgil, 105
Volney, Constantin, 137, 138; *Ruins*, 14, 141, 143, 155 n.19
Voltaire, 8, 9, 11, 22, 23, 159, 160, 161, 168; his influence on Barlow, 155 n.18; *Philosophical Dictionary*, 143

Wade, I. O., 43
Walker, Benjamin, 109–10, 125
Walker, D. P., 108 n.9
Walpole, Horace, 91
Walters, Robert, 48 n.24
Warburton, William, 62, 78 n.4, 130
Ward, Ned: *History of Clubs*, 123
Warner, John, 152 n.1, 153 n.9
Warville, J. P. Brissot de, 137; *Le Patriote François*, 152 n.2
Watson, Richard, 159, 160; *Apology for the Bible*, 158; *Letters to Thomas Paine*, 170 n.1; "Reply to Paine," 170 n.1
Webbe, John, 90, 91 n.3
Webster, Charles, 46 n.15
Westfall, Richard, 21, 23, 42
Whiston, William, 23, 94, 100, 102, 103, 163, 169
White, John, 85, 87
Whitefield, George, 165
Whitman, Walt: "Song of Myself," 151

William III (king of England), 44
Williams, Glyndwr, 47 n.23, 84
Williams, Jonathan, 118
Winans, Robert, 92 n.6
Wittgenstein, Ludwig, 153 n.10
Wodrow, Robert, 45 n.4, 108 n.10
Wolff, Christian von, 29
Wollaston, William: *Religion of Nature Delineated*, 98
Wollstonecraft, Mary, 137, 156–57 n.24; *Vindication of the Rights of Woman*, 154 n.15
Woodress, James, 153 n.5; *Yankee's Odyssey*, 152 n.1
Woolston, Thomas, 63
Wren, Sir Christopher, 130

Yolton, John: *Thinking Matter*, 45 n.2

Zionism, 169